Inside

Indonesia's

Big Bang

INSIDE
INDONESIA'S
BIG
BANG

*A Canadian Policy-Maker's First-Hand
Look at Governance Reform and
International Collaboration*

Mark Gilbert, PhD

First published in 2026 by

Halifax, NS, Canada
www.ocpublishing.ca

OC Publishing is based in Kjipuktuk, Mi'kma'ki, the traditional territory of the Mi'kmaq.

Edited by Anne Louise O'Connell and Jon Tattrie
Cover and interior design by David W. Edelstein
Cover photo by Said Alamri on Unsplash

ISBN 978-1-989833-58-2 (Paperback edition)
ISBN 978-1-989833-59-9 (eBook edition)

CONTENTS

Part 3 After the Tsunami: Quiet Years for our Partnership (2001-2006)   105

Part 4 Back on Track: Our partnership grows (2006-2009)   123

Part 5 Doubling the Effort: Project Leaders Ask for More Canadian Input in Implementing Reforms (2010-2015)   153

PREFACE

*"A man practices the art of adventure when he breaks
the chain of routine and renews his life through reading
new books, travelling to new places, making new friends,
taking up new hobbies and adopting new viewpoints."*

– Wilferd Peterson, American author 1900-1995

In December 1993, I received a phone call that offered a rare opportunity to expand my world view and open doors that until now had
remained closed. The president of the Institute of Public Administration
of Canada (IPAC) was organizing small teams of Canadian public servants familiar with the workings of local and provincial governments.
The teams would undertake exploratory missions to Southeast Asian
countries interested in strengthening local governments to identify
areas where IPAC might work with them in making improvements. I
was a member of the IPAC Board of Directors and had local government experience, which along with IPAC's interest in having regional
representation on the mission, were reasons I was asked to participate.

Indonesia was my destination. I went back year after year and hosted
Indonesian missions to Canada until 2014. Initially, I was part of a four-
person IPAC team. As the Canadian member composition evolved, I
took on the responsibility of team lead and Nova Scotia became the
provincial lead on the IPAC-administered, Canadian-government
funded project.

The governance structures in Canada and Indonesia are quite different. Canada is a federal state where the national and provincial governments share power and responsibilities. Indonesia is a unitary state with all powers vested in the national government. The centralized system of government suited the Dutch when they colonized Indonesia. It also suited the post–World War II Indonesian government that wanted to make sure the archipelago held together as a single nation. The centralized model and President Suharto's "New Order" goal of promoting economic development weren't compatible when it came to growing opportunities for exports brought about by globalization. Delays and uncertainties surrounding permits and approvals for the movement of goods was an impediment, as were the deficiencies in public services that supported the economy. Indonesia has over 17,000 islands, more than 250 million people and covers an archipelago that spans 5,100 kilometres from east to west and 1,800 kilometres from north to south. There would be economic advantages to transferring some of the decision making to the local level. Indonesian businesses and citizens especially welcomed changes that would reduce the wait times for licences and permits.

Canadian experience with the decentralization of power and responsibility made IPAC, along with its members drawn from the three orders of government and academia, a logical choice for a partnership with a nation moving toward decentralization. The Suharto government had no interest in decentralizing power so its focus was solely on administrative decentralization as a way to improve the way public services (including the issuance of licences and permits) were provided.

After five years of working with IPAC on administrative improvements in areas such as one-stop shop service centres, local government enterprise management, and improved revenue generation, Indonesia experienced a financial crisis and a change in leadership, which created one of the many challenges we were to face during tumultuous times. Each new president (there were five of them during the time we worked together) promoted political decentralization and most of the public service responsibilities were transferred, through national laws, to district and city governments. It happened quickly. This was unfamiliar territory for the elected and appointed heads of local governments as well as for the Department of Home Affairs and other ministries responsible for overseeing the transition. They were eager to learn more about how Canada dealt with decentralization issues, knowing it would contribute to the creation and implementation of decentralization laws. Over the next fifteen years our cooperation with Indonesia revolved around projects related to good governance (training for councillors, transparency, accountability), developing service standards, exploring alternative methods of service delivery, improving central-local government relations, building financial management capacity, and identifying service areas (health, education, fire, infrastructure) where we could use Indonesian–Canadian public service teams to make specific improvements.

This book is a reflection on the achievements of our joint efforts over a twenty-year period, which covers five Canadian and Indonesian cooperative government funding agreements, and the impact that political transitions and natural disasters had on the project. It follows the pace of the decentralization initiatives, which accelerated during the "Big Bang" period when reform laws were passed before regulations and structures were in place that were necessary for their implementation.

This story has never been told. As I'm the only person who was a regular participant in the study missions to both Indonesia and Canada, I believe I have the experience and, equally important, the inclination to tell it. The collaboration is unique in its positive, peer-centred approach to international development. It creates cultural awareness and gave the Nova Scotia participants, including me, an opportunity to expand their world views. I enjoyed it and found it meaningful. I want people to view Indonesia as more than just another developing country and also to reflect on the opportunities international work and travel offer for personal growth.

The Canadian/IPAC/Nova Scotia role was to share knowledge and showcase Canadian practices through roundtables, workshops, and site visits. It included providing technical assistance to improve public service delivery and standards as well as governance in a decentralized model where most services are provided by local governments with central governance oversight. Apart from IPAC staff who administered the project and accounted for the Canadian International Development Agency (CIDA) funding, the Canadian public sector participants, both those who went on missions to Indonesia and those who participated in Indonesian missions to Canada, were volunteers. We had a peer-to-peer relationship with the Indonesian government officials and worked collaboratively as equals. Most of the Indonesians and Canadians involved were public servants or academics eager to learn and exchange knowledge, so the peer-to-peer format worked well.

The achievements and results of our cooperation were more difficult to measure than some of the other government-funded projects. Our program didn't build schools, dig wells, provide education or vaccines to school children, or develop manuals or policies. The Indonesian government wanted something broader from our cooperation. Indonesia was interested in ideas and examples of innovations in service provision and good governance, and we offered to share the related experiences and practices that Canada had acquired from over a century of working in a decentralized governance system. Initially, we measured our inputs and activities, and later Indonesian local government heads were able to provide concrete examples of how they applied Canadian practices in their cities and districts. Research published in the *Journal of Southeast Asian Economics* a few years after our project ended dealt with the impact of two decades of decentralization reforms in Indonesia and I was able to learn more about the progress of the reforms where IPAC / Nova Scotia had been involved. Some of the reform initiatives had come closer to achieving their goals than others.

There were three individuals involved from beginning to end who provided the continuity needed to keep the project moving forward. Agung Mulyana was the coordinator for the Indonesian Ministry of Home Affairs during the early years of the cooperation and stayed involved when he moved to other government ministries. Jeffrey Ong served as a program officer at the Canadian embassy in Jakarta, and I represented the Institute of Public Administration of Canada (IPAC) and Nova Scotia. During our two-decade association, we became friends as well as colleagues.

The program gained momentum in its final years. Our Indonesian colleagues made plans for us to build on its success. The Canadian embassy in Jakarta encouraged us to take it to the next level through a bilateral agreement with full-time resources in Indonesia. Neither happened at that time and the reasons are part of the story. However, the relationships that we built have endured and in 2024 Indonesian colleagues were talking about finding a way to renew our cooperation. The many achievements of our work together were highlighted in a presentation made by the Indonesian project leader during the IPAC annual conference in Edmonton in the final year of the program. He went well beyond his allotted time. There were other, less tangible benefits that were not included in Yusharto Huntoyungo's presentations that are also part of this story. They were the ones that were more personal and kept us engaged–building friendships, acquiring knowledge, broadening personal horizons, and the exposure to new cultures, people, and places.

PROLOGUE

Borobudur Temple, Indonesia, on a Saturday in February 1997

Standing at the top of the Borobudur Monument in Central Java, I look out over the Kedu Plain. It's 9:30 in the morning and the sun, which rose three hours ago, is halfway between the horizon and its zenith. It has taken me some time to reach the temple's "Realm of Formlessness." First I had to climb the temple steps and walk around the terraces set between walls of relief panels and outward-facing Buddha statues. Along the route I passed through the "Realm of Desire" and then the "Realm of Forms" before reaching the steepening stairs that led to this final stage of enlightenment. I'm not here to become enlightened–not that I wouldn't benefit from the experience–but because it's part of a weekend program our Indonesian hosts arranged between weekday meetings.

Most everything I can see beyond the temple is a shade of green—mountains, hills, tropical vegetation, and open fields. Looking to the northeast I'm disappointed that it's too hazy to see Gunung (Mount) Merapi, Indonesia's most active volcano that's part of the Pacific Ring of Fire. The temperature is in the high twenties but it's not uncomfortable here in the open air 300 metres above sea level. Ibu Lies Kurniawati, an Indonesian colleague who organized the weekend stopover in Yogyakarta, says we should honour the pilgrim/tourist tradition of touching a Buddha statue inside one of the seventy-two stupas on this level and have a wish granted. This suggestion takes me out of the present moment and I think about the appropriate wish.

This is the fourth time I've come to Indonesia as part of a Canadian team. We are here working with Indonesian colleagues to grow the economy though decentralization and improved public administration practices. Our work to date has been on administrative decentralization, as President Suharto is not interested in sharing political control and we have to be careful not to step out of line. The earlier missions to Indonesia and Canada under our program, which is sponsored by the Government of Canada, were spent learning about one another's system of government and priorities. We've agreed that our first area of cooperation will be one-stop shops that have services similar to ones offered by our province and municipalities. On Monday our team will go to Gianyar, Bali, to provide an assessment of a one-stop shop that recently opened there.

I feel very at home here in Indonesia even though it's not like my home in Canada at all. The humid air is heavily scented from lush tropical growth and kretek cigarettes, and no one here has a cold-weather wardrobe or central heating. It's the nature of the Indonesian people I've met that makes me comfortable. They are warm, gracious, and gentle, and value harmony, courtesy, and family. Our Indonesian colleagues can find humour in most any situation and are very social. These are qualities and values that I either share or would like to possess.

My thoughts shift to the task at hand. What should my wish be? Something related to this decentralization project, to a broader global goal, or to something more personal related to myself, or someone close to me? A long life for our Indonesia–Canada cooperation is the winner. With a first project and lots of goodwill, we're building momentum and I don't want it to end.

PART 1

Different Cultures and Common Goals: Our Work Begins (1994-1997)

"Coming together is a beginning, keeping together is progress, working together is success."

– Henry Ford

O n a chilly mid-December morning a container ship navigated its way through Halifax Harbour sea smoke. I watched through my office window as it passed McNab's Island and headed toward open water. My eyes went back to the spreadsheet on my desk, but my mind was thinking about the ship's next port of call. I was restless. Having worked hard to get established in my twenties, then enjoying the benefit of a stable career path in my thirties, I was ready for something new. But it shouldn't be so new and different that I'd lose the benefit of all I'd acquired to date. My phone rang and interrupted my thoughts.

The call was from the president of the Institute of Public Administration of Canada (IPAC), a professional association for government administrators and academics. Jim Beaulieu and I were both on the board of directors. The last board meeting had taken place in Ottawa a few weeks earlier and Jim and I had a brief conversation about the institute's growing interest in international projects and my interest in participating in one of them. The Canadian government was already working with the Federation of Canadian Municipalities to share Canadian public sector expertise abroad and they agreed to fund exploratory IPAC missions to determine if there was a role for IPAC in improving governance and public service delivery in developing countries. The previous year Jim joined two other IPAC board members for an exploratory mission to Southeast Asia. Three countries there were interested in decentralizing to promote economic development and were willing to discuss involving Canadian / IPAC expertise in their initiatives. Afterwards I regretted that Jim and I hadn't had a longer conversation. I had spent the past two decades working in local government (both in city government departments and with the provincial ministry that provided advice and oversight to municipalities), and I had a good idea of what would be involved in transitioning service delivery and decision making to local governments. I was more than curious about how it could play out.

Jim wasted no time getting to the point of his call. He said he was organizing teams of two to undertake exploratory missions to the three countries that had showed interest in working with IPAC. He asked if I would like to be part of the Malaysian team.

I took a deep breath and steadied my voice before readily accepting. Jim would accompany each team. He asked if I could recommend a second member. Yes, I could. I had a colleague, Bill Hamilton, who was a seasoned town manager with an interest in international development that I could vouch for. Would I contact him? Yes! When I called Bill he was so overwhelmed by the out of the blue news that he was lost for words. I waited what seemed like a long time for his most affirmative response.

Our employers, the province of Nova Scotia and Town of Bridgetown, were both supportive of our participation in the exploratory mission. Nova Scotia had an active IPAC chapter, and the province was interested in strengthening commercial ties with Southeast Asia. As Bill and I made our preparations, the ground shifted[1] when Jim called again, this time to say the Malaysian government had a change of heart and decided not to participate. Before I could respond to this disappointing news, he added, "But I am reassigning you two. You can join the team going to Indonesia and I'm adding Bill to the one going to the Philippines." And that was the beginning of my twenty-year involvement in local-government reform and capacity-building initiatives in Indonesia. Jim hadn't met Bill, but he chose his reassignment well as Bill's extroverted nature and boundless energy endeared him to our Filipino partners, who shared these qualities. I was more comfortable with the quieter more formal approach adopted by our Indonesian colleagues.

Mission preparations dominated the next two months. I had my tropical country vaccinations and filled a prescription for malaria tablets. I made attempts to learn more about the world's fourth-most populous country and found that the international community didn't pay

---

1 This was the first of many unexpected changes that I would experience (and roll with) through my work on international projects.

much attention to Indonesia[2]. The internet was in its infancy and I had no online access to information. The reading material I found was limited to a Canadian government booklet on working in Indonesia, and an Indonesian tourist guidebook from the local library. A few days before leaving I saw an article in *The Economist* about the need to decentralize approvals for moving Indonesian trade goods so that the economy could grow.[3] My parents were sponsoring an Indonesian child at the time through one of the NGO programs and I read the letters they received. A colleague invited my wife and I over for a slide show her husband had put together. His photos were taken during a project he had worked on in Indonesia and we saw tropical scenes filled with smiling people. I took his suggestion to watch *The Year of Living Dangerously*, a movie about an Australian reporter working in Jakarta who covered the military coup that brought Suharto to power in the mid-1960s.

My excitement grew as the February 26, 1994, departure date approached. Bill left for the Philippines a week earlier. We had been talking on the phone every day before he left, and I missed sharing preparation stories and mission expectations with him. My mind and body were in overdrive—Jakarta was eleven time zones away and tropical. I had no first-hand knowledge of the country and had never met an Indonesian. I couldn't wait to start.

Indonesia 1994: Not the Year of Living Dangerously

In February 1994, it took three days to fly from Halifax to Jakarta via Toronto, Vancouver, Hong Kong and Singapore if you went by local times—a bit over thirty hours if you add up the time spent on airplanes

---

2   In his book *A Nation in waiting: Indonesia in the 1990s* published in 1994, the year of my first mission to Indonesia, Adam Schwarz provides three reasons why this is the case. First it's a young country, having achieved independence only after WWII. Second, it did not spawn a canon of romantic literature by its colonial ruler. And the third is that for most of its national life Indonesia has managed to sidestep the great conflicts of the industrialized world.

3   Administrative decentralization (more administrative decision making at the local level) would drive the early years of our cooperation.

and waiting at airports. I left Halifax on a cold pre-dawn Friday morning and arrived at Hong Kong's Kai Tak Airport early on Saturday evening. The plane touched down after navigating the tight space between mountains, skyscrapers, and clotheslines that contributed to its reputation as the sixth most dangerous airport in the world[4]. This was my first visit to an Asian city. After checking in at a Nathan Road hotel, I put on a pair of walking shoes and joined the crowd. The streets around the glitzy shops and round-tabled restaurants were teeming with activity. The fast moving, dense, pushy crowds reminded me of a Saturday afternoon on Montreal's St. Catherine's Street. When the hustle and bustle became overwhelming, I took a stroll along the quieter waterfront. The air was cool and couples sat close together on benches, taking in the view of Hong Kong Island and watching the Star Ferry.

The Malacca Strait was dotted with cargo ships when the plane made its descent into Singapore the next day. On the one-hour flight to Jakarta's Sukarno-Hatta airport I had a bird's-eye view of the Java Sea and its many islands, and then a closer look of the rice fields on the outskirts of Jakarta. A small part of a country that stretches 5,100 kilometres from east to west (similar to the width of Canada, which is 5,514 kilometres), straddles the equator, and has over 240 million people who speak 300 languages and live on or near its 17,508 islands.

The modern (at the time[5]) Soekarno-Hatta airport, named after Indonesia's first president and vice-president, was unlike any airport I had seen. It was an airport in a garden, where tropical plants filled the spaces between corridors and the connected boarding pavilions had Javanese steeped roofs. The floor and wall tiles were the colour of red soil and long windows filled the corridors with light. Indonesia is located in the Malay Archipelago and the diversity to be found within the world's largest group of islands was evident in the display of wooden carvings representing Indonesian art and culture.

There was a moneychanger near the luggage carousel and I bought Indonesian rupiah from him at a rate of 1,500 to one Canadian dollar.

---

4   Kai Tak Airport closed in 1998 and was replaced by Chek Lap Kok International Airport.

5   Terminal 1 opened in 1985 and the larger terminal 2 in 1991.

It was the most expensive rupiah I would ever buy. The Asian financial crises and other global events would result in major decreases in its value.

I cleared immigration and walked through the airport doors into humid 28 degrees Celsius heat. The fragrant spicy aroma from kretek cigarettes caught my attention. My taxi pulled up and porters rushed forward to load my bags in the open trunk. I waved them away, got in the back seat, and the car moved along slowly in heavy traffic. Street vendors lined the route selling food, consumer items, music tapes, and bottled water. They were mostly men and boys, and they wore long pants and flip-flop-style sandals. The older men wore plain or patterned shirts and traditional songkoks (*peci* caps). The younger ones were dressed in T-shirts or colourful shirts and caps. This was my introduction to the Indonesian preference for modesty in dress regardless of the weather.

A uniformed young woman with an infectious smile opened the tall glass hotel doors and I entered the Borobudur Hotel's air-conditioned lobby. I felt relief from the heat and humidity. The lobby and meeting rooms were grand. My room, decorated with small Indonesian statues and prints, was basic and comfortable. The only piece of fruit I recognized in the welcome basket was a miniature-sized banana. The *rambutan* (hairy fruit) and *salak* (snake fruit) looked mysterious. At the back of the hotel there was a landscaped tropical garden, an asphalt surface walking / jogging track, and an almost Olympic size pool[6]. The hotel had been recommended by Canadian embassy staff because it was near the Ministry of Home Affairs (Delam Negeri).

That afternoon I met the other members of the IPAC mission for an update and strategy session. Jim Beaulieu was the only one I knew. He was in his early fifties with dark hair and eyes and a solid build. When not wearing his IPAC president's hat, Jim was deputy minister for the province of Manitoba department responsible for municipal affairs. In professional settings Jim was direct and to the point. He liked being in

---

6   The story often told was that the hotel owners were concerned the government might commandeer the pool for training its elite athletes so deliberately made sure it was a few centimetres short of fifty metres in length.

charge and welcomed a good argument. He was also an ideas man and proactive with a global perspective. I would learn a lot working with him. Socially he was inclusive and friendly.

Sue McLellan, also in her fifties at the time, was born in Newcastle, UK, and had lived in Malaysia while working on her doctorate. She spoke Malaysian, which is similar to Indonesian, the country's official language. Sue was slim and fair skinned. She had ginger hair, an infectious smile, a robust laugh, and was capable of a British formality, which she rarely used. A former Ottawa lobbyist, she was between jobs when we met. Sue was recruited because she understood the Indonesian culture and language. Her knowledge and interest were invaluable in getting our Canadian – Indonesian cooperation off to a good start.

Louis Dussault, a lawyer with the Quebec Ministry of Municipal Affairs, was in his late forties. He was tall and fair, professional, thoughtful and easygoing. Jim thought it was important to include representation from both English and French Canada and Louis had responded to a call for a project volunteer Jim had put out to his ministry. Louis spoke both French and English and liked to travel. He was also a good shopper and thanks to him I never came home empty-handed.

At age forty-four I was the youngest member of the team. Most of my career to date had been in local government and at the time I was working as a municipal finance and governance advisor with the Nova Scotia government. I was also completing a doctorate and my thesis topic was on local government finance.

Jim had been in touch with the Canadian embassy staff and through them had arranged a Monday morning meeting at the Indonesian Ministry of Home Affairs Planning Bureau. We pooled our limited information about the Republic of Indonesia. Sue shared some Indonesian history. She told us Indonesia was made up of over 1,000 ethnic groups and had over 300 languages. Indonesian, a standardized form of Malay used in the archipelago, is both the common and official language. Indonesia became an independent nation in August of 1945 and Sukarno its first president. He introduced "Guided Democracy," which was based on the Indonesian values of discussion and consensus. In the mid-sixties there was a failed military coup that was suppressed by Major General

Suharto. This was followed by the mass killing of communist support-
ers, after which Suharto became president. Suharto introduced what he
called the New Order. It was committed to maintaining political order,
economic development, and the removal of mass participation in the
political process. It included a political role for the military. In addition
to defence-related activities, it was allocated a specific number of seats
in parliament and permitted to raise revenues through businesses which
it owned and operated. Jim added that there was a Ministry of National
Development Planning, referred to as Bappenas, responsible for central
economic planning for the nation.

The Transparency International Corruption Perception Index,
founded in 1993 by former employees of the World Bank, gave
Indonesia an unfavorable score and Sue had heard stories from her
and her husband's colleagues about corruption within the civil service,
whose members often expected payment for cooperation. I shared
the information from The *Economist* about the need to decentralize
the permit and approval processes to expedite trade and development
opportunities. Jim said that when he had visited our embassy in Jakarta
last year, staff there had said they would follow up with the Indonesian
government on potential areas of cooperation with IPAC. Sue had visited Jakarta when she lived in Malaysia and commented on the warmth
and hospitality of the residents. She told us, "Don't hesitate to go walking outside the hotel. The locals may want to talk or walk with you, but
it's a safe place."

Now for what we didn't know in 1994, but that I do know now.
At the time of our first mission in 1994 the Indonesian economy was
doing well under President Suharto's New Order. It offered stability
and development in return for restricted freedoms. An example of the
latter occurred later that year when *Tempo* magazine, the Indonesian
version of *Time*, was banned. The country was governed by the five
principles, referred to as Pancasila, taken from the 1945 constitution.
They included social justice, a belief in one God, guided democracy,
and unity. Unity was an issue in 1994 as citizen and rebel groups in three
of the Indonesian provinces (East Timor, Aceh, and Irian Jaya) were
pushing for freedom from Indonesian rule and the economic dominance

of Java. The issue was exacerbated by the government's transmigration policies, which altered regional demographics[7].

The centralized system of governance was a carryover from the Dutch colonial days, as was the dominance of Chinese in business and commercial activities. Civil society was weak, and in practice there was a one-party system under Golongan Karya (Golkar). Civil servants were expected to support the party. Corruption involving civil servants, police protection networks, the awarding of contracts, and other unethical activity, was widespread. The president's family were involved in businesses, many of which required government permits or approvals, and family members were reported to be extremely wealthy. Private and public monopolies were widespread. The military had a dual function. One was defence and security, the other was direct involvement in politics and development that included commercial activities. Something else we didn't know in 1994 was where any future cooperation with IPAC would fit with all of this.

Our discussion continued over an evening meal and when I got back to my room, a major thunder and lightning storm was underway. I awoke around four in the morning to the sound of the Fajr call to prayer coming from the Istiqlal mosque. My sleep was disturbed again a bit before 6 a.m. by another call from the muezzin to sunrise prayers. There was no doubt I was in a foreign land. Indonesia's constitution recognizes six religions[8] but nearly 90 percent of Indonesians are Muslim. Our hotel was within walking distance of the East Asia's largest mosque located in the country with the world's largest Muslim population. The Periplus Travel Guide published earlier that year referred to religion in Java as a gentle blend of Islam and Adat[9]. Adat refers to the influence of local customs and traditions, which in the case of Indonesia include tolerance and a spiritual attitude toward reality.

---

7   The transmigration initiatives moved people from densely populated areas like Java to less populated regions. One of the consequences of these programs was to change the ethnic composition of the receiving regions.

8   Muslim, Protestant, Catholic, Hindu, Buddhist and Confucianism.

9   Periplus Java Travel Guide p. 66

Home Affairs: Dalam Negeri

On Monday morning, Bob Woodhouse from the Canadian embassy met us at the hotel and accompanied us to a meeting at the Ministry of Home Affairs (MOHA or Home Affairs). Bob occupied one of the senior rotating positions at the embassy.

Louis Dussault and Susan McLellan on the day of our first visit to Home Affairs, Jakarta, March 1994.

The embassy van had three rows of seats, and as Louis and I had never been to Jakarta before, we assumed the role of junior team members and climbed into the back row. The van's route was circuitous, the day sunny and hot, and the streets shaded by lowland tropical trees. The Home Affairs block of offices featured a multi-storied main building and several low-rise buildings. The office configuration of private offices for senior officials, cubicles and open work areas for everyone else, plus conference rooms, would not have been out of place in Canada. The offices had air conditioning, worn wooden furniture and vinyl or leather sofas. We made small talk with Bob as we waited in the reception area. If the meeting went well, we planned to invite the Indonesian officials we met there to join us in Canada in the spring.

The two senior Indonesians at the meeting were Pak[10] Soetjitro, head of the Bureau of Planning, and Pak Tambunan, head of the Finance Directorate. Pak Soetjitro was a small man with black hair. Pak Tambunan was of medium height and build with receding gray hair, and spoke a bit of English. They were both close to the mandatory retirement age of sixty. Their willingness to discuss ideas and make plans for a future cooperation enabled us to move forward. Both men would participate in future missions to Canada in the 1990s but they did not play an active role in initiating projects, or moving them along. It was Agung, the third Home Affairs official in the room, who made things happen.

Thirty-eight-year-old Agung Mulyana was Sundanese (West Java), of medium height and build, with a full head of black hair, good posture, and good looks. He was married to Lili (the daughter of a former governor) and they had two sons. Paying no heed to the "two is enough" government policy that promoted small, prosperous families, they later added a daughter to their family. Agung held a master's degree in planning from the University of Queensland and he and his family were fluent in English. He joined our meeting as the interpreter for the two senior ministry officials. Agung would remain dedicated to our cooperation until the end.

With Sue and Agung as our interpreters, we discussed similarities and differences between our governance structures and potential project ideas. Jim told our hosts that IPAC was interested in sharing Canadian public sector knowledge and expertise that would aid Indonesia in improving governance and service delivery. The approach would be peer-to-peer, meaning that we would work together as professionals, and the cooperation would be structured to meet Indonesian needs. A memorandum of understanding and a visit to Canada later in the year were suggested as a way to move the cooperation forward.

The IPAC team was informed by Pak Tambunan that during the colonial period the Dutch introduced a system of strong centralized

---

10 Pak is the Indonesian word for Mister - Ibu is the word for Missus.

government. When Indonesia became an independent unitary state it kept this system as a way of maintaining control and holding a diverse nation together. The Indonesian constitution gives all power to the national (central) government. The central government decides where and when functions can be delegated to other levels of government. This can be changed at any time through the passage of national laws. At that time in 1994, the Indonesian central government appointed the leaders of provincial and local governments and often had central government staff assigned to local governments (provincial, city and district) to implement national policies and provide national services.

Pak Soetjitro said the term "administrative decentralization" (also known as deconcentration) is the one that best applies to the method of public service provision Indonesia was interested in at the time of our meeting. It refers to a transfer to lower-level central government authorities, or to other local authorities who are upwardly accountable to the central government[11]. It does not transfer power from the central to the local governments. Our hosts also identified the five levels of government in Indonesia: national, provincial, regions/cities, subregions, and villages. We were told that the military had a dual function (political and protection) and generated income though its commercial operations. Economic development was centrally planned rather than subject to market forces.

Jim Beaulieu explained our federal system of government in Canada, where both the federal and provincial governments each have designated powers and responsibilities under the constitution. In Canada, provinces have the same absolute control over their local governments as the Indonesian central government does with its subnational governments. Most public services are the responsibility of provincial and local governments, and they determine most service standards. The federal government will sometimes mandate minimum service standards when federal funding is involved. All levels of government

---

11   Ribot J. 2002, *Democratic decentralization of natural resources: Institutionalizing popular participation*. World Resources Institute, Washington, DC.

have merit-based hiring systems. The military does not share political power. Governments support economic development that is driven by market forces.

Pak Soetjitro told us that Indonesia was interested in promoting administrative decentralization as a means to improve the economy and the Canadian experience with decentralized services could be beneficial to Indonesia. This was in line with the promotion of decentralization in developing countries being promoted by international organizations as a part of structural adjustment programs[12]. We were informed that a five-day visit to South Sulawesi had been arranged and Agung would accompany us. After a few more days of meetings and discussing ideas for future projects, we were ready to set out. One of the project ideas, studying local government amalgamation in South Sulawesi (municipal amalgamations were mandated in several Canadian provinces in the 1990s), went with us.

Jalan Jalan—Hello Mister

I used any free time I had in Jakarta to go exploring on foot. I felt like I was walking into a sauna each time I ventured out. My starting point was usually the Lapangan Banteng Park, located across the street from the Borobudur Hotel. It is home to the Irian Jaya Liberation Monument, a freedom memorial statue depicting a gigantic, wild-haired man breaking from his chains. I knew it represented freedom from colonialism but only recently learned it was not commissioned until 1963 after the final Dutch colonial possession (West Papua New Guinea) had become part of Indonesia. The locals call it the Incredible Hulk. As Indonesia had spent several centuries under Dutch influence and Dutch control, I expected that a considerable Dutch influence would remain. This was not the case. The architecture and layout of the former Dutch administrative and military hub of the city, and buildings in some

---

12   Kusno, A. *Shifting modalities in urban government.* Chapter 2 in Governing Urban Indonesia, Indonesian Update series, The Australian National University, ISEAS Publishing, Singapore 2024 p.26.

other areas of Dutch colonial administration, were the only noticeable reminders of the former colonizer's presence. Dutch-style cuisine was available but not ubiquitous and English, not Dutch, was the preferred Western language.

Walking through the park I was constantly being called to with the words, "Hello Mister." If I said hello back, then a series of standard questions would follow. "Where you from Mister? Where you going? Are you married? Where you stay?" Sometimes people would want to accompany me or offer to be a guide. Edward was one of them. He was a small outgoing Indonesian man, in his late twenties, who spoke a bit of English and had no steady work. He joined me on my walk and asked the usual questions. It was a hot day and he helped me purchase a bottle of water from a street vendor. I bought one for him too. He asked if he could come to my room and I said the hotel didn't allow guests. When it was time to leave, I handed him some rupiah bills and thanked him for his company. His eyes filled with tears as he said, "I am not a beggar," and he refused to take the money. I realized then that he wanted to be treated as a friend and I had misread the situation. I'd have to be more careful about this in the future.

Sulawesi Amalgamation Studies Pitch

Sue, Louis and I left for the airport early on a Saturday morning to meet Agung for our flight to Ujung Pandang (more commonly known as Makassar). The Canadian government had selected Sulawesi, an island of gangling appendages that give it a strange shape and long coastline, as the geographic focus for Canada's development cooperation program. Sulawesi (once known as the Celebes) is one of the four Greater Sunda Islands that collectively account for most of the Indonesian population. It is third in size (Sumatra and Kalimantan are larger), about three times the size of Nova Scotia, and with 19 million residents, third in population (after Java and Sumatra). Sulawesi is just east of the "Wallace line" that separates the bio-geographical zones between Asia and Australia. Several species of birds, fish, and animals (like the anoa, a dog-sized buffalo) are endemic to the island. Makassar[13] is its largest city and the gateway to Eastern Indonesia.

When we arrived in Makassar, Agung took our return tickets and had them confirmed. Otherwise, he said our return tickets might not be valid. A driver from the University of Guelph-led Sulawesi Regional Development Project (funded by the Canadian government) met us at the airport and took us to a harbourfront hotel. On Sunday morning the driver took us north toward Maros. The route was lined with large piles of coconuts for sale, small businesses with sliding metal doors, and *becak*[14] drivers waiting for passengers. A culture of entrepreneurship was evident at intersections where street vendors, either out of necessity or family traditions, sold snacks, drinks, household items, and garments. The Pettakere Caves (limestone) are a short distance from Maros and we saw twenty-six red and white hand prints that are over 35,000 years old. The caves are surrounded by lush vegetation and steep hills and a mountain stream flows nearby. There was a covered rest area near the entrance and we sat there awhile, listening to Agung as he talked about the human bones that suggested the caves here were also a probable burial site.

On Sunday afternoon we had what Indonesians refer to as a "free program," meaning you're on your own. I wanted to see more of Makassar and thought renting a bicycle would be a good way to cover more ground. I couldn't find a bike rental shop so I went exploring on a bicycle borrowed from one of the hotel kitchen staff. It had been Sue's suggestion to check with them. Her knowledge of the country and approach is one of the reasons the project got off to a good start.

Sitting on a hard bicycle seat I got a closer look at the six-foot-thick walls that protected the seventeenth-century Dutch fortress called Fort Rotterdam and pedalled over narrow foot bridges into residential neighbourhoods. The children called out, "Hello Mister." The adults

---

13 Going forward I use the name Makassar for the city that has also been called Ujung Pandang(UP). It was called UP during the 1990s but is more commonly referred to as Makassar in the 21st century. It is Indonesia's fifth largest urban centre.

14 A three-wheeled bicycle with a passenger seat found in many parts of Indonesia. In Jakarta the *bajaj* (a motorized three-wheeled, fume-belching box) is more common.

Agung Mulyana at the Pettakere Caves,
Sulawesi March 1994

looked surprised to see me and were neither welcoming nor rude. I asked Sue what I should offer as payment for the use of the bicycle and her advice was, "Whatever you would pay at home." The bicycle owner was thrilled to receive the equivalent of $20 in rupiah and I used Sue's advice from then on. Later I watched the sunset over the harbour from my room. It happened quickly. The sun dropped and it was dark.

On Monday we made the five-hour drive by jeep to Enrekang. Agung sat in the front with the driver while Louis, Sue and I squeezed in the back seat. Agung was reserved and didn't share any of his opinions about the government—standard practice for public servants during the Suharto era. We didn't know if it was because public servants in Indonesia were discouraged from talking politics, because he didn't want to portray the government in a negative light, or that Indonesians aren't open with foreigners until they've gained their trust. However, he did comment on all the satellite dishes we saw on rooftops during the drive, observing that exposure to international programing would result in greater public demands for change. I learned later that the Indonesian government had launched satellite services in all parts of

Indonesia in the 1970s, but broadcasts were limited to a government channel. A few years before our drive to Enrekang, private stations were given licences (the first one went to one of Suharto's sons) to broadcast on the satellite network.

The route stayed close to the coastline of the Selat Makassar, passing through rice fields and limestone outcroppings on the way to the port city of Parepare. Then we turned northeast into the mountains with brown-water rivers that reminded me of the ones flowing into the Bay of Fundy between Nova Scotia and New Brunswick. Children, at an age when they appear to be all arms and legs, swam and played in the water.

In Enrekang we had our evening meal at the home of Remi and Linda Gauthier, the couple working on the CIDA-funded Sulawesi Regional Development Project. The project focused on rural development and capacity building in planning agencies in Sulawesi's four provinces. Assistance was provided by teams of advisors contracted and managed by the University of Guelph[15]. The first phase ran from 1984 to 1990 and the second phase would end the following year in 1995[16]. The photos taken outside that night show the colour green dominating the landscape and the telltale signs of tropical heat encroaching on the space between clothing and skin.

We spent the night at the governor's guesthouse, a rustic dwelling with the constant hum of tropical insects to keep us company. There was no air conditioning and the high level of humidity made sleep difficult. In the morning, we met with local government staff to pitch the idea of an amalgamation study of the regions' local governments as a joint project. They greeted us with smiles and offered us sugared tea and small cardboard boxes filled with food, including sticky rice wrapped in banana leaf. Yes, they liked our idea to work together on

---

15 Francis Harris Cummings Project planning and administration lessons from the Sulawesi Regional development Project. Canadian Journal of Development Studies January 14(1): 137-166 1993.

16 Later in the year a University of Guelph review of the project that was critical of the Indonesian government resulted in President Suharto terminating the project. This was an early reminder that our cooperation was limited to administrative matters and if we strayed beyond that we would not be welcome in Indonesia.

an amalgamation study. Sue knew they were being polite and yes didn't really mean yes. Louis and I were inexperienced in the cultural nuances and thought we had a promising potential project. Agung said he would pass on their expression of interest to the governor's office. That was the last we heard about it.

It was the holy month of Ramadan and both Agung and our driver were fasting during the day. To pass the time on the long drive back, Louis reminisced about Quebec and talked about his favourite French-Canadian foods (sugar pie was top of the list) and his summer cottage on the St. Lawrence River. When we arrived back in Makassar, Sue suggested we give the driver a gift of money to celebrate the holidays and family time that would soon follow. He was appreciative and I received another valuable piece of advice about helping those who help you.

In the evening Agung said we would take a break from meeting government officials and have a different Indonesian experience. Night had fallen and the Makassar waterfront was overflowing with people who had come out to eat following a day of fasting. Agung navigated his way through the crowd and we followed close behind in the clove-scented night air until he reached an unoccupied table on the kilometre-long esplanade. Food stalls shaded by tall palm trees lined one side and picnic-style tables with a sea view competed for the space on the other side. We were barely seated when Agung sprang into action, giving orders to the young men standing close by to bring us drinks and food from the stalls. His tone with the workers was neither polite nor rude but matter of fact in keeping with a society where it is common for middle-class families to employ servants to help with household chores. The food was plentiful and our appetites were sated by *nasi goring* and *nasi uduk* (rice dishes), *gado gado* (Indonesian salad), *satay*, *rending* (spicy meat), *bakso* (meatball soup), *gudeg* (a vegetarian dish with a jackfruit base) and *ayam goreng* (fried chicken). The spices in some of the dishes made my eyes water and I especially liked the peanut sauce that covered the *gado-gado*. One of Agung's helpers brought bottled water and soft drinks.

The remainder of the mission was spent at meetings in Makassar and Jakarta learning more about Indonesian public-sector issues and discussing potential areas of cooperation. The Canadian team had a debriefing session at the end of each day. Sue added colour by sharing the passing remarks she overheard Indonesians make to each other during the meetings and her cultural observations on body language and facial expressions. One remark she shared that made us laugh was that we dressed like movie stars. There was nothing she observed that would have a negative impact on our work. Sue suggested we refer to the IPAC team as "The Bintangs." Bintang is the word for "star" in Indonesian and also the name of a popular Indonesian beer. It fit with my "this is a big adventure" view at the beginning of the project. Over the next twenty years my attitude and approach would evolve to something broader and more meaningful.

This was the first time in Jakarta for Louis and me and we wanted to see more of the city. On a free morning, we took a Jakarta highlights tour. I was fascinated by the melodic, soothing music of the Indonesian *gamelan* orchestra playing in the lobby of the Hotel Indonesia where we gathered for the tour. The dominant percussive instruments were metallophones played with mallets, and hand-played drums. The tour took us to the Dutch administrative area, to the old harbour, and made an unnecessarily long stop at a large gift shop. The last stop was the National Museum of Indonesia, located on the west side of Medan Merdeka (Freedom Square). The tour van passed through a throng of vendors crowding the entrance. One of them was selling dart blow-guns. As we exited the van he blew a dart that whizzed by us and hit a nearby tree. It was friendly fire meant to draw attention to his wares. Point taken. One evening Louis suggested we go to a *rijsttafel* restaurant featured in a Jakarta guidebook. It was in a colonial style building filled with Dutch memorabilia. *Rijsttafel* (rice table) is a meal consisting of small plates filled with Indonesian dishes plus rice. It was also good way to sample Indonesian food but this time the setting was more sedate compared to the hustle and bustle of Makassar Esplanade food stalls.

On our last day in Jakarta we met Jeffrey Ong, an Indonesian employed by the Canadian embassy in Jakarta. Jeffrey is serious, hardworking, articulate and a decade younger than me. He would become our main Canadian embassy contact and play a large part in our cooperation with Home Affairs in the years that followed. Along with Agung and me, Jeffrey would be involved for the duration of the project. We also met Dr. Bernard May at his GTZ (German Aid Agency) office located in the MOHA compound. Bernard had spent many years working in Indonesia. He was welcoming and open and through him we were able get a better idea of Indonesian politics and priorities, saving us from suggesting areas of cooperation that wouldn't be of interest to our Indonesian colleagues and focusing on ones that would.

Before leaving Jakarta I bought a Periplus Travel Guide to Java[17] published earlier in the year (1994). An American anthropologist and her husband[18] wrote the section on being Javanese titled "Equanimity, Etiquette and Self-control." They write that "to be Javanese is not only to be adult (infants are too emotionally fragile), but to have achieved the proper degree of self-control, balance, bearing and grace that in the Javanese scheme of things distinguishes them from animals, infants, the mentally impaired and most foreigners." My Western upbringing encouraged a degree of aggressiveness and confrontation and standing up for your rights to settle disputes when you felt wronged. I think Agung and other Javanese and Sundanese Indonesian colleagues felt "distinguished" from me on a couple of future missions when I expressed my frustration in a very non-Javanese way. During this mission I was too busy taking everything in to get upset. Bill Hamilton, who worked on the IPAC project in the Philippines, and I often asked ourselves, and each other, why things that would bother us at home didn't faze us when we were overseas. We came up with a number of possible reasons but thought the most likely one was that our expectations were different at home and abroad. An example was a meeting not starting on time. At home we were often irritated (as were others) by the delay but in Southeast Asia it was part of the mystery of a different culture and our colleagues never showed any frustration.

---

17 Java is home to 60 percent of all Indonesians but makes up only 7 percent of its land mass. The seventy-three million Javanese live on the eastern two-thirds of the island. The Sundanese live in West Java and in the recently created Banten province in the far west of Java. Pisanni p3 and p 356.

18 Nancy Smith-Hefner (Boston University) and Robert Hefner.

I was in good spirits when the IPAC team left Jakarta. Although we didn't have a confirmed project when we left Indonesia we did have a commitment from Home Affairs colleagues to come to Canada in May.

The Culture of Rice-Indonesians in Canada (1994)

A few months later, Jim Beaulieu invited all our Southeast Asian IPAC partners (current and potential) to Canada. The eleven participants from Indonesia, the Philippines and Malaysia started the study tour in Winnipeg and then went to Quebec and Nova Scotia. IPAC staff had told me that one of the Indonesians would be accompanied by his wife. When they arrived in Winnipeg I was surprised that it was Agung, the junior member of the group. I had observed the organization hierarchy based on rank and age in the Indonesian public service and had expected a senior official's spouse. The mission was timed to coincide with the IPAC board meeting in May so that our colleagues could become more familiar with IPAC and meet the board members. There was no similar organization in Indonesia. Jim was a good host and wanted to make the group feel welcome. He arranged meals at popular restaurants that specialized in French and Italian cuisines. After the first of these "hard to find rice" meals, our two senior Indonesian guests said they were tired and declined the invitations. Afterwards they went out for Chinese food. We learned that if rice was not served our Indonesian colleagues would say they hadn't eaten.

The group spent a few days in Quebec City where Louis Dussault introduced them to local government structures and issues in Canada's French-majority province. The final stop was Halifax to see how things worked in Nova Scotia[19]. I thought I had the food situation under control. An IPAC regional lunch was arranged and Dr. Alex Brillantes, a participant and respected University of the Philippines academic, was the guest speaker. I ordered rice for the soup-and-sandwich buffet

---

19 Unlike provinces in Indonesia's unitary state, provinces in the Canadian federation are each responsible for determining the responsibilities and powers of their local governments.

Winnipeg was the first stop on the May 1994 mission to Canada. Participants were from Indonesia, Malaysia, and the Philippines.

Right to left: Soetjitro, Tambunan, Agung and a participant from Malaysia in Winnipeg, May 1994.

lunch but noticed the Indonesians didn't put any rice on their plates. Perplexed, I asked Agung later why no one had eaten the rice. He said it hadn't been served with four accessories (Indonesian dishes) and so no one had looked for it. It had been placed at the far end of the table. We had better but limited success with the meal Bill Hamilton had hosted for the group in Bridgetown, an Annapolis Valley town. The rice was visible but not sticky enough to be a hit.

We took the group to the Habitation, the fortress overlooking the Annapolis Basin that seventeenth-century French explorer Samuel de Champlain had built for a New World colony. He established a social club for food and entertainment referred to as "The Order of Good Cheer." The buds were on the trees and the earth had started to warm when each of our guests was officially welcomed into this order and received a certificate. The sun stayed with us on the evening drive back to Halifax and Filipino Jojo Delles regaled us with stories from his earlier visit to the Canadian north. At that time my colleagues and I had little knowledge of, or interest in, the territories and viewed them as places of cold winter darkness where non-natives stuck it out for a few years to make some money. Jojo's experiences provided a different, more favourable impression of a beautiful land occupied by people with a unique culture that respected the environment. This view would soon resonate with many Canadians.

My wife, Lise, joined me on the weekend trip to the Annapolis Valley and we both met Agung's wife Lili for the first time. She is a petite, intelligent woman with a serious look that belies a quiet sense of humour. Lili told us she owned a successful consulting company and that her income gave Agung the freedom to pursue a career in the public sector. She said she had responsibilities as the wife of an Indonesian official and that included accompanying her husband on international missions. As Lili was financially independent, she was able to cover her travel costs and her command of the English language enabled her to fully participate in activities.

The Annapolis Valley weekend provided an opportunity to build relationships. Filipinos Jojo Delles and Alex Brillantes became IPAC project colleagues, and it was the beginning of a long friendship with Agung and Lili. Unfortunately, the two delegates from Ipoh were not able to persuade the Malaysian government to partner on a project with IPAC. However, the mission did provide opportunities for the participants to learn more about government in Canada and help them to identify specific areas of cooperation.

Decentralization and One-stop Shops (1995-1997)

The annual missions to Indonesia and Canada continued over the next three years. The IPAC team met with local government officials in Sidoarjo, East Java, January 1995. In the photograph, Jim Beaulieu who led the mission is on Sue's right.

CIDA agreed to cover IPAC's costs related to the cooperation and a high-level memorandum of understanding was signed in Jakarta in January 1995[20]. Annual action plans were prepared and signed in Jakarta each year during the IPAC mission. Each year we held our breath, hoping the action plan would be signed and the project would continue. The workplans were important for IPAC as it enabled it to demonstrate to CIDA, the funding agency, that the project was active and valued by the Indonesian government. The workplans were prepared by Home Affairs staff after we had reached agreement on the projects and timelines. Signatures were added at formal meetings arranged by Home Affairs.

On one of these earlier missions (1995), we didn't know if we

---

20 The stated purpose of the MOU was to strengthen cooperation for improving efficiency and effectiveness of services provided by local government on the administrative decentralization initiatives. It included twelve articles.

would have a workplan completed in time to take back to Canada with us. The IPAC team had returned to Jakarta from North Sulawesi where discussions regarding a possible municipal amalgamation study project had taken place. Both Louis and I had recently been involved with municipal amalgamation projects in Canada, and we were eager to share this knowledge. Indonesia had fewer local governments than Canada and it was only later we realized studying consolidations as a means of improving services was of little interest. The discussions were probably arranged as a courtesy to IPAC as it was one of our suggested areas of cooperation. When the responsibility for service delivery was later decentralized, the number of local governments actually increased as local interest groups lobbied for access to the resources that came with greater independence and autonomy. Once back in Jakarta we were energized from what we perceived to be encouraging discussions in North Sulawesi, a bit wired from a near runway miss when we transferred planes in Makassar, and looking forward to developing our annual workplan with Home Affairs. We waited at the hotel the next day for a call that never came.

The next morning, I picked up a copy of the *Jakarta Post* in the breakfast room and was surprised to see Agung had written a letter to the editor complaining about the long wait time to have a phone line installed at his home. It was good to see him advocating publicly for service improvements. Sitting around the breakfast table we were troubled that we still hadn't heard from Home Affairs. We were scheduled to leave Indonesia later that day and didn't want to go back empty handed. At Sue's initiative we arranged for a taxi and went unannounced and uninvited to the Home Affairs office block. Our first stop was the GTZ office where we talked with Dr. May about the situation. He sympathized with our frustrations about finalizing plans during short mission time frames. He suggested we resolve the situation by going to the Home Affairs offices and asking to meet. Louis, Sue and I walked up the stairs to Agung's office. If he was surprised to see us he didn't show it. He welcomed us and, using his white board, we prepared a project workplan and timetable for our cooperation. It set out a framework with details to be added during the mission to Canada later in the year.

We left not knowing why the initiative to finalize the workplan fell to us. Perhaps Agung had other pressing issues and would have reached us later. Maybe he had forgotten we were leaving that day. What mattered was that he had reacted positively to our showing up unannounced at his office and we accomplished what we set out to do.

Afterwards we walked back to the hotel in the midday heat and traffic and had *gado-gado* for lunch. Louis and I praised Sue for her advice—without it the project would have stalled. At checkout time I experienced the usual shock of seeing such a big number, over a million rupiah, on the bill. It worked out to less than seven hundred Canadian dollars for a three-day stay that included meals and access to the business centre.

There was a lot to learn about one another's governance systems and priorities. Information sharing and program planning received a lot of attention in the early years of our cooperation. In 1995 we spent several days in a Halifax boardroom with Agung and three Indonesians who were new to our program. Edi Suhadi and Kausar worked for Home Affairs. Misbach held a senior position with the province of West Java. One of the reasons Misbach had participated was to meet with the Nova Scotia Ministry of Intergovernmental affairs to further explore a sister province agreement between Nova Scotia and West Java. The planning meetings were lively ones. Indonesians like to reach a consensus on issues and Edi Suhadi was a likeable contrarian who made vigorous arguments to support his points of view. At times they were difficult to follow and Agung would use the phrase "what Edi is trying to say" as a preface to explaining Edi's point of view. Agung was patient with him, and Sue enjoyed the drama. By Thursday afternoon we had agreed on a workplan where one-stop shops for improving public service delivery were front and centre.

The number two priority was the sister province partnership between an Indonesian and Canadian province (West Java and Nova Scotia). A third, and smaller project, was exploring ways to generate local government revenue. Under the authoritarian rule of President Suharto, the scope of our work for the next three years remained confined to administrative decentralization. The president was still

Sue with Agung, Misbach and Edi Suhadi in a boardroom at
Summit Place, Halifax developing a plan for our cooperation,
October 1995.

not interested in sharing or delegating political power to Indonesian provinces and local governments. He had come to power following a period of political unrest which culminated in the failed military coup in 1965 referred to as the 30 September Movement. Suharto's "New Order" committed to achieving and maintaining political order, economic development, and the removal of mass participation in the political process. Thirty years later he was not about to change course but did support administrative improvements that would help to grow the economy.

Montreal was the first stop on the 1995 mission to Canada and the IPAC team joined our Indonesian colleagues on a visit to a one-stop shop. That visit would end up shaping our cooperation for the next few years. Access Montreal had been set up as a one-stop shop for city services and recently received an Institute of Public Administration of Canada (IPAC) award for its initiative. Citizens could apply for licences and permits, have services connected or disconnected, and report problems all by calling or visiting a single location. Agung had told us that in Indonesia the process was so time-consuming and unclear that people found informal sector employment by being paid by well-to-do Indonesians to stand in multiple long lines to get or renew licences and permits. His initial solution was to replicate a brochure he had seen in Canada that provided detailed information for citizens applying for licences and permits. Now he saw something better.

To move the one-stop shop initiative forward Agung said he would like to bring thirty Indonesians to Nova Scotia for a 1996 October mission to learn more about one-stop shops in Canada and accelerate their use in Indonesia. This was a good project for administrative decentralization as it focused on improving service delivery. I thought it would be a totally new initiative for Indonesia but that turned out not to be the case. Other donors had already worked directly with a few local governments to set them up. Instead, we were involved in promoting the benefits of one-stop shops, demonstrating the wide range of services they could cover, and later providing assessments of existing ones and making suggestions for improvement.

By 1996 one-stop shops were widely used by both provincial and local governments in Canada. They often used the word "access" (e.g. Access Nova Scotia) to identify them to the public. The term "single window" was also used, and in some cases the service would extend to all government (federal, provincial, municipal) requirements.

There had been four Indonesian participants in the 1995 mission to Canada and Sue McLellan and I had made the local arrangements with IPAC approval. When the time came to organize the 1996 mission to Canada Sue had started work with the British High Commission in Ottawa and was no longer actively involved in the project, and I was a few months into a new job as CEO of the Nova Scotia Municipal Finance Corporation (a municipal infrastructure bank reporting to the minister of Municipal Affairs). For a group of thirty requiring accommodation, ground transportation, field visits, and rice at every meal, I needed help. I approached a colleague, Jack Novack, who was program director with the continuing education group at Dalhousie University that offered local government certificate and diploma programs. To meet the budget, his group did some contract work as well. Jack and I put together a plan and IPAC approved it. IPAC contracted out the work

Agung and Bill Hamilton. Halifax Autumn 1996.
Bill participated in the IPAC – Philippines partnership.

associated with local arrangements and the organization of a seminar on one-stop shops with local speakers to Jack's group. I arranged for the field visits to provincial and municipal one-stop shops.

Another organizational challenge was that because our cooperation was new and somewhat tentative, there was always uncertainty around the timing of the missions. Dates often changed after we had a program in place as a result of travel approval delays or evolving Indonesian government priorities. This happened in 1996 and we had to adjust all the local reservations, speaker dates and field visits to accommodate a one-week delay.

The study mission included seven officials from Home Affairs. The other participants represented local government pilot program districts that were interested in single-window service delivery. Pak Tambunan was the senior Indonesian government participant but he wanted to leave early so Agung assumed the leadership role. Agung's wife, Lili, was the only spouse to join the group. A breakfast buffet suited to Indonesian tastes was provided at the Radisson Hotel in downtown Halifax. The aroma of rice, eggs, roasted vegetables, chicken, and spices greeted me when I met them each morning in the breakfast room. Agung always brought packets of sambal hot sauce with him to add to his food when he came to Canada as he found the food too bland without it.

A two-day seminar on one-stop shops took place on the Dalhousie University campus. The presenters at the seminar were from both provincial departments and municipal governments in Nova Scotia. It included sessions on what was needed to implement more one-stop shops in Indonesia and identified obstacles to be overcome. Agung took on the role of interpreter as many of the Indonesian local government officials didn't speak English. We invited local municipal administrators to one of the seminar luncheons and took photographs, one of which accompanied an article on our Indonesia–Nova Scotia cooperation that was featured in an issue of IPAC's *Public Sector Management* magazine.

The seminar offered the first opportunity for meaningful communication during presentations. At earlier meetings with local and provincial governments in Sidoarjo, Manado, Enrekang, and East Java, our presentations were basically an exchange of information about our systems of government and service provision. Statistical information dominated the Indonesian presentations. The presentations were translated and finding common areas of interest where we could work together was limited. The thirty Indonesians were selected for their interest in one-stop shops and were engaged in the discussions following each of the presentations. I learned a lot about the challenges they faced and the services that were one-stop shop priorities. To me, it was similar to holding a seminar for Canadian local government officials and I was comfortable participating. This topic-focused seminar provided information that could be used to accelerate the adoption and improvement on one-stop shops in Indonesia.

Volunteer drivers drove rented vans for visits to municipal and provincial one-stop shops. I joined Agung and six others for a tour of Access Nova Scotia, the provincial one-stop shop in Kentville (an Annapolis Valley shire town) that linked service information for all three orders of government. For example, if you wanted to open a business you could see the federal, provincial and municipal licences, permits and other requirements. Information on government

Nova Scotia local government and IPAC representatives were invited to meet the 1996 Indonesian study mission participants at a luncheon held at Dalhousie University in Halifax.

incentives for specific types of businesses was also part of the information package. We arrived early, parked the van, and went to a nearby Tim Horton's for coffee. It was a warm, sunny October morning and the participants were in no hurry to leave when it was time to walk the two blocks to the one-stop shop. I wanted to be on time and when the group made casual conversation as they sauntered along the sidewalk,

I showed my frustration by shouting at them to hurry up. This was done in a very un-Javanese way that no doubt distinguished me (not in a favourable way) from my Indonesian colleagues. I was learning that punctuality was not as high a priority with Indonesians as it was with me, and I'd need to be more patient. The group was warmly received when we arrived five minutes late.

A few months later (February 1997) I went to Indonesia with Neil Balcom, a province of Nova Scotia one-stop shop specialist. We were there to follow up on what the Indonesians said was a productive one-stop shop seminar held a few months earlier in Halifax. There were already a few donor-funded one-stop shops in Indonesia but there was no standard model used by Indonesian local governments and there were major differences in their one-stop shop resource and service capacity. We had seen one in Central Java that offered only a few services and was only a marginal improvement to the licence–separate service model. Agung and his colleagues wanted to accelerate the establishment of one-stop shops in local governments, standardize services offered, and encourage the adoption of best operating practices. To showcase the work that had already been done while looking for ways to improve the service, Home Affairs asked us to undertake an assessment of the local government one-stop shop in Gianyar, Bali. It was one of Indonesia's best and Agung had arranged for us to go there as the *sekwilda*, or district secretary, had participated in the previous year's seminar on one-stop shops in Halifax and had implemented ideas from the study mission. Gianyar Regency (population 320,000) is situated in the centre of Bali and is a major arts and tourism centre. When we arrived (accompanied by junior Home Affairs staff) we saw the one-stop shop was located in an attractive, spacious two-storey building with a tiled roof and a combination brick and adobe exterior. The parking lot was filled with motorbikes and vans. The customer counter area was built of a wooden base with designs carved in it and marble counters. It was interesting that they had taken the time to make the area visually appealing. The floor was tiled and there was natural light through a wide row of windows near the top of the wall. We were given a tour by an official named Made (two syllables) and then Neil spent a few hours

The one-stop shop in Gianyar, Bali, February 1997.

Interior of one-stop shop in Gianyar with Neil, Lies and Fauzi at the counter.

collecting the information he needed for his assessment. I was told this one-stop shop had been funded by an international donor. A few weeks later Neil completed his report and provided copies to IPAC and Home Affairs. It was generally positive and included a few recommendations for improvement. Gianyar's one-stop shop was a good model for other local governments wishing to establish one. Indonesian interest in one-stop shops continued and in future years we visited more of them but were asked only for general observations rather to than carry out more in-depth evaluations. In 2011, Home Affairs and IPAC organized a second workshop / seminar on one-stop shops. This time it was a larger, high-profile event and held in Jakarta rather than in Nova Scotia on the Dalhousie University campus.

One of the project ideas discussed during our planning sessions was a sister province agreement between an Indonesian and Canadian province. It would have two parts. One would be sharing public sector knowledge on decentralization. The other would be to generate economic activity through business ventures. The Canadian embassy staff in Jakarta had suggested a province in Sulawesi be selected as Sulawesi was the focus of Canadian aid to Indonesia at the time. Jim Beaulieu suggested Nova Scotia become involved as it was a Maritime province and Indonesia was a country of islands. Home Affairs chose the province of West Java so we agreed on pursuing a sister province arrangement between West Java and Nova Scotia. At the time a number of Nova Scotia companies were doing business in Indonesia and the Canadian federal government was facilitating business opportunities. The Indonesian cabinet minister of industry, Tungki Ariwibowo (now deceased), was a graduate of a Halifax university and promoted these commercial ties. When we met in Bandung in 1996 to discuss the partnership, Misbach, a senior West Java administrator who had participated in the 1995 mission to Canada, was at the first meeting and contributed to its positive tone. The second meeting (1997) was with the governor's staff and translation was required. Agung was unavailable to join us and our Home Affairs translator was shy and not as effective as Agung in moving the discussion forward. However, we agreed to meet again. The Asian financial crisis, which is discussed later, resulted in the initiative being put on the back burner. When we were ready to resume discussions, a western section of West Java had been taken to create a new province called Banten. The Indonesian government thought a sister partnership with Banten province (which borders Jakarta) would be a better idea.

Our Indonesian colleagues found the program format with seminars and field visits useful and requested we use it for the October

1997 mission that focused on revenue generation. Agung and Timbul Pudjianto[21] led over thirty participants, most of whom were from local governments. Local governments in Indonesia received most of their revenue in the form of grants from central government. Own-source revenues were limited to minor taxes, user fees and contributions from their local government enterprises. The group was looking for ways to increase own-source revenues. In addition to generating ideas for new revenue sources, setting and collecting fees for permits and services was also part of the agenda. As any Indonesian reforms were limited to administrative matters the material provided about the reliance on own-source revenues, such as property taxes, by Canadian local governments was educational but not something Indonesia would be able to make use of at this time as it would require legislative changes. The information on calculating user fees and on obtaining additional revenues from local government enterprises had a more immediate relevance as they could possibly be achieved through administrative changes. After the two-day seminar was finished there were field visits to meet with local government financial officers.

Cross-Cultural Learning Continues (1994-1997)

The Canadian and Indonesian participants used these years to learn more about the other country and its people. First impressions are important and we both made efforts to showcase interesting places. A convenient way to do this was to include different locations in the work program. On our first mission Agung had accompanied us to meetings in South Sulawesi and we took advantage of a free weekend to see the Pettakere Caves and explore Makassar. In the three years that followed I joined the IPAC team on trips to Surabaya, East Java; Manado, North Sulawesi; Bandung, West Java; and several spots in Central Java and Bali. The Indonesian mission participants to Canada saw Winnipeg, Montreal, Quebec City, Halifax, Peggy's Cove, and visited the Annapolis

---

21 DG Regional Financial Management, Ministry of Home Affairs.

Valley and South Shore of Nova Scotia. They often added side visits to the Indonesian embassy in Ottawa, the Indonesian consulate in Toronto, and Niagara Falls.

While both Canada and Indonesia were former colonies of other countries that used our natural resources for their benefit, there were differences in their paths to independence. In Indonesia the native population accounts for 95 percent of the total; in Canada it is less than 5 percent. Canada's European settlers started coming to what is now Canada in the early seventeenth century, attracted by the economic opportunities and a temperate climate. They soon outnumbered and later marginalized the Indigenous population and then gained their independence through peaceful means from the mother country. European interest in Indonesia began with the Portuguese in the late sixteenth century, and it was centered on the spice trade. The Dutch soon replaced the Portuguese as the dominant European country in many parts of what is now Indonesia. Initially they set up a trading company called the Vereenidge Oste-Indische Campagnie (VOC)[22]. The VOC went bankrupt in the late eighteenth century, the Dutch crown took over its assets, and within a few decades colonized what it referred to as the Netherlands East Indies. Over time the Dutch expanded the colony's territory to include most of present-day Indonesia. Europeans were less interested in moving to tropical Indonesia than to more temperate climates and there was no shortage of local labour, so the settler population remained small. It was more a Dutch occupation than a Dutch settlement and the local population were not encouraged to speak Dutch. To gain self-rule, Indonesia's Indigenous population had to fight for independence against a foreign occupier. Agung told us about Indonesia's road to independence when he accompanied us to meetings in Surabaya, Indonesia's second city.

---

22 On page 100 of his book, *A Brief History of Indonesia: Sultans, Spices and Tsunamis,* Tim Hannigan observes that corruption throughout the VOC had become so endemic that it had become officially normalized: to obtain an administrative post, a junior company merchant might be expected to make a payment to the appointments board totalling almost ninety times the value of his monthly salary.

The City of Heroes / East Java

During the drive to the governor of East Java's office, Agung told us why Surabaya is called the "City of Heroes." In 1942 Japan invaded Indonesia and replaced the Dutch as its colonial master. When World War II ended with the defeat of Japan in 1945 the Dutch and their allies attempted to recolonize Indonesia. This wasn't what Indonesians wanted. The Battle of Surabaya followed from local reaction to the raising of the Dutch tri-color flag on top of a Surabaya hotel. Young Surabayans climbed the pole and removed the blue section of the flag, leaving only the red and white colours of the Indonesian flag. The youth groups formed a resistance movement and fought with the British for control of the city. The events culminated in a bloody three-week Battle of Surabaya in November 1945. Dutch and allied forces levelled the city and the residents fled to nearby communities. The battle drew international attention to Indonesians' resolve to remain independent. Revolutionary Heroes Day is celebrated in Indonesia on November 10 and a 41-metre obelisk called Heroes Monument, dedicated to those who died in the battle, has been on display in Surabaya since 1952.

East Java province covers more than a third of Java Island, is about the size of Nova Scotia, and has more people than all of Canada. Agung took us to meet with officials at the governor's office and at local government municipalities, where we exchanged presentations on our systems of government and explored areas of future cooperation including local government amalgamations. White-feathered and red-combed roosters (caged or as statues) were common sights around government buildings. In Kabupaten Sidoarjo, Jim made the main Canadian presentation, Sue translated, and Louis and I shared our experience in conducting amalgamation studies. It was my first time speaking to a group of government officials in a foreign country and I kept looking for reactions as Sue translated. There were smiles and nods when it was done but no comments. Afterwards we took a group photo—the Canadian men dressed in suits and ties and all the Indonesians in open-collar beige uniforms with nametags except for the senior administrator, who wore a brown uniform. Sue stood out in her floral print skirt suit. Agung arranged for us to stay at a hotel in downtown Surabaya and when we went out that evening boys with shrill whistles helped us cross the busy streets. There was a large furniture store I found intriguing that had bulky, beautifully crafted pieces made of solid dark wood and embellished with intricate Arabic designs. I also went into a map store and bought a large map of Sidoarjo as I was encouraged by the reception we received there.

North Sulawesi - Independence Holdouts

Our project work took us to Manado and other parts of prosperous North Sulawesi. It was the first time an Institute of Public Administration of Canada team had been north of the equator in Indonesia and to a region that was predominantly Christian. Many of the people there had not supported independence from the Dutch in 1949 and for a while the region was nicknamed "the twelfth province of Holland," at a time when Holland had only eleven. We found that at this point in time, the people there were now proud to be Indonesian.

We were accompanied by Andre and Ardi, two accommodating junior Home Affairs officials we hadn't met before. They were pleasant and professional. Andre was a native of North Sulawesi and was proud to be accompanying us to his home province. We had hoped to have more senior officials from Home Affairs joining us as their presence would have encouraged local commitments in specific areas of cooperation, which we needed if our work in Indonesia was to move forward. On the other hand, we were pleased that Home Affairs had arranged for us to be here and had set up meetings for us.

Manado is located along the coastline of an inlet of the Celebes Sea and surrounded by mountains. In one of the most beautiful parts of Indonesia we found our negotiating skills tested in a hotel with over-priced rooms that were, in a word, depressing. The furniture was old and damaged, it had a musty odor, the air conditioner was broken and there were cockroaches. The initial ask was US$200 (much higher than our rate in Jakarta). After a heated exchange in which we distinguished ourselves from the Javanese, we agreed on US$55. The hotel was operated by the Sahid group. A few days earlier Sue had seen a letter in the *Jakarta Post* which shared an unfavourable view of the hotel chain, and I was puzzled as to why this hotel had been chosen for us. Indonesia had an international reputation for corruption but we hadn't experienced it before. Were we now?

The meetings with provincial and local government officials were a combination of courtesy calls and information sharing. Driving from office to office we could see the area was prosperous. Jim hadn't joined this part of the mission and as I was on the IPAC Board of Directors I made our opening remarks and explained Canada's system of government. Sue translated. Louis and I sought out areas where we could work together such as exploring local government amalgamation in North Sulawesi. My biggest challenge surfaced at a midday meeting with the City of Manado *dinas* (a sectoral local government agency). The speakers' table was set on a raised platform where a whiteboard, which I was using for my presentation, had also been set up. The tropical heat and humidity were overwhelming, and I could feel my energy ebb. The fifty uniformed staff in attendance constantly fanned themselves with sheets of paper and most of them didn't seem to be paying much attention to what I was saying. Sue was translating and I felt my message wasn't getting through. The heat and the absence of a common language was frustrating and although I knew the most we could realistically expect from the meeting was goodwill, I had hoped it would lead to more. I felt better about it once we were back in the air-conditioned van.

On the drive to Kabupaten Minahasa (the Land of Smiling People) we passed horse-drawn taxis sporting canopies. After the meeting we were taken to a bountiful lunch at a roadside restaurant where food was brought to our picnic tables. There was no end to it—fish, rice, meat and vegetable dishes, and fruit including *durian* with its foul smell but delicious taste. An alcoholic drink called *cap tikus* made from palm tree flower stocks capped off the meal. The serving of alcohol reminded me I was in one of Indonesia's few predominantly Christian provinces.

Bali: Island of the Gods

No discussion of Indonesia is complete unless there's a reference to Bali, Indonesia's most popular tourist destination, also known as the Island of the Gods. Bali is a small island similar in size, but not shape, to Prince Edward Island, Canada's smallest province. There were many Hindu kingdoms in Indonesia between the fourth and fifteenth centuries, but Bali is the only part of Indonesia that remains predominantly Hindu. The Balinese are friendly and tolerant and the island has fabulous scenery, a vibrant culture, and offers lots of outdoor adventures. My first trip to Bali was on holiday with my wife Lise before the start of our third IPAC mission[23] in 1996. The previous Christmas I received a Bali guide book and read it over the holidays. At the time I thought Bali couldn't be nearly as wonderful as presented in the book. It turned out to be better. We hired a car and driver who took us to ancient temples, markets, and places of natural beauty such as Lake Batur, a crater lake in a volcanic mountain setting, the seaside temple at Pura Tana Lot, and Ubud, the cultural hub of Bali. We watched traditional performances—the Barong Keris Dance and the Kecak Fire Dance.

It was all wonderful except for the visit to Ubud's Sacred Monkey Forest Sanctuary, home of the Balinese long-tailed monkey. I had always thought of monkeys as helpful and good—in the Sanskrit epic the *Ramayana* they help Prince Rama rescue his wife Sita from the demon Rahwana. In the Barong dance they are playful. It was my first visit to a monkey forest and it started out well. A wide pathway wound its way through tall green-leaved trees, past moss-covered temples, walls, and statues, and over quiet streams. Birds chirped and monkeys chattered and screeched. I was standing with my hands in my pants pockets enjoying the heat and the earth smell of damp moss when an adult monkey approached. He growled and then grabbed at my front pockets. I was

---

23 This was the first mission without Sue McLellan, who had recently accepted a position with the British High Commission in Ottawa.

under attack and didn't know what to do. A passerby shouted for me to take my hands out of my pockets. I did and at the sight of my empty hands the monkey turned away. He thought I had food in my pockets. I've been wary of monkeys ever since.

The few days in Bali provided a different view of Indonesia beyond what I had seen in Java and Sulawesi. The following year I was back in Bali, this time for the assessment of the one-stop shops in Gianyar Regency. On Sunday afternoon Neil and I along with staff from Home Affairs flew to Denpasar Bali and checked into the Natour Hotel in Kuta. Kuta Beach is a popular destination for Western tourists, especially Australians. It's sandy, five kilometres long, and beautiful. The thing that didn't feel right to me about it then was the contrast of scantily clad, beer drinking Westerners on a beach in the midst of a modest, conservative Indonesian community. I wouldn't think twice about this scene on a beach in North America or some parts of the Caribbean but it felt out of place here.

After sunset I joined my colleagues for an early evening walk on Kuta Beach. After we turned around and started walking back, a group of young men came up quickly behind us then kept on going. I was taken aback by their speed and energy and realized how vulnerable we could have appeared to them in other circumstances. After dinner at the hotel, we listened to a three-piece band playing old rock and roll. Neil Sedaka's *Oh! Carol* was one of their favourites and we sang along.

The next day we drove to Gianyar and finished up in time to return to Denpasar before dark. On the flight back to Jakarta I read a letter to the editor of the *Jakarta Post* about a twenty-year-old British university student named Peter who had been bludgeoned (and died later) on Kuta Beach. It took his friend three days to locate him in a Denpasar hospital as he had no identification. The aggressors were thought to be antisocial persons from other parts of Indonesia, not Balinese. The writer extended condolences to Peter's family and commented "grief shared is halved." That comment stayed with me and I used it years later when I sent a card of condolence to the parents of a young man in Halifax who like Peter had died much too young.

Yogyakarta / Central Java Weekend Interlude

Yogyakarta is another Indonesian favourite for both tourists and Indonesians. It's a provincial-level autonomous region and referred to as a special territory, or sultanate. Located in the centre of Java, it was given this status at the time of Indonesian independence because of the then-sultan's support in the struggle for independence, when the internationally unrecognized new republic moved its capital from Jakarta to Yogyakarta for safety reasons. For people interested in Javanese history and culture who want to learn the Indonesian language, it's the place to go. During the 1997 mission Neil Balcom and I had a free weekend between sister-province meetings in Bandung and a one-stop shop assessment in Bali. Yogyakarta is located between these two locations so Home Affairs arranged for us to spend the weekend there and had two junior officials accompany us. Lies (pronounced as lease) Kurniawati, a member of Agung's staff, organized the activities along with her colleague Radi. Lies came from a well-to-do family in Gorontalo (Sulawesi), was in her thirties and widowed. She had a child (who became a physician) whom she didn't like to talk about with us and she would deflect any questions with a demure laugh. Lies had long wavy hair, darker skin than the Javanese, a slim figure, and wore glasses. There was something about the set of her jaw that reminded me of my childhood piano teacher. When she travelled with us she liked to wear Western-style clothes—blue jeans, plaid shirts, polo tops. Her demeanor was typical of many Indonesian women working at Home Affairs in the 1990s—deferential to those (mostly men) in the hierarchy, passive in meetings, obedient in following instructions, relaxed among peers, and fun loving outside of formal settings. This demeanor evolved in Indonesia, as was evidenced by a 2019 delegation of three women from West Java province who came to Dalhousie University in 2019 to discuss a training and education partnership. They were forthright, confident and very much in charge.

Our Home Affairs guides organized a busy weekend that took in all the highlights of this popular tourist area—the eighth-century

Borobudur Temple (one of the seven wonders of the ancient world), the nineth-century Prambanan Hindu Temple, Mount Merapi, and Parangtritis Beach (in the domain of the Queen of the Southern Ocean) on the mystic southern coast. The Keraton, or sultan's palace, forms a model of the Javanese cosmos in miniature. We went in the heat of the afternoon and spent most of the time in the pavilions away from the open courtyard. Court retainers, who serve the court or sultan, dressed in *batik* guarded entrances and gateways and our timing was right for watching a group of five bare-shouldered elderly women walk slowly and ceremoniously across the courtyard to bring tea to the sultan. It felt like we had gone back in time to a far-off land. Four carried the tea and accessories and the fifth carried what appeared to be a large parasol, though it may have been some symbolic part of the ritual. If we'd visited earlier in the day we would have caught the *gamelan* (an Indigenous orchestra made up of mostly gongs and other metal instruments) rehearsal. In the evenings we went to the Malioboro section of the city to see the Ramayana Ballet, had meals at the food stalls, listened to street musicians, and did a bit of souvenir shopping. One evening Lies had a street artist draw portraits of Neil and me and gave them to us as gifts. I look more Indonesian, especially around the eyes, in mine than I do in real life and he shaped my lips into something close to a cruel sneer.

During our weekend in Yogyakarta Lies asked a street artists to draw Neil and I. This was the result.

Lies and Radi stocked up on *salak* (snakeskin fruit) and *rambutan* (hairy fruit) so we could snack in the van when driving. Lies bought *durian* when we stopped for lunch. An Indonesian saying is that *durian* tastes like heaven and smells like hell. It is not allowed in some hotels and confined public spaces. Lies had the *durian* sliced and cut into portions, which we ate at an outdoor table. After eating a piece, Neil turned to our Indonesian driver sitting next to him and said, "I don't like the taste of *durian*! Do you?" The response was a tactful, "Indonesians like *durian*," that avoided disagreement. I was learning that Indonesians prefer harmony and would sometimes be indirect when choosing words. The word *belum* (not yet) instead of a straight no is an example. On our second mission the IPAC team took a taxi to the Jakarta airport to catch a flight to Surabaya. The driver asked where we were going and Sue asked in Indonesian if he had been there. "Belum," he replied. A Canadian would have answered with a direct "no" rather than a more harmonious "not yet." I've started saying "not yet" more, sometimes in the way it would normally be used in Canada, but also for things I would never want to do. If my tone is right the latter usually gets a laugh.

When observing Lies as our capable and quietly confident tour director I was impressed with her kindness toward others. An older thin, frail man interceded unnecessarily to help park the van in a tight space. He had a whistle and used it along with dramatic arm gestures. It was time consuming and I reacted in a non-Javanese way, gripping the inside door handle, sighing impatiently, while thinking, *Enough already, why can't we just park and get on with our day*? Lies thanked him and passed him a handful of rupiah. She quietly tipped everyone who helped us whether we benefitted or not. Obviously, I was still learning the Javanese ways.

Neil and I were so taken with the wonderful hospitality shown to us by Lies and Radi in Yogyakarta and Bali we offered to take them out to dinner in Jakarta. They chose a Japanese restaurant at the Hotel President in the business district. The top-floor restaurant had a spectacular view of the Jakarta skyline and many of the diners were well-dressed Chinese. Radi's husband and Fauzi, our Home Affairs driver, joined us. No alcohol was served. When presented with the bill Neil and

I were expecting something close to what we would pay for a similar meal for six without alcohol in Canada. My pulse quickened when I saw an amount equivalent to our weekly per diem allowance. This restaurant was more exclusive than I thought. Afterwards the Indonesians became the hosts and took us to a karaoke bar not far from the restaurant. Lies arranged for a private room and Fauzi programmed the songs; mostly Western pop tunes (*Oh! Carol*, *Hotel California*, Beatles songs) and romantic Indonesian songs (*Widuri* was a favourite). We all sang. The final song of the evening was *Auld Lang Syne*, even though it wasn't New Years Eve.

Jakarta Hospitality

Whenever there was free time in Jakarta I liked to explore the city by cab or on foot. Fatahillah Square sits at the heart of the former Dutch administration capital, and the surrounding Dutch colonial buildings have been restored. Sunda Kelapa, or old harbour, is the site of the East India Trading Company post where the Ciliwung River meets the sea. Domestic commercial sailing fleets were still using the old port in the 1990s and I watched stevedores unloading lumber, probably from Kalimantan. Monas (national monument), Jakarta's most visible landmark, is in the centre of Medan Merdeka (Freedom Square), a large park at the heart of Jakarta. My first impression upon viewing the scenes from Indonesian history housed in the base of the monument was that the period of Dutch colonialism did nothing that benefited the lives of Indonesians. The author of *Jakarta Inside Out* takes a different view when he refers to the dioramas as depicting watershed moments in Indonesian history through the eyes of the paranoid Suharto regime— arguably the greatest re-writers of history ever.[24]

The National Museum and the shopping areas were on my list of places to see. The Pasar Baru (New Market) was within walking distance of our hotel. Getting there was part of the Indonesian experience.

---

24 *Jakarta Inside Out*, Daniel Ziv, Equinox Publishing (Asia) Pte. Ltd Jakarta, 2002 p. 98.

My usual route when walking there with the IPAC team from the Borobudur Hotel went through Lapangan Banteng (Cattle Square), past the West Irian Monument (a.k.a. the Incredible Hulk), the Supreme Court and the neo-gothic cathedral, a mad dash across two busy intersections with no traffic lights, past a row of food carts and street paintings, up a flight of metal stairs, and across the bridge over the canal. By then we are at the gated south end of a long market street named Jalan Pasar Baru and sweating profusely after ten to fifteen minutes of Jakarta heat. Established in the 1820s, it became the busiest shopping district in Jakarta until the malls took over, similar to the transition from downtown to shopping mall trend in North America. It's still a lively place. The street is lined with two- and three-storey buildings and there is a multi-storey shopping centre at its north end. There is an assortment of stalls, kiosks and food vendors set up in the middle of the street and at street corners. The shops sell textiles (materials and clothes), crafts, footwear (there was a shoe store called Canada and another one called Toronto), gold, silver, art, jewelry, food, and most anything else an Indonesian living in Jakarta would want to buy. I liked the smell of damp earth, fried rice and *kretek* cigarettes, as well as the flapping of sandals, the laughter, and non-aggressive crowds.

On our first visit there Jim, Louis and I had our evening meal at a Macdonald's restaurant as we weren't sure if Indonesian food at Pasar Baru would agree with us. We chose a window seat overlooking the street and then wished we hadn't as a group of hungry children gathered on the other side of the window. On the walk back to the hotel we were approached by a group of male sex workers who said we were handsome, and they would like to come to our hotel. When we shared the story with Sue at breakfast, she jokingly said the reference to us being handsome was a reflection of an Indonesian culture that avoids giving offence so we might want a second opinion. We took the ribbing all in good fun.

There were two occasions when Indonesian hospitality extended beyond the workplace. On the final evening of our third mission (which included spouses) to Indonesia, Agung hosted a dinner for us at an outdoor venue that served local dishes. He was the sole Home Affairs representative and his wife Lili accompanied him. They brought their wedding pictures to show us. We were awed by the beauty of their colourful regional wedding costumes and with the young couple in the photos. Agung took charge of the menu and several dishes were placed on the long table. I was glad that we were developing something more than a working relationship with at least one Indonesian from Home Affairs.

In the fourth year of the project, I was invited to the home of an Indonesian colleague for the first time. Edi Suhadi, the contrarian from the October 1995 mission to Canada, invited me to dine with him and his wife at their home. They sent their driver, who carried a letter of introduction, to my hotel. Edi's house was surrounded by cement walls and barbed wire like the other homes in the area. It was an attractive two-storey property with three rooms (reception, kitchen / dining room, den / office) and a bath downstairs. The bedrooms were upstairs and a verandah overlooked a large backyard. The floors were covered in white tiles, and the walls were plain. The refrigerator was tall and narrow. I hoped I wouldn't be asked to help rearrange the beautiful, but bulky, wood furniture. Sweet tea and banana fritters were served before the main meal of rice with fried chicken and *gado-gado*. We ate in a traditional Javanese style, using our hands and rinsing them in finger bowls. Afterwards we had a conversation on the verandah and Edi demonstrated his yoga abilities by doing a headstand. Before leaving Edi and I exchanged small gifts. I received Bugis silk (for my wife) and a Sumatra tie clip.

Southeast Asia Conference and Stopovers

The IPAC team's learning and travel experiences from the project were not limited to Indonesia. One of our activities was an international conference on decentralization held in Manila and organized jointly by Institute of Public Administration of Canada and the University of the Philippines' Local Government Academy. Manila had a totally different feel from its Indonesian neighbour. Many of the people there spoke English and dressed in a Western style—lots of T-shirts and jeans. Armed security officers stood at the doors of shops and restaurants, including a McDonald's.

Jim Beaulieu arranged for a number of Canadians to speak at the conference, and I made a presentation on generating local government revenues. Paul Thomas, a respected Canadian academic and editor of the IPAC academic journal, was the keynote speaker. Paul liked to include a bit of humour in his talks and told the story of a speaker introduction he received from a nervous woman who said, "I'd like to introduce Paul Thomas our next speaker, who deserves no introduction." Except for the Canadians present, the audience remained stone faced. Humour doesn't always translate well even with a common language.

There were stopovers in other Asian cities and Louis and I spent nights in Seoul, Bangkok, Hong Kong, and Singapore. On one occasion I arranged a meeting with a senior manager at the Scotia Investment Banking Centre in Singapore to discuss local government financing in the region. My day job focused on financing local government infrastructure in Canada. I was eager to understand how it worked in Southeast Asia, thinking it could be an area of focus for our cooperation in Indonesia, a country with lots of public infrastructure that needed to be built or improved. The term that later became popular in Canada when referring to this need is "infrastructure deficit."

Nova Scotia Weekends

Our Indonesian colleagues also learned more about Canada, and Nova Scotia in particular. Nova Scotia has a rich and rocky colonial and Canadian history that spans four centuries. We provided a taste of it during the initial mission when we took the group to the Habitation on the shores of the Annapolis Basin.

When Agung brought thirty Indonesians to learn more about one-stop shops we organized a Saturday bus trip to Lunenburg, an historic town on Nova Scotia's South Shore. Sue came down from Ottawa to join us for the weekend activities and we were all thrilled to see her.

She shared two pieces of news. The good news was that she enjoyed her work at the high commission. The sad news was that she had cancer. She said, "I'm not going to let that keep me from enjoying the weekend activities with all of you." And it didn't. This was Agung and Lili's third Canadian mission and by now they were becoming familiar with the Nova Scotia lifestyle. They boarded the bus wearing jeans and sweat-shirts; Agung's had "Halifax" written on the front and Lili's had puffins. Lili wore her hair long and they looked like a couple enjoying a holiday with friends. I liked the image. We stopped at Peggy's Cove and took photos before arriving in Lunenburg. Mayor Laurence Mawhinney, also an executive member of the Federation of Canadian Municipalities, met with the group and talked with them about service provision and finan-cial issues facing Canadian municipalities.

Agung and Lili on the Lunenburg Waterfront, September 1996.

Afterwards we took a guided walking tour of Old Lunenburg (a UNESCO World Heritage site). In addition to visiting places of interest on the waterfront and along the town's streets, the guide arranged for a tour of the historic St. John's Anglican Church. Lies Kurniawati was among a small number of Indonesians who were not comfortable setting foot inside a Christian church. Most of our Indonesian colleagues were Sunni Muslims. Over the years we made efforts to accommodate their prayer schedule (five times a day with exceptions while travelling) and find locations for them to attend Friday prayers. The Dalhousie campus was one of them.

On the bus ride back to Halifax we took the motorway to save time. The Indonesians began laughing. The autumn colours on the trees caught their attention and some were yellow, the colour of Indonesia's ruling Golkar party. The joke was that the trees were voting for Golkar. Agung took the reference to Golkar as an opportunity to share an incident that took place at Canadian customs when the group arrived. One of the non-English-speaking participants who was new to international travel was asked how much money he was bringing into the country. Four million, he replied. The immigration officer asked what it was for. He replied it was for hotel and meal expenses. The official said, "Don't you have a credit card like a Visa or a gold card?" "Yes, I do," he said and took out his wallet and showed his Golkar Membership card. At this point Agung intervened and explained that the figure provided was in Indonesian rupiah and the equivalent of US$2,000.

The bus motored along the highway, bordered by miles of forest on both sides, prompting the question, "Where are all the people?" With a small population relative to our land mass and lots of empty spaces to build highways there's often not much to see beyond the trees on our trunk highways. To our Indonesian colleagues it was like driving through a no man's land.

A farewell dinner was held at the Radisson Hotel after we returned from Lunenburg. Our Indonesian colleagues dressed Western style when participating in the daytime activities on mission to Canada and wore uniforms when we worked with them in Indonesia. For evening events such as dinners and socials some of our colleagues liked to wear *batik* shirts and blouses. The male Indonesian participants dressed for dinner in either sports jackets with open-necked shirts or formal *batik*. Agung was the exception as he was still wearing his Halifax sweatshirt (but with black slacks). Was he becoming more Canadian with each mission? The female Indonesian participants wore jackets or blouses with skirts or slacks. I wore a *batik* shirt purchased in Jakarta. Lise, Lili, and Sue all wore dresses. Each of the Indonesian participants received a certificate confirming their participation in the One-Stop Shop Seminar. Agung called out each recipient's name and I presented the certificates. Small gifts were exchanged. Lise and I each received Indonesian puppets.

An exchange of gifts was part of the mission's 1996 farewell dinner at the Radisson Hotel in Halifax. Lili, Agung, Lise and I pose for a photo holding the Indonesian puppets we received.

The gifts we gave came either from the Nova Scotia Protocol Office or Jennifer's of Nova Scotia, a shop that specializes in Maritime gifts. They were appreciated but it was the certificates that were treasured. The value of these certificates was demonstrated the following year when one of the participants, Ramba Pahan, was inadvertently left off the list and showed deep disappointment bordering on shame when he was overlooked. He received his certificate the next day before leaving for the airport.

The farewell dinner at the Raddison Hotel marked the end of Sue's involvement with the project. We kept in touch after she returned to Ottawa and underwent cancer treatments. She sent me an Indonesian cookbook with recipes for the dishes we had enjoyed during our missions and continued to offer advice. She died the following year after her short, courageous battle with cancer. I can't say enough about how her experience, language skills, and cultural awareness contributed to getting the IPAC – Indonesia cooperation off the ground. Sue was always upbeat and I would miss her both as an inspiration for the project and as a friend. By this time Agung and I had become the informal leaders of the project.

South Shore Exploring with Agung and Lili

There was no partners program as part of the missions to Canada and Lili was the only spouse to ever join the group. Lise and I were growing closer to Lili and Agung so when I was in Kentville with Agung, Lise took Lili to Mahone Bay, a popular tourist town on the South Shore. Summer items were on sale and Lili visited every store in town. She left with a large shopping bag of gifts decorated with symbols of Canada. That evening we invited Agung and Lili to our home for dinner. Agung showed me his way of preparing sticky rice (*nasi putih*). He washed and drained the rice and placed it in a pot. Water was added (double the volume of rice), the rice was brought to a boil, the heat was reduced, and it cooked for twenty minutes with water added as needed and no stirring.

The following year on a Friday afternoon in October when the other participants were preparing for the long flight home to Indonesia, Lise and I picked up Agung and Lili and drove down Nova Scotia's South Shore, further than Mahone Bay this time. It was dark by the time we stopped for a meal at Wong's Chinese restaurant in Liverpool where we knew there would be rice on the menu. Afterwards we travelled along the Lighthouse Route to Summerville Beach and checked in at the Quarterdeck, a white-sand beachside resort.

Early the next morning we went for a beach walk. Agung was

An unofficial spouses / partners program. Lise and Lili drove to Mahone Bay to check out the scenery and the shops. September 1996

barefoot and even though the sun was warming the sand, he found it cold underfoot. He made hopping movements to avoid the cold, which we found funny and had a good laugh. He said "Indian summer" was his favourite time of year in Nova Scotia.

We packed up and continued along the Lighthouse Route to Shelburne. A couple we knew, who had a daughter living in Southeast Asia, joined us for lunch at a Chinese restaurant on Water Street. After lunch we experienced our only tense moment of the weekend. While touring the historic Loyalist town, I turned the wrong way onto one-way Dock Street. I realized the error immediately and backed up on the side street intersection just as two men in a pickup truck came up the street. The driver rolled down his window and both men berated us (me) for our stupidity. At one point I thought they were going to get out of the truck, run amok[25] and assault us. Agung and Lili stayed still and quiet during this outburst of road rage. This was a new experience

---

25 Amok, or running amok, is derived from the Malay word mengamok, which means to make a furious and desperate charge. Captain Cook is credited with making the first outside observations and recordings of amok in the Malay tribesmen in 1770 during his around-the-world voyage.

for them. I had never experienced or heard of road rage in gridlocked Jakarta, where it can take hours to drive a short distance in rush hour traffic. After the incident we continued our tour and conversation as if nothing had happened. I couldn't find the words to explain the aspect of our culture that enabled this behavior and Agung and Lili preferred to ignore the incident and maintain harmony (*rukum*).

Taking stock: A Boost for International Cooperation

By the end of 1997 IPAC had been working together on administrative decentralization with the Government of Indonesian for four years. CIDA was now willing to establish a three-year International Cooperation Agreement with IPAC. It would allow our work to continue in Indonesia and another half dozen IPAC partner countries. It's now time to take stock.

Our IPAC team had a limited understanding of Indonesian politics and priorities at this point. We had learned about its colonial and post-independence history and knew that both involved a highly centralized form of government. Within this unitary state, there were twenty-seven provinces (referred to as local government level one), 305 local governments level two (cities and regencies), 3,844 sub districts, and 65,852 villages. Indonesian independence was based on the five principles of Pancasila, or unity in diversity, which were monotheism, civilized humanity, national unity, social justice, and deliberative democracy. The highly centralized governance model was standing in the way of economic development, which was controlled through central planning. The Government of Indonesia was interested in learning about the decentralized model for public service delivery used in Canada. We were aware that corruption and military involvement in politics were two areas of concern, elections were not free and fair, and we were not to advocate for legislative reforms. We had no first-hand knowledge of what the government considered to be its major priorities, nor had we gained the level of trust of our Indonesian colleagues needed for this discussion. Even if we had their trust, they would be reluctant to level with us in the current political environment and risk being seen as dis-loyal. We fared better in terms of learning about the culture and history, thanks to Sue's prior experience in the region and the in-country travel that was part of our annual mission programs.

The objective during our initial missions was to explore ways we could work together to implement administrative decentralization reforms in Indonesia. Our attention centered on service delivery through the implementation of, and improvements to, the one-stop shop model. IPAC provided workshops and field visits to one-stop shops in Montreal and Nova Scotia and undertook an assessment of the one-stop shop in Gianyar. The second project involving a sister province part-nership started out well with general discussions but was stalled by the economic and political fallout from the 1997-1998 Asian financial crisis. A mission with thirty participating Indonesians dedicated to revenue generation had been successful from a learning and exposure point of view but meaningful change in this area would require political reforms that were beyond the scope of our cooperation. The local government amalgamation studies were a non-starter. The groundwork was laid for future areas of cooperation involving knowledge sharing and tech-nical assistance. The IPAC international programs were peer-to-peer, meaning that public servants in Canada worked with public servants in other countries in areas of shared interest and expertise. This appealed to our Indonesian colleagues as they were able to work with Canadian practitioners. Our annual action plans provided flexibility as Indonesian priorities evolved and our Home Affairs colleagues, who set the priori-ties, appreciated this feature of our cooperation.

Agung and I had built a good working relationship and I was get-ting helpful information and advice from Jeffrey Ong at the Canadian embassy in Jakarta. In these early years, communication between mis-sions was difficult as we hadn't started to use email to correspond with Indonesian colleagues. The eleven-hour time difference limited our ability to schedule phone calls. Using a land line, I would call Agung on his cell phone around 9 a.m. AST when it would be evening in Jakarta to discuss our upcoming missions. We also used our fax machines.

Sue MacLennan's departure from the project left a local language and knowledge gap that was hard to fill. Louis Dussault became less involved due to additional work responsibilities during a Quebec government restructuring. Jim Beaulieu remained involved but had limited time available for the project. He had left the Manitoba government and set up an international consulting company that took most of his time. I took on the Canadian side of the leadership as I was the only one both willing and in a position to make the project a priority. It was also a good fit for my education and background in local government finance and administration and local-central government relations. Nova Scotia welcomed the opportunity to be the provincial lead on the IPAC—Indonesia partnership.

On the Indonesian side Agung was our most dedicated and reliable contact. When he wasn't available to accompany us in Indonesia he kept in close contact with those who did. In our early years there were a number of changes in senior positions (secretary general, head of Planning Bureau, head of Centre for Management of Overseas Cooperation) at Home Affairs that made Agung's involvement even more important.

There was a bit of culture shock experienced by mission participants on both sides. It caused some disruptive behavior behind the scenes but fortunately didn't detract from the work.

I felt I was learning and growing from my involvement in the project. My term on the IPAC Board of Directors ran from 1992-1998 and I was able to share my experiences with other board members involved in similar peer-to-peer CIDA funded IPAC projects in Africa and the Philippines. I was also a member (and later chair) of IPAC's International Committee, which provided me with insights into international project work.

The annual missions to Indonesia were rewarding from both a professional and personal perspective. I learned more about governance in Canada through comparisons of what I learned about Indonesia. I still hadn't grasped the significance of some of the things I was exposed to in Indonesia like the involvement of the military in politics and business that appeared so unusual to a life-long resident of Canada. Over these years I saw my uninformed pre-involvement view of Indonesia change.

It evolved from one of a tropical country prone to natural disasters with rich soil, exotic spice islands and too many ethnic groups to count, to a more informed, mostly positive view of a beautiful country with a rich culture, history and civilization that had a long way to go to reduce inequality and improve the quality of life of its poorer citizens.

Our project may have played a small part in promoting Canadian unity. In 1995 there were calls for more autonomy by provinces in both Canada and Indonesia. Louis Dussault, the Quebec member of our IPAC team, joined us in Nova Scotia on the last day of the program planning meetings. It was a warm evening, so Louis and I took a walk along the Halifax Harbour boardwalk after dinner. A provincial referendum on Quebec independence from Canada was taking place later in the month and it was expected to be close. I didn't know how Louis would vote but I did know Quebec culture and history were important to him. Looking out along the harbour he shared his thought that "Canada is such a wonderful country I would not want to see it break up." Louis never mentioned how he voted but the stay-in-Canada side won the referendum by a narrow margin.

PART 2

Winds of Change: Turmoil Sparks Potential New Program Areas (1998-2001)

"Show me the heroes that the youth of your country look up to, and I will tell you the future of your country."

— Idowu Koyenikan

Agung and I are in the backseat of a Bluebird taxi driving north on a crowded Jakarta side street. It's February 24, 1998, and the late afternoon traffic is heavy. The driver is taking a shortcut through a narrow street that could pass for a lane. Parked cars, oncoming traffic, orange, three-wheel smoke-belching taxis called *bajaj*, and pedestrians compete for the limited space. The scent of *kretek* cigarettes and damp earth permeate the air in 28° Celsius temperatures. The rain has stopped but large puddles encroach on the sides and middle of the street. Our driver is patient and eventually we're back on a main road. Our return trip from meeting with the director of the Institute of Government Studies in South Jakarta is nearly over. We're not far from Monas (National Monument), the landmark near the Home Affairs headquarters. Louis and Lies left in another taxi at the same time. Agung is quieter than usual and alert to our surroundings. He tells me, "This is not a good time for the IPAC team to be in Indonesia." I ask why and he replies, "The Asian financial crisis had caused a major devaluation of the rupiah, there's public unrest and a lot of uncertainty as to where this will lead. It's already having a major impact on affordability and people are worried."

We've just begun the next phase of our cooperation and, although I don't know it yet, it's going to change in unexpected ways.

A Time of Political Transition

The results of the early years of our cooperation confirmed that Canada and Indonesia (through Home Affairs, the Institute of Public Administration of Canada, and Nova Scotia) could work together. We were already cooperating in three areas[26] that were within the

---

26 One-stop shops, sister province, and revenue generation.

administrative decentralization boundaries and would support economic development.

The next phase of our cooperation was arranged through a three-year International Cooperation Agreement between IPAC and the Canadian International Development Agency (CIDA). The goal of the agreement (1998-2001) as it related to the Indonesia– IPAC, and Nova Scotia cooperation was to support Indonesian government initiatives on decentralization, public sector reform, and capacity building. Our partnership emphasized sharing knowledge and experience in the area of administrative decentralization, supporting Indonesia in improving public services, and building a long-term relationship. Our Indonesian colleagues asked us to work with them on improving local government enterprise management, local government finance, good governance, and public sector training and education. As the decentralization effort gained momentum the need for different kinds of Canadian expertise increased. Our mission teams went from the same individuals in the early (planning stage) years to including others with specific knowledge or skills related to the individual projects. Our program was peer-to-peer and priority areas of our cooperation were still determined by Home Affairs.

I expected the activities of the three-year agreement would follow the pattern we had already established by expanding our work in existing areas and adding others where we could make administrative improvements to streamline processes or provide services. It didn't work out that way at all.

This period saw the first major political change since Suharto took control and became Indonesia's second president thirty years earlier. Indonesia faced an economic crisis and as a result there were changes in government leadership and policy direction. This included opening the door to political reform and decentralization.

These changes were triggered by the Asian financial crisis of 1997-98 that Agung had expressed concerns about. The economies of Southeast Asia were dependent on exports and foreign investment and the countries there needed US dollars to meet their financial obligations. When the United States increased its interest rate, the American dollar appreciated as did the currencies linked to it. The Thai baht was one of them. When it severed its link with the dollar, the currency devalued. This resulted in capital flowing out of the country and later the region including Indonesia, which had a large US dollar-denominated debt. The International Monetary Fund (IMF) intervened and ended the crisis by providing loans to stabilize the economies that were impacted. As this was unfolding, in keeping with past practice, Suharto was re-elected president for another five-year term (his seventh) by the People's Consultative Assembly in March 1998.

Shortly after Suharto's re-election, the IMF, which was providing a bailout package with set conditions, directed the Indonesian government to cut fuel subsidies. It did so on May 4, 1998. Later that day students responded by rioting in Medan, Sumatra's largest city. On May 12 students protested in Jakarta and four of them were killed by security forces. Non-student mobs ran amok in Jakarta looting and destroying property (hotels, shops, banks, homes). Glodok, the commercial heart of Jakarta's Chinatown, was one of the areas targeted. Except for guarding large hotels and a few Western chains, security forces made no attempt to subdue the mob. President Suharto returned from a Group of 15 Summit in Cairo on May 14 and order was restored by the army. Protests continued and a few days later demonstrators arrived at the Indonesian parliament. Suharto resigned as president on May 21, 1998 and was replaced by vice-president B.J. Habibie.

President Habibie instituted a number of democratic reforms that allowed greater media freedom, the formation of new political parties, and the release of political prisoners. He endorsed decentralization and promoted regional and local autonomy to empower provincial, city and county/regency governments. Two provinces, Aceh and Irian Jaya (now Papua) were granted special autonomy status in the areas of governance and fiscal policy. The economy improved but the rupiah remained weak.

The political and economic fallout from the Asian financial crisis impacted our project in two ways. The first is that it opened the door for us to cooperate on political reforms. Up until now our mandate was solely related to administrative decentralization by encouraging more efficiency in service delivery through initiatives like the one-stop shops and local government enterprise management. Going forward we could also work with Home Affairs in implementing political reforms. This would require training for elected officials from local governments with new responsibilities and accountabilities such as meeting established service standards and evaluating service delivery options. Major changes were coming and IPAC, Nova Scotia, and I all wanted to be part of it.

The second way our cooperation was impacted was by the change in size and composition of the Indonesian missions to Canada. There were only four participants in the August 1998 mission and they were all from Home Affairs and sponsored by the IPAC program. There had been thirty or more participants in each of the previous two missions to Canada, the majority of them from (and sponsored by) Indonesian local governments. For the 1996 and 1997 IPAC missions the exchange rate was roughly 2,000 rupiah to US$1. In 1998 it took over 10,000 rupiah to purchase one US dollar. Sponsoring delegates to a Canadian study mission during an economic crisis with a currency in free fall was far from the top of local government priorities.

Inception Mission Possible – International Cooperation

Agung, Lies and Home Affairs staff in Jakarta during the quiet days before the protests that led to Suharto's resignation in May of 1998.

The renewed program started with an IPAC inception mission to Indonesia. It took place in mid-February 1998 between two crucial dates—the issuance of the January 6 budget statement and the resignation of President Suharto on May 21. Louis Dussault and I were joined by Cathie McDonald who came to help Home Affairs plan an international workshop on local government enterprise (LGE) management in Jakarta[27]. Cathie had recently retired from the City of Toronto and had experience organizing conferences and workshops. She was tall and fair, an experienced traveller and a welcome addition.

The rupiah had lost 80 percent of its value against the US dollar since our 1997 mission. The Borobudur Hotel rates were still quoted in US dollars so there were no cost reductions for the IPAC budget, but the hotel was feeling the impact of the economic crisis nonetheless. The occupancy rate had dropped to 25 percent.

Agung was concerned about our security during this period of turmoil and accompanied us the whole time. As it was an inception mission there were more courtesy calls than usual at the ministries of Home Affairs, Finance, and MENPAN (Ministry of State Apparatus Utilization and Bureaucratic Reform). Agung organized and chaired a lunch meeting with Canadian embassy staff, which included Jeffrey Ong, before accompanying Louis and me to Bandung by train. Agung always travelled light, but I hadn't mastered the art of doing so in 1998. I had two large suitcases and was losing patience as I struggled to navigate them through the station stairs and turnstiles. Before I reached the point of clearly distinguishing myself from the Javanese, Agung quietly look one of my suitcases and carried it on the train.

We spent the night in Bandung and met the next day with the vice-governor of West Java to discuss our sister province initiative. Agung made the introductions and kept the discussion moving forward. We exchanged information about our provinces and countries and identified common industries such as agriculture, fishing, and marine activities, and public service priority areas where we could cooperate. We agreed

---

27 Due to delays caused by the Asian financial crisis and 9/11 the workshop would not take place until March 2003.

to prepare a letter of intent to develop a sister province agreement before the IPAC team left Indonesia. When we arrived back in Jakarta Lili was waiting for us at the train station and drove us to our hotel. On Friday we met with Agung to discuss post-secondary education for public servants and with Dr. May at GTZ to ask him for his thoughts about the international local government enterprise workshop.

Cathie spent the next week planning an agenda for the workshop on local government enterprises. Agung arranged for Louis and me to meet Ryaas Rasyid, director of the Institute of Government Studies. We travelled in two taxis: Agung and me in one, Louis and Lies in the other. This is when Agung told me that he was worried about our safety during this unsettled period in Indonesia and said, "I wanted to postpone our mission but was overruled."

I spent the next day at the hotel business centre working on a West Java proposal. Agung attended the signing of the MOU and 1998-1999 workplan where the Indonesian officials projected a business-as-usual approach. In reviewing the events leading up to and following our 1998 mission I've concluded that Agung was right to be concerned. We were there during that short interval between the January 6 budget statement when the rupiah was falling and runs on supermarkets were taking place, and President Suharto's re-election a few days after we left Indonesia. I was focused on the inception mission and moving our cooperation forward, so I didn't think much about being in danger. Home Affairs staff had always managed our schedule and I trusted them to keep us safe. I was concerned about the hardships Indonesians were facing from the steep drop in the value of the rupiah and its negative impact on prices and the economy and less concerned about my safety

New Secretary General Takes Lead Role

Our annual missions continued though it took a few years before the number of Indonesians participating in missions to Canada was back to pre-Asian financial crisis levels. Improving local government enterprise management was an Indonesian priority in the early part of our

International Cooperation Agreement, and Agung and Timbal led a four-person mission to Canada in the late summer of 1998 to learn more about the Canadian experience. In Calgary we showcased LGE management through presentations and site visits. In Halifax we focused on local government enterprise management issues related to water services. Profitable local government enterprises were an important source of Indonesian local government revenues and the mission participants were looking for ways to make them more efficient. We discussed what the change in Indonesian presidents would mean for our project. It was still early days but our Indonesian colleagues expected that more autonomy and responsibilities would be given to Indonesian provinces and local governments.

During the 1998 mission the Indonesians took part in their first Institute of Public Administration of Canada annual conference, which was held in Montreal. The keynote speaker's address fit with the new public management practices that were in vogue during the 1990s. In his slide presentation he championed the value of renewal and used a forest fire and regrowth analogy to make his points. He was an excellent speaker but the content wasn't new to me. When I saw Agung after the session he was calm and relaxed. He said he was inspired by the presentation and liked the forest fire analogy. He was already thinking about how he could apply the new public management ideas to local government enterprises in Indonesia.

Five months later an IPAC team went to Indonesia to work on the LGE project. The rupiah was now trading at 3,700 for a US$1 (or 5,461 to the Canadian dollar). This was close to double the 2,000-to-US$1 exchange rate at the time of our 1997 mission but a major improvement from our 1998 mission rate of 11,000 to US$1. Because we were not in Indonesia during the worst of the financial crisis and the subsequent unrest, our group had no first-hand knowledge of the impact it had on the city and its residents. We knew that the number of people living in poverty had increased, and that hefty price increases for essentials had caused hardship and aggression. We were aware that businesses relying on imports had shut down and some banks had closed. Ethnic Chinese, who control a disproportionate share of the country's wealth, had become targets of violence across the country. However, by the time the IPAC team arrived in February 1999 the government had stabilized the economy and an export-led recovery was underway.

The 1999 mission built on the work we had done in Nova Scotia in October 1997 when a large number of Indonesian local government officials participated in seminars and field visits related to local government revenues (which included LGE profits). I asked two Canadians with local government enterprise experience to participate. Blaine Rooney and Francis Leong had met with, and organized activities for, Agung and his colleagues during the late summer 1998 mission and had a good understanding of the issues. Both were middle aged and had travelled internationally. Blaine was the CFO of Halifax Water and Francis held a similar role with a City of Calgary local government enterprise. Blaine and I had worked together on securing infrastructure financing for Halifax Water when a major water treatment plant was built and we were involved in alternative service delivery discussions on its ownership and operations. I knew Francis through the Government Finance Officers Association—we were both members and had met at the 1998 annual conference in San Francisco. Francis organized the Calgary portion of the 1998 Indonesian mission to Canada.

The first item on the 1999 mission program our Home Affairs colleagues had prepared was a meeting with Siti Nurbaya. She had recently been appointed secretary general, a position she would hold for the next five years. Dr. Nurbaya is originally from Sumatra and was the first secretary general we had met with who was fluent in English. The first things I noticed were her fashionable glasses and her high energy. Her tone of voice was often command-like. "Pak Mark I want to tell you this," she would say to me, using the Indonesia phrase for "Mr." She moved with authority and when we saw her in Jakarta she always appeared to be in the middle of something urgent. She took her work seriously and looked out for Lies and other female members of her staff. Her willingness to lead the next mission to Canada boosted the profile of our program.

We had our first post-Suharto meeting with Jeffrey Ong, the program officer who we met on the first mission. Jeffrey continued to be our main contact at the Canadian embassy and he had a good working relationship with Agung. Jeffrey worked under a series of rotating Canadian managers. They often attended our meetings in Jakarta but Jeffrey was always our "go to" person. Jeffrey was also our link with the Canadian ambassador in Indonesia, who regularly participated in the opening sessions of our future international workshops and seminars held in Jakarta. The first of these was in 2003. Three others followed in 2006, 2009, and 2011. The support, information and continuity Jeffrey provided were a major factor in the ongoing success of our cooperation with Home Affairs. Without a full-time presence in a country experiencing a major political and policy transition, we relied on Jeffrey's information and insight to provide a Canadian government perspective on Indonesian politics, programs and priorities.

The IPAC team spent an hour and a half with Jeffrey learning about the current situation in Indonesia. He provided details about how Western governments, including Canada, were making financial investments toward a smooth political and economic transition in Indonesia. After two days of meetings in Jakarta with Home Affairs, other ministries, and GTZ, it was time to take our local government enterprise (LGE) show on the road. The mood in the capital was upbeat and there was a general optimism that President Habibie would continue to press ahead with a reform agenda that would enable local governments to better serve the needs of the people. On a Friday evening in February Francis, Blaine and I packed our bags and headed the Jakarta Kota train station where we met Lies and other Home Affairs staff.

Riding the Night Trains—Central and East Java

The first thing I noticed when boarding the night train to Banyumas, Central Java, was that several of the train windows remained damaged from the 1998 riots. The other passengers were Indonesian and they didn't seem bothered by this so I adopted the same attitude. Banyumas local government staff were waiting when the train pulled into the station at 3 a.m. and drove us to the Dynasty Hotel. After breakfast we went to

*Banyumas waterfall where village boys jumped from the rock cliff
to the water below. February 1999.*

City Hall to make presentations on LGE management in Canada, visited
the local water company, a one-stop shop (with manual systems), and
the municipal hospital (an LGE) where a traditional Indonesian lunch
was served. The hospital had a garden setting with several small, low-
rise buildings. The relaxed atmosphere and dedicated staff impressed us
as did the care provided by visiting family members who brought meals
for the patients.

On Sunday, Banyumas staff arrived with vans to take us on a tour.
The first stop was the water reservoir. Access was along a mountain
ridge where a pipeline had been installed and the path was slippery. Lies
preferred fashion over function and her stylish shoes caused a couple

of slips but thankfully no injuries. Our last stop was at a park with lush vegetation situated below a waterfall. The village boys provided entertainment by riding the falls or jumping off the rock cliff into the water below for money. One of our Banyumas guides held up some small denomination rupiah notes and a pre-teen boy jumped into the water. After all the years I had spent in local government in Canada, my first thought was about liability issues if something went wrong. The jump was successful. The boy happily received his money and then offered a repeat performance.

Shortly before midnight we boarded the overnight train to Surabaya. Our tickets were economy class. The train was full, but the seats were well spaced and wide enough to make me feel I wasn't being crowded. A few of the passengers fell asleep right away and began to snore loudly. I couldn't sleep and my mind wandered as the train passed through the darkness of the tropical countryside. I watched the daybreak as the train came to a halt at a colonial style railway station outside Surabaya. It could easily have fit as a tropical setting for a 1920s Somerset Maugham novel. A stocky, agile, sweat-scented, barefoot, bass-voiced hawker with newspapers under one arm walked up and down the aisles of the train shouting "*Jawa Pos, Jawa Pos.*" Workers were busy in the rice fields and cars meandered their way along in the heavy morning traffic as we entered Surabaya at 6:30 a.m.

Surabaya city staff drove us to the Utami Hotel. There was just enough time to shower and have breakfast before our first meeting. The meeting was with the local government water enterprise. Next we went for a budget presentation and tour at a hospital LGE, then, to a local government one-stop shop and finally a luggage factory. Blaine, Francis and I made presentations at each location (except the luggage factory where we were given a tour instead) based on the Canadian experience with local government enterprises.

We went back to the hotel to change for dinner and for the first (and only) time, two Indonesian civil servants asked us for money, first Francis and then me. We told them we had no cash and kept the incidents to ourselves. One of them told me he needed extra money to compensate for getting up early to meet us at the train station. We felt this was a bit rich after we had spent a sleepless night on hard train seats.

I sent a message to Siti Nurbaya via Lies saying no more night trains. The following morning, we, and the half dozen Home Affairs staff accompanying us, boarded a Jakarta-bound train for a ten-hour ride. The railway line ran through the northern side of Java, usually inland and some distance from the coast. Although we travelled in daylight through a fertile area with varied landscape, the demands of the previous days had dulled our inquisitiveness, so we read and slept. The train passed through Semarang, a Central Java port city and commercial hub on the Java Sea. Outside of Semarang the route approached the coast and heavy waves appeared in the Java Sea. The water was brown near the shore and clear in the distance. Within a few days we had covered the width of Java by train twice, under night skies through the southern part and accompanied by cloudy skies through the north.

There were two parts to our local government enterprise management project. One was sharing information with Indonesian LGE managers through an international workshop in Jakarta, and in 1998 IPAC (Cathie MacDonald) and Home Affairs (Eko Subowo) began making plans. The second was using a peer-to-peer format, and Blaine Rooney and Eko Subowo agreed to work together on ways to improve water LGE management in Indonesia. The LGE initiative stalled when Home Affairs attention turned toward political reform and regional autonomy.

Legislation was introduced in 1999 that transferred responsibility for the delivery of most public services to local government (law no. 22/1999), codified fiscal decentralization and funding (law 25/1999), and covered other fiscal issues related to decentralization and local autonomy. The legislation passed into law and in many cases was enacted before the accompanying regulations and guidelines for implementation were put in place. Our Indonesian colleagues half-jokingly referred to this as the "Big Bang," which I interpreted as a sudden forceful beginning of radical change. There was an immediate need to prepare local government councillors for their new role and responsibilities under political decentralization. The international LGE workshop and related LGE initiatives were put on a back burner until 2003.

A Canada Mission Without Agung

Home Affairs wanted to ensure that the elected local officials who would be responsible for the delivery of most public services understood their role and what was expected of them. Clean government (the Indonesia euphemism for no corruption) at the local level was a national government priority. IPAC organized two study missions on this topic.

The size of the September 1999 study mission to Canada reflected the post-Suharto era interest in moving the Indonesian reform agenda forward. In May 1999 Agung had sent an email to tell me he had been assigned to manage a rural development project, financed through the Asian Development Bank (ADB). The three-year project would establish food banks for 30,000 villages, savings and loan facilities for 45,000 villages, and develop rural markets in 30,000 villages (there were 66,500 villages in Indonesia at the time). Agung's plan was to enhance management capacity in villages and provide seed money and working capital. He joked that his role was like that of a midwife in helping the birth process. A year later, in May 2000, Agung sent another email to "share his happiness." He had been installed as the new head of an international organization tasked with promoting rural development and alleviating poverty in Southeast Asia affiliated with the Centre on Integrated Rural Development for Asia and the Pacific. Its acronym, SOCSEA, is an abbreviation of the sub-regional CIRDA office in southeast Asia. SOCSEA conducted training and research and Agung wrote that he hoped IPAC could become involved. His emails always provided an update on his children's studies and references to his missions to Canada. He referred to Halifax as his second city.

The 1999 mission to Canada was the first Indonesian mission without Agung, and I would miss his wise input. He was always calm, cool and collected. When a caterer forgot to exclude pork from a tray of sandwiches, he calmly informed me they could not eat the food (we reordered). At our formal farewell certificate presentation dinners, he was self-assured, charming and humorous. He was serious at times, enthusiastic at others, and comfortable in formal settings. I hoped things would run as smoothly under Siti Nurbaya's leadership. Dr. Nurbaya was from Sumatra where people are known to be direct and expressive in contrast to the Javanese culture that favours equanimity, etiquette, and self-control.

The Canadian side of the cooperation was now firmly grounded in Nova Scotia and IPAC referred to it as the Indonesia-Nova Scotia partnership. As the program activity grew so did its profile and the involvement of Nova Scotia government officials. I had joined the project as an IPAC volunteer. Now I was coordinating the Indonesia-Nova Scotia partnership under the Government of Canada-funded IPAC International Cooperation Agreement program. The province of Nova Scotia's support for the project and my role in it remained constant.

There were nineteen participants in the study mission. Five of them were from Home Affairs and their travel was funded under our program. The others were from Indonesian local governments who sponsored their travel. Six were women. A representative from the Canadian International Development Agency (CIDA) joined us. We continued our work on the administrative side of decentralization but now we were able to look at the political side as well. In addition to presentations on local government service provision and financial issues, there were discussions on the role of the elected officials and laws governing their conduct. Former Nova Scotia premier and Dartmouth City mayor John Savage, Dalhousie University President Tom Traves, and Deputy Minister of Municipal Affairs Patricia Ripley participated in a seminar on the roles and responsibilities of elected officials, held at Dalhousie University. Nova Scotia civil servants, municipal administrators, and Indonesian delegates also made presentations[28]. Our program was gaining a higher profile in Nova Scotia.

Dr. Nurbaya gave a presentation on decentralization reforms in Indonesia. In the seminar photos she is wearing a grey sports jacket over a white blouse with a printed Indonesian-coloured (rust, black, beige, orange) scarf positioned in the manner of a loosened tie. Her relaxed,

---

28 Seminar local arrangement costs were covered by IPAC and the Canadian speakers volunteered their time.

Siti Nurbaya (bottom left) and her mission colleagues pose for a photo on the Dalhousie University campus during the September 1999 workshop on the role and conduct of elected officials.

Dr Siti Nurbaya made a presentation at the 1999 workshop.

energetic delivery demonstrated she was used to making presentations. She was an advocate for these reforms and often used enthusiastic hand gestures to emphasize points.

Shortly after Dr. Nurbaya and her colleagues returned home, Abdurrahman Wahid (usually referred to as Gus Dur) became the president of Indonesia through a vote by the MPR (People's Consultative Assembly). A national election had been held in June and over one hundred million votes were cast. Golkar, the party of Suharto and Habibie, came in second place with 20 percent of the vote. The PDI-P (Indonesian Democratic Party) received the largest percentage (37 percent) but it was Gus Dur, the leader of the third-place party PKP (National Awakening Party) that received 17 percent of the votes, who was chosen to lead the country in October 1999. At that time the president was elected by the People's Consultative Assembly and Gus Dur was chosen as a moderate after the PDI-P and Golkar parties were unable to garner enough support for their candidates. He was impeached less than two years later on July 23, 2001. During his term he created a Ministry of Regional Autonomy[29] to support the decentralizing agenda and appointed M. Ryaas Rasyid (formerly director of the Institute of Government Studies) as its minister. In a December 2002 working paper on "The Policy of Decentralization in Indonesia"[30] prepared for the international studies program for the Andrew Young School of Policy Studies, Dr. Rasyid provides background information on the policy, explains the framework of regional and local autonomy and shares his assessment of the implementation problems and prospects.

A second Indonesian mission to Canada on clean government and related topics such as transparency and conflict of interest took place

---

29 The following year the ministry was integrated into the Ministry of Home Affairs.

30 The paper concludes that the prospect of decentralization policy in Indonesia can only be bright if the central government is willing to strengthen its leadership, maintain its commitment to supervise the implementation, correct some of the unnecessary and improper decisions, and consistently prepare all the regulations and technical guidelines for local government. If not, I cannot imagine how messy the relationship between the central and local governments would be. The mood for autonomy is now very high in almost every region and locality, and therefore the central government should manage this policy and consistently.

the following year. Siti Nurbaya was the designated lead, but her participation was cancelled at the last minute due to pressing issues at home. Pak Marwan assumed the leadership. Lies Kurniawati was the only female participant. A seminar on good governance topics related to political decentralization (procurement, ethics, public engagement, and codes of conduct for elected and appointed officials) was held on the Dalhousie University campus. Earlier in the year, the new Indonesian president had dismissed ministers who he alleged were involved in corruption, and two corruption scandals[31] involving the president were in the news. Home Affairs wanted to address decentralization concerns about nepotism and corruption during the transition. Local presenters and seminar participants included Dalhousie President Tom Traves, former federal cabinet minister Stewart McInnis, former Nova Scotia premier John Savage, Anna Allan, who led UNSM (the elected municipal councillors association), and two provincial deputy ministers. The Indonesian delegates were from Home Affairs or its training institute (IPDN) and one of them was the speaker at the seminar luncheon.

Stewart McInnes (former federal cabinet minister), Anna Allen (President of the UNSM) and Dr. John Savage (former Nova Scotia premier and former mayor of Dartmouth) participated in the 2000 Clean Government workshop held at Dalhousie University as part of the Autumn 2000 Indonesian mission to Canada.

---

31   Buloggate and Bruneigate.

Dalhousie President Tom Traves made opening remarks at the 2000 workshop held on the Dalhousie University Campus.

Lies and Marwan sharing a laugh at the 2000 workshop.
Humour is a big part of Indonesian culture.

After the program in Halifax was completed, I accompanied the group to Montreal. Nicolas Roy, a colleague from the City of Montreal I had met at an "Africities" conference in Namibia earlier in the year, organized a program for the group. It began with a meeting with Mayor

Pierre Bourque at City Hall. Afterwards we meet with city staff to discuss good governance practices in Montreal.

The outcome of these two missions to Canada was a request from our Indonesian colleagues to include the education and training of newly elected Indonesian local government officials in the next phase of our cooperation. It would begin with orientation sessions.

Academic Night Riders and a Program Evaluation

The 2000 IPAC mission to Indonesia focused on another Home Affairs initiative under the International Cooperation Agreement. It related to cooperation between Canadian and Indonesian universities to improve public sector education and training in Indonesia after the "Big Bang."[32] Local government officials were going to be responsible for delivering most of the public services and this required the appropriate managerial and technical skills. University-level courses and programs would help to fill the gap and Dalhousie University had experience in teaching about governance and administration in a decentralized country.

I asked Keith Sullivan, director of the Dalhousie School of Public Administration, to participate. Keith is tall with a neatly trimmed brown beard mixed with grey and has an outgoing salesman's personality. He is a few years older than me and was accustomed to international travel. Keith joined the mission to explore the possibility of a public sector capacity building initiative through university cooperation. This time I flew out of New York (JFK) where I had gone to make a presentation on local government finance in Canada at a World Bank conference on sub-national credit markets[33]. I met Keith at Hong Kong's Lantua

---

32 The Big Bang refers to the rapid passing of laws on decentralization before the regulations and capacity to implement them was put in place. This was Indonesia's second Big Bang. The first was when it declared independence in 1945 when a constitution, a head of state, a parliament, a government, something resembling an army, and the start of new administrative apparatus were all realized in less than two weeks (Revolusi: Indonesia and the Birth of the Modern World. David Van Reybrouck p. 278).

33 My participation in this conference led to an invitation to the 2000 Africities Conference where I met Nicolas Roy. He arranged the City of Montreal portion of the October 2000 mission.

Airport and we flew to Jakarta. There was a message from Lies waiting for me at the Hotel Borobudur. It said our program arrangements were complete and she would meet us in the hotel lobby in the morning.

On Monday, Keith and I participated in meetings with Home Affairs, the Canadian embassy (Jeffrey Ong), and GTZ (Dr. May and Gabe Ferrazzi). Gabe is Canadian and worked with Dr. May at GTZ. He is an energetic, outgoing man who speaks Indonesian, has a PhD, and is a decade younger than me. Gabe also did sessional teaching in rural planning at the University of Guelph where he lived with his wife and family. I was impressed by Gabe's knowledge of Indonesia and its reform goals and challenges and appreciated his willingness to share it with us. I had started corresponding with him by email in 1997 and we met for an evening meal whenever we were in Jakarta at the same time. It was helpful to have another Canadian perspective on what was happening in Indonesia and Gabe kept abreast of developments there through his work and contacts. I was always glad to see Gabe waiting in the lobby when I walked through the open glass doors at the Hotel Borobudur at the end of a workday.

On the evening of the first day of the mission, Agung joined us for dinner at the hotel and I treated. When Agung included his family in our meals he always insisted on paying. Even when I told him he was my guest he would make an arrangement to cover the bill before I knew what was happening.

The next day Keith and I met with Siti Nurbaya and visited a one-stop shop in nearby Tangerang. In the earlier years we had worked together on improving service delivery through one-stop shops and Home Affairs liked us to see how the initiative was progressing. That evening Gabe Ferrazzi joined Keith and me for Chinese food at Pasar Baru. We were now up to date on what was happening (or not happening) in Indonesia. With President Wahid's party only having a small percentage of the votes in parliament, his first cabinet included members of the various political parties. His election, which took place four months before our mission, was followed by two administrative reforms that abolished the Ministry of Information and the Ministry of Welfare. Like former President Habibie he also wanted to reduce the military's involvement in economic activity and politics[34]. In January and February 2000 President Wahid made several international trips.[35] There was uncertainty about his reform agenda and how his presidency would survive. Our public sector education discussions were more focused on administration and program development than politics so we heard nothing that would negatively impact our mission.

Over the next few days Keith and I met with colleagues at three Indonesian universities[36] to discuss ideas for cooperating on university courses and programs in public administration. Some of the faculty heads spoke English and in other cases faculty members were our interpreters. One popular idea was what the Indonesians called a sandwich program where the first and last years of a program would be spent in one country and the middle years in another. The result would be a joint degree from an Indonesian and a Canadian university. We were impressed with the university colleagues we met, and they were all interested in exploring program opportunities with Dalhousie University and IPAC. The main hurdle we faced was the financing. The IPAC program could facilitate meetings such as the ones we were having but did not have a budget for funding a joint degree program. In order to attract Indonesian government funding the initiative would need a strong local champion with influence. It took time to get an initiative like this off the ground. A decade later we were able to introduce an academic cooperation arrangement between IPDN (the degree-granting institute for training public servants that is part of Home Affairs) and Dalhousie University in our Indonesia-Nova Scotia cooperation.

Lies and her coworker Nita were assigned to accompany us at these meetings and make the travel arrangements for Yogyakarta and Malang. They didn't assume a leadership role. Although we were meeting senior

---

34 The military were allocated seats in both the Indonesian parliament and the MPR (People's Consultative Assembly) and also involved in running businesses. This providing funding for equipment and supplies and also opportunities for personal enrichment.

35 Wikipedia, retrieved April 19, 2020.

36 The three universities were University of Indonesia, Gadjah Mada, and Brawijaya University.

people, we continued to be accompanied by junior Home Affairs staff, and I would have preferred at least one senior Home Affairs staff person accompany us to demonstrate the importance the ministry placed on our cooperation. This time the fieldwork involved a different night travel experience. We had flown to Yogyakarta for our meetings at Gadjah Mada University so Keith Sullivan and I were surprised to learn that a mini bus would take us to Malang, East Java, for our meetings at Brawijaya University. The mini bus pulled out of the hotel parking lot at 7:30 p.m. and arrived in Malang eight hours later at 3:30 a.m. It was a harrowing drive. The driver took the eight-hour timeline as a challenge. His speed was excessive and we had many close calls with oncoming vehicles on rough narrow roads. Keith and I bounced around in the last row of seats and tried unsuccessfully to nap.

After a day of meetings and discussions about university cooperation, our Brawijaya University colleagues hosted an official evening dinner at our Malang hotel. I struggled to stay awake and alert to show an appreciation for their hospitality. One of the challenges with these two-week missions was adjusting to the eleven-hour time difference. Another was that IPAC team members were practitioners with full-time work who scrambled to finalize their office work while preparing for the mission. We were exhausted by the time we got on the plane[37]. I often wondered what motivated Home Affairs to organize our transportation modes and travel times the way they did. Was there a subtle message? Were they testing our commitment to the project or our resilience? Our junior-echelon colleagues that accompanied us on field trips appeared quite accepting of the arrangements and had mastered the ability to sleep during night travel.

Keith and I were impressed with the interest and ideas for cooperation expressed by the universities we met with. We hadn't made a selection yet but would be willing to work with any one of them. All we needed was a source of funding.

---

37 In the early years under the Management for Change / International cooperation Agreement which lasted until 2000 we were permitted to follow the travel guidelines for federal employees and travel business class on flights of nine hours or more. From 2001 onward we were required to fly economy class.

The next time my work with the Nova Scotia Municipal Finance Corporation took me to Toronto I also visited the IPAC office to meet with the executive director and the director of international programs. Joe Galimberti (executive director) and I discussed the direction of our Indonesia cooperation. Joe thought now that political reform was on the table in Indonesia, our resources would be better focused on practitioner-to-practitioner projects rather than academic cooperation which required a type of funding unavailable under our program. I accepted his advice and we put the academic initiative on hold. One of the goals of the broader program was to use our cooperation to leverage opportunities for other Canadian organizations and businesses. If Keith and I, or our Indonesian colleagues, could find donor funding for a separate academic initiative, that would be fine with IPAC.

There was a second part to the February 2000 IPAC mission. IPAC had a new director of international programs. Marie Fortier-Balog had retired and been replaced by Mary Shenstone. Mary was the first Institute of Public Administration of Canada staff member to participate in a mission to Indonesia, and she was there to undertake an evaluation of our cooperation. I joined Mary for the project evaluation session with Siti Nurbaya and her staff. Mary had a set list of questions. Dr. Nurbaya had positive responses to all of them. However, the responses were mainly one-word affirmations and didn't include many examples or details. Had Agung been included in the evaluation session he would have been able to provide more information and context. At this stage all positive feedback was welcome and it enabled us to move forward.

Indonesia welcomed another new president in July 2001 following the impeachment of Gus Dur owing to what was said to be his erratic leadership. She was Megawati Sukarnoputri, daughter of Indonesia's first president, and head of the PDI-P, which had won the most votes in the 1999 June elections. In September of that year a Nova Scotia deputy minister joined me on the mission for the purpose of moving the sister province agreement along. Decentralization and political autonomy had resulted in a number of requests for new provinces and local governments. In 2000, a section of West Java bordering Jakarta was hived off to form Banten province and Home Affairs asked us to hold discussions with Banten rather than West Java on a sister province agreement. That was the final mission under the International Cooperation Agreement. The mission began with meetings with Home Affairs staff, the Canadian embassy, Bappenas, and the first of several scheduled meetings with Banten province. Then on September 11, 2001, which coincided with day two of the mission, terrorist attacks were carried out against United States of America, and our program agenda came to a halt. I watched BBC and CNN, both available in my hotel room, and quickly discovered that BBC was providing the most useful coverage as it focused on what was happening rather than interviews with incoherent, emotionally distraught Americans. When I called home, I learned flights enroute to the USA had been diverted to Halifax and other east coast airports and that volunteers were helping accommodate them. Home Affairs pressed pause on our mission agenda and our work came to a standstill. I contacted our travel agent to see what our return flight options were and a few days later we were headed home. When I got back to Halifax everyone was talking about their experiences with community support for the diverted flights. I had spent those same days far from home at the Borobudur Hotel, watching the news and waiting to see what would follow.

Side Trips Lead to Insights and Surprises

The Asian financial crisis and the changes in Indonesian national leadership occurred shortly after the new International Cooperation Agreement was approved. The missions to Indonesia and Canada continued to include some in-country travel. Travelling to other locations added to our regional knowledge and cultural understanding. It also helped us build relationships and trust. Weekends provided an opportunity to do some exploring on our own or with Canadian and Indonesian colleagues. Also, they were a bit of a breather from the intensity of some of the sessions.

Showing a Backpacker Around Jakarta

In early 1998 I saw another side of Jakarta on the weekend when Ed Stoddard, a Canadian family friend and journalist, made his first visit to Indonesia. He had come to write a story about orangutans in Kalimantan and wanted to see the capital before heading to Banjarmasin. We spent the weekend exploring Jakarta and Louis and Cathie often joined us. On Friday afternoon we had a pricy poolside drink beside the Borobudur Hotel pool before walking to Pasar Baru for dinner at a Chinese restaurant. The bill for the four of us was 130,000 rupiah or US$12, which shows how far the rupiah had fallen in value.

The next day I showed Ed around the Jakarta I knew. We started at the old port (Sunda Kelapa) where cement and lumber from Kalimantan was being loaded on boats. A slim, middle-aged Indonesian man with a black moustache who wore a fisherman's peaked cap offered to row us to the fish market in his wooden boat and we accepted his asking price. We walked along the streets of what was the Dutch administrative centre during colonial times, past the centuries-old stucco two-storey former city hall that's now a history museum, and stopped at the entrance to Café Batavia. The two-storey building overlooking Fatahillah Square was a colonial military residence, then an art gallery, and now a restaurant. We went inside to see the pictures of the rich and famous, provocative prints and posters, and other works of art, and then found a humbler establishment nearby where we had *gado gado* and spicy chicken. Later as we made our way to the National Museum, the guards in the street in front of the Presidential Palace used what the Indonesians refer to as gentle persuasion to keep us off the sidewalk by making gestures with their arms and hands.

Cathie, Louis and I saw how inexpensive Jakarta accommodation could be for the flexible traveller when we visited Ed at a hostel in Jalan Jaksa, Jakarta's backpacker neighbourhood. For a few dollars a night he was travelling rough and meeting lots of interesting people. We had dinner with Ed at the Café Margot in Jalan Jaksa and enjoyed the laidback, party atmosphere reminiscent of our student days in the 1960s and 70s.

Fast forward to the following year (1999) when we arrived on our first "post-Jakarta 1998 riots" mission. Not everything was back to normal. Check-in staff at the Hotel Borobudur cautioned us not to go out after dark. Later on, I saw the impact the rioting had caused at Pasar Baru, the shopping area we frequented within walking distance of the Hotel Borobudur where I had taken Ed to for an inexpensive meal the previous year. I'd always enjoyed the crowded market atmosphere and felt safe being there. This time, in the aftermath of the May 1998 riots, it looked less inviting. Rioters had looted and burned some of the shops and the fire damage was still visible. Some shops had not reopened.

Ancol with Agung

Jakarta was peaceful again during our 1999 mission and on the last day Agung and Lili picked me up at the Borobudur Hotel. They drove us to Ancol (North Jakarta) where we had lunch with Home Affairs staff and colleagues I had worked with over the past six years. Our table was beside a high aquarium and there was a lot of joking and laughter.

After lunch Agung checked us in at a resort on the Java Sea. The first thing I noticed were the palm trees, two of which were anchoring a large hammock. There were two connecting rooms: one upstairs (mine) and one downstairs for Agung, Lili and family. I was left with a block of free time when Agung and Lili went to pick up the children. On my walk to the art market a small boy tugged my arm and asked for money. Caught off guard I said no and kept walking. He persisted by tugging my arm with one hand and patting his stomach with the other. I was touched by the scene and gave him money. This made him very happy, and he waved thank you several times. It made me happy too.

During the twenty-four hours we spent together Agung and I talked about reforms in Indonesia and PhD programs. He highlighted some of the major issues involved in the electoral reform process, Golkar (the governing party up until 1998), and the past practice of requiring civil servants to vote at polls set up in the workplace. Now that Suharto was no longer president there was greater interest in political reform and civil servants, like Agung, felt more comfortable talking about the need for change. We talked away as we ate our breakfast on the patio overlooking the Java Sea, enjoying our time together with Agung's happy family. Even though it was warm, Lili and Agung wore long sleeves and long pants. Open sandals provided some relief from the heat. After breakfast they drove me to the airport for my flight to Canada via Bangkok.

Lili, Adimas, Anissa, and Agung during our stay in Ancol, Jakarta, February 1999.

This marked the end of Agung's direct involvement in what our Indonesian colleagues referred to as our cooperation[38] but he would continue to support and promote our projects. Agung wanted to contribute to the well-being of Indonesians in a major way. The Indonesian reforms and our cooperation were a sideline project for me, one that I found stimulating and enjoyable, but my career path was in Canada. I was working as a municipal advisor in 1994 when I received Jim's call to join the first mission. In 1995, I became CEO of the Nova Scotia

---

38 In Canada we called it the Nova Scotia – Indonesia IPAC project.

Municipal Finance Corporation (a provincial crown corporation) and in 1996 completed my PhD with a thesis focused on local government finance. Agung's career was with the Indonesian government. He was ambitious (often joking that he would be a government minister one day), hardworking and dedicated to improving the quality of life (and public services) for Indonesians. He sought opportunities where they were available and moved on to positions unrelated to our cooperation, but we stayed in touch.

Mount Bromo Sunrise

Our hosts accompanied us on a few side trips during the off hours of the 2000 university cooperation mission. Lies and Nita showed Keith and me the local sites and culture. In Yogyakarta we shopped at Malioboro and saw an evening performance of the Ramayana Ballet. In Malang they (and the university) arranged a visit to a market, an apple plantation, shopping at the local Sarinah (department store) and a becak (three-wheeled pedal rickshaw) ride. I was so tired from our nocturnal mini bus drive I only remember the apple plantation where we sampled the tart yellow-green Malang apples. I wasn't expecting to see apples growing in the tropics even if some regions, like this area of East Java, have a cooler climate.

Our colleagues at Brawijaya arranged a late-night outing to Mount Bromo. Keith, Lies, Nita and I boarded yet another mini bus and joined Professor Bambang Swasto on a midnight drive to the Bromo-Tengger Region. We had come to see the sunrise. Watching the sunrise from the top of Gunung Penanjakan is popular with both tourists and locals. The initial plan was to hike to the top of the mountain but Lies and Nita didn't have the proper footwear so we went by Jeep instead. We bought toques, gloves and hot drinks at the mountain-top stalls and sat on sheltered east-facing benches. It was 2° Celsius and there was a strong wind. At 5 a.m. an orange patch appeared in an overcast sky. There was peacefulness in the visible light. A few minutes later I could see the volcano's smoking plumes in the distance. The crowd stirred but remained quiet and it felt like something bigger, perhaps supernatural, was being shared. People were in no hurry to leave. Our group came down the mountain, mounted Java ponies and followed the long narrow sulphur-scented trail over volcanic ash and rock to the top of a crater. In the dim light of an overcast day, we watched smoke rise from the Bromo volcano.

Walkers make their way down the mountain after watching the sunrise from the top of Mount Bromo, Tengger Region, East Java, February 2000.

We returned to the Jeep and four hours later we reached the airport in Surabaya, arriving with only minutes to spare. As we prepared to board our flight to Jakarta, Keith asked Nita if her last name was Chinese. This question angered her and her expression hardened. Her tone was aggressive when she asked, "Do I look Chinese?" Keith apologized for asking. I've often been asked when travelling if I'm Dutch; an Acadian friend was asked if he's Portuguese. We both find it amusing. Nita's hostile reaction may reflect Indonesian resentment toward wealthy Chinese business people who enjoy a disproportionate share of the country's wealth. Another lesson learned, but not without hard feelings.

It was Lies Kurniawati who had arranged or facilitated most of our non-work activities up to this point. The places she took us to deepened our knowledge of Indonesian culture and history and my commitment to our cooperation. Once we left Jakarta for meetings in other parts of Indonesia it was never clear to me who was paying for what except the IPAC team didn't pay for transportation or admission fees. Lies may have covered some of the extras as Agung had told me her family in Gorontalo was well to do. This was the last time Lies would accompany us on in-country travel. The new CIDA-funded program starting in 2001 would result in Jakarta-based (rather than field-based) activities for the next few years. When in-country travel started again, more senior colleagues would accompany us.

Strikes and Flights in Canada

Our Indonesian colleagues saw more of Canada through this phase of our program. They spent time in Montreal during the 1998 IPAC annual conference and I was glad Agung was there to attend the annual meeting and hear IPAC President Jacques Bourgault refer to my outwardly calm and steady manner when he presented my certificate of appreciation for serving six years on the IPAC Board of Directors. Perhaps I was developing a more Javanese style of self-control and balance than I realized. After the conference we hosted the group in Halifax. I had met Agung's children, but he had never met mine, so I was glad my daughter Carla was able to join us for one of our dinners on the Halifax waterfront.

A decade later when Carla was working for the Government of Canada and Agung was deputy head of BNPP (Indonesia's national agency for border management), they corresponded on border-management issues related to their work.

Sahat Marlitua, who would replace Agung as our designated project coordinator for a brief period, was also a mission participant.

Indonesian and Philippine delegates at Halifax's Historic Properties in September 1998. It was an opportunity for my daughter Carla (second from left) to spend time with Agung and the other participants.

He was Sumatran, in his thirties, and distinguished himself from his Javanese colleagues through his eagerness to express his emotions and thoughts without restraint. We were all anxious on the day in 1998 when the Indonesians were due to leave Halifax. Air Canada pilots had gone on strike in September, disrupting air travel. I made plans with Agung to take the group to the airport on a Saturday morning (their scheduled departure day) and help with any needed alternative flight arrangements. When it was time to leave the hotel, Sahat was not there, and no one knew where he had gone. There was no way to reach him. Agung told the rest of us to go ahead and he would wait for Sahat to return. They arrived at the airport an hour after the rest of us. Agung told me Sahat (who offered no explanation) had gone shopping that morning.

The rescheduling of flights was more difficult for Indonesians who didn't have United States travel visas as they could not transit through the USA. Timbal Pudjianto was one of them. He stood with me at the airline counter as we waited . . . and waited . . . for the agent to find a non-USA routing for him. Finally, she nodded and we heard the chugging sound of a dot matrix printer and watched as Timbal's ticket came through. He smiled and said, "This is the happiest sound I have heard since the day my daughter was born."

Anne's Green-gabled Island and a Prime Minister's Funeral

Siti Nurbaya was the first secretary general to lead a mission to Canada under our program and I was thrilled she had shown such an interest in our cooperation. The final activity of the Siti Nurbaya-led 1999 mission involved a road trip. IPAC rented three vans and arranged for the Indonesians to visit the 12.9-kilometre Confederation Bridge linking Prince Edward Island to mainland Canada and tour its operations centre. The bridge had opened in 1997 and our colleagues were eager to see it as there was interest in building a bridge between Java and Sumatra, the two most populous islands in the 17,000 island Indonesian archipelago. Afterwards we drove to Charlottetown, the provincial capital, for a rice-based lunch (having learned that lesson more than once). There was a discussion among the participants regarding where to go next and some suggested we break into three groups and each group could pick the tourist spots on the island they wanted to visit before going back to Halifax. Some wanted to know more about Anne of Green Gables, a beloved fictional character used to promote tourism in PEI. Lies called this "the three kings' solution." I didn't like it as it would be hard to maintain responsibility for the group and the other volunteer van drivers would have to adjust their own schedules. The three kings' suggestion was dismissed, and after a walking tour of the city known as the birthplace of Canadian Confederation we all drove back in tandem over the Confederation Bridge. By this time, it was raining hard, visibility was poor, and wind rocked the vans. My wife Lise had joined us, and we took turns driving one of the vans. Soetjitro was in our van and informed me he was uncomfortable having a woman drive in these harsh conditions. He didn't say why.

On the way back we stopped at the Tim Hortons in Stewiacke (a town that bills itself as the halfway point between the equator and North Pole) for a break and refreshment. We lined up in single file in front of the order counter (Tim's style) and each person was asked to pay as they placed their order. This casual arrangement contrasted with Javanese formality and upset Ibu Ngadisah[39]. She informed me it was bad manners to order and pay this way. She said the proper way was to have one person act as host and take care of both the order and the payment. This was a reminder that I needed to be sensitized to the fact that Canadian society was structured differently than Javanese society—the former more egalitarian and casual, the later hierarchal and formal.

There was an incident involving local entertainment the Indonesians pursued on their own one evening that may be too culturally sensitive to include, but suffice it to say that the learning regarding cultural differences continues on both sides.

The following year when we included meetings in Montreal, Nicolas Roy arranged a preferred rate for us at a recently opened boutique hotel. It was a high ceiling, former bank building located across the street from Notre Dame Basilica. My wife Lise accompanied me and when we came down for breakfast the morning following the meetings we saw Lies Kurniawati sitting alone. She told us her seven colleagues had taken an early morning train to Ottawa to make a previously unscheduled visit to the Indonesian embassy. They travelled light, leaving their luggage at the hotel with instructions for her to take their baggage and meet them at the airport that evening. Lies felt as a junior member of the group she had no choice but to comply. She laughed and tried to make light of the situation.

After breakfast, Lise, Lies and I walked over to the Place d'Armes Square and waited as preparations were made for the funeral service of Pierre Trudeau, Canada's fifteenth prime minster, which was being held at Notre Dame Basilica. Later in the day Lies joined us in witnessing a historic moment as we watched the service from one of the screens set up in the square.

---

39 She later was appointed rector at the IPDN Jatinangor campus.

As evening approached, Lise and I waited with Lies as she arranged for the twenty-four suitcases to be loaded in vans for transport to the airport. She tipped everyone involved, boarded one of the vans, and waved goodbye to us from a side window. The next time I saw her I asked how it had all worked out. "All twenty-four suitcases made it back to Jakarta," she replied. However, the incident didn't sit well with Siti Nurbaya, especially as the mission agenda included codes of conduct and appropriate behaviour for public officials.

Getting the Job Done: The First Seven Years

When the International Cooperation Agreement ended in late 2001, the Canadian government, IPAC and the partner countries (including Indonesia) were satisfied with its achievements and wanted it to be extended. Although there would be more changes in Indonesian political leadership, the decentralization reform initiatives would continue. Our cooperation had weathered the Asian financial crisis, the social unrest and a change of government in Indonesia, and the months of global uncertainty that followed the 9/11 terrorist attacks.

At the beginning of the program, we were tasked with supporting Indonesian government initiatives toward decentralization, public sector reform, and capacity building. Canada would share knowledge and experience in areas of administrative decentralization and build a long-term relationship with Indonesia. The areas of cooperation that Indonesia identified at the beginning of the agreement were (1) local government enterprise management, (2) local government finance, (3) good governance, and (4) public sector training and education.

It's time to take stock again. I'm comfortable reporting that we made progress in numbers one and three, made attempts at number four (it would happen eventually) and that we didn't specifically target number two. However, finance is a topic that covers every aspect of public administration (always follow the money) so it was indirectly part of all our projects. There wasn't much data available that could be used to measure progress in these areas other than the number of people participating in the program activities in both Canada and Indonesia, and the positive verbal and evaluation form feedback we received. I can attest the participants were attentive and engaged.

Once the new Indonesian president (Habibie) signalled a change of policy direction, which included the "Big Bang" commitment to decentralize most public services and transfer the responsibility for providing them to local governments, the priorities of our Indonesian colleagues shifted. Political decentralization was now part of the reform. The earlier interest in local government enterprise management became less immediate. Preparing local government councillors and staff for their new responsibilities became the priority. Our program had the flexibility to accommodate changing priorities.

Annual work plans were still prepared. We were now communicating by email and no longer having formal work-plan signing ceremonies during our missions, as it was now easier to exchange information and materials by email between missions.

Siti Nurbaya's involvement in, and support for, our work enabled us to move forward on our areas of cooperation. Working initially with Agung we had built a foundation on which to grow. The program started out with administrative reform initiatives (one-stop shops), improved financial management, and local government enterprise management, and now included political reforms related to decentralization and the strengthening of local government finance and services. It was exciting to witness and, in a peripheral way, be part of these reforms. At this point I had developed a good relationship with both Agung and Jeffrey Ong. Lies was a good coordinator and I could count on her. A disadvantage of not speaking Indonesian was that our team members (now that Sue was gone) were not able to communicate at the relationship-building level with senior Indonesian public servants who didn't speak English. Over time this became less of an issue as English-speaking Indonesians, many of whom did graduate studies in English, moved up the ranks.

Indonesia appeared to be on a path to major public sector reform but that brought uncertainties. Would the momentum continue? Would priorities change? How would obstacles be handled? Was there still a role for an IPAC peer-to-peer program? In Canada we knew the political players and what to expect from them. I relied on Jeffrey Ong and Home Affairs colleagues to provide those assessments in Indonesia.

Personally, I was learning more about Indonesia and becoming more committed to the work we were doing. Although I was gaining more international project experience and a global perspective through the project, I was also more aware of lacking the language skills that would have made the experience richer. Growing up in Nova Scotia, there was little incentive to learn other languages and as an adult my studies were directly related to establishing and advancing a career. On the initial mission to Indonesia, I purchased an English–Indonesian dictionary and practiced a few words with the hotel staff. A few years later I found an Indonesian university student in Halifax willing to help me learn Indonesian but this was during a busy period in my life and I didn't make much progress.

I was also learning more about Canada through the involvement of people in other provinces and by participating in meetings and workshops that covered areas that were not part of my regular work. In 2000, I joined the Board of Directors of the Government Finance Officers Association of the United States and Canada (GFOA) and co-chaired its Committee on Canadian Issues. This also increased my knowledge of local government issues and trends in Canada. It was helpful when organizing study missions and looking for speakers and relevant Canadian projects / methods of service delivery to showcase to our Indonesian colleagues.

PART 3

After the Tsunami: Quiet Years for our Partnership (2001-2006)

"Whether it is a tsunami, or whether it is a hurricane, whether it's an earthquake—when we see these great and fatal natural acts, men and women of every ethnic persuasion come together and they just want to help."

— Martin Luther King III

The view from Naval Hill in Bloemfontein, South Africa, is like the one from the top of the Borobudur Temple in Central Java, Indonesia, in some ways. They both overlook a fertile and somewhat flat terrain, the inland plateau known as the highveld in South Africa, and the Kedu Plain in Indonesia. Prominent peaks in the distance are a common feature, with the volcanic mountain near Borobudur and *koppies* in the Free State. They both attract visitors—Naval Hill because it is the home of the Franklin Nature Reserve and offers a clear sky panoramic view of Bloemfontein and the surrounding area, and Borobudur because it is an ancient temple that offers a spiritual experience. But it's the differences I'm thinking about in June 2005 as I jog along the Naval Hill Trail. I stop at a lookoff point and breath in August winter air that's so dry that the office staff have been complaining about noses bleeds. The dominant scent is mimosa flowers not *kretek* cigarettes. It's taken a while to adjust to the aggressiveness of the Afrikaners, so different from harmony-seeking Indonesians. South Africa is in the process of righting the wrongs of an apartheid system based on race, whereas Indonesia's focus is on economic prosperity through decentralization and local autonomy. I'm here in Bloemfontein because I've taken a two-year break from my work in Nova Scotia, including the Indonesia project, to be a part of local government capacity building project in post-apartheid South Africa.

There's also been a break in the IPAC-Indonesia project during the time I've been in South Africa, this one due to Mother Nature. Hurricanes and snowstorms in Nova Scotia resulted in cancelled and postponed missions to Canada, and the immediacy of the Indonesian relief effort following an Indian Ocean earthquake and tsunami put the IPAC—Home Affairs cooperation work on hold for over a year. My work in South Africa will be over in a few months and I'll be moving back to Canada and picking up the lead on the Indonesia project again. I'm looking forward to it.

New Developments at Home and Abroad

By 2001, the economic and political upheavals of the late 1990s had settled and we resumed work on Indonesian project priorities. IPAC's International Cooperation Agreement: Management for Change ended in 2001 and was replaced with another CIDA Partnership Branch funded program. The Public Sector Capacity Building for Governance and Social Development Program (MSOP) ran until 2006. It was the second of four Canadian-government sponsored IPAC programs that included Indonesia as one of the project partners. The goal of the new program (MSOP) was to foster responsive democratic governance and an enabling environment for sustainable social development and poverty reduction. Its objectives were related to government capacity building, gender equality, social development and increased Canadian international awareness.

Indonesia developed implementation plans and regulations for several of the decentralization laws that were initiated in 1999, as well as new ones approved in 2003 and 2004. An initiative referred to as the "grand design" to coordinate the reforms at the regional / local level was accepted. This followed the "Big Bang" that I referenced earlier, which is what Home Affairs colleagues called the decentralization laws that were approved prior to developing the capacity needed for implementation.

There were changes in Indonesian leadership during MSOP but not in decentralization policies. Megawati Sukarnoputri, who was chosen as president in July 2001 by the MPR (People's Consultative Assembly), remained in office until the 2004 election, which was won by Susilo Bambang Yudhoyono (SBY). He was the first Indonesian president to be elected directly by the people.

In 2001, the Institute of Public Administration of Canada appointed Ann Masson as director of international programs. Ann is a couple of years older than me and had a long career with the government of Ontario. She came to IPAC on a secondment and then stayed on after her retirement from the province. A petite blond, small but mighty with

Ann Masson was appointed IPAC director of international programs in 2001. She remained in that position for the remainder of our cooperation with Indonesia.

a business-like presence and a dash of colourful fashion sense, Ann was hard working and tireless in her efforts to promote IPAC and share Canadian public sector know-how with other countries. We didn't always share the same perspective on issues, but I enjoyed working with her and found her supportive. She was innovative at times and rulebound at others. Her job was a difficult one as she had to manage relationships with CIDA, the provincial volunteers, the partner countries, and the IPAC board. In relaxed settings she was good company and had many interests. Her husband was originally from France and her two sons were close in age to my daughter.

The first time I met Ann at her IPAC office in Toronto we discussed staff resources for project support. I thought the IPAC office should be doing more. Ann had limited staff capacity and wanted IPAC's provincial international program partners to provide these resources. This became less of an issue as IPAC international work expanded and its program funding increased. The topic that took most of our meeting time was the preferred way to identify and measure the results of the Indonesia—Nova Scotia cooperation. The CIDA (Canadian International Development Agency) Partnerships Branch was providing the funding for all the IPAC partnerships and this funding was linked to results. The achievements and results of our cooperation with Indonesia were more difficult to measure than some of the other CIDA-funded projects which were more specific. Instead of concentrating on one aspect of health care, early child development, or communications policy, our project involved supporting an entire public services decentralization effort. Priorities and hot spots shifted during implementation of the "Big Bang" reforms as new information became known. Ours was a peer-to-peer program with one of the world's largest countries that was transitioning from a centralized to decentralized governance structure. Indonesia was looking for macro (not micro) level input from us. Our Indonesian colleagues wanted exposure to the Canadian way of providing public services, financing them, and setting standards.

The international donor community is well represented in Indonesia both because of its size and status, which was "developing country" at the time of the initial IPAC mission in 1994. Since then, Indonesia has transitioned to an emerging market economy and reached middle-income country status. This creates a lot of work for those employed at Home Affair's Centre for Overseas Cooperation. The world's major country and donor agencies have a strong, continuous presence there. IPAC did not but this didn't stop our cooperation with Home Affairs from eventually becoming one of the ministry's favourites. The IPAC program was based on government needs and priorities and the control remained with our Indonesian colleagues. The IPAC program didn't have the resources to build and develop one-stop shops in Indonesia, but it could provide models for developing them and an assessment of how established ones were performing and meeting their objectives.

Indonesian Central Government Downloads Services

The qualities, abilities and commitment to the reform process of the Indonesian public servants we worked with also supported a macro (big picture) approach to our cooperation. During this period (2001-2005) the groundwork was prepared to implement the laws and regulations that would make decentralization a reality. In 2004 three important decentralization laws were passed that dealt with local governance, finance, and national development / planning. Other than regulation and setting standards, the national government transferred most responsibilities associated with all but six functions to local governments. The national government retained 1) foreign policy 2) national defence, 3) national security 4) judicial 5) religious affairs and 6) national fiscal and monetary policy. This meant local governments would be fully or partially responsible for health, education, and transportation as well as the services assigned to local governments in Canada. The assigned local government functions were deemed obligatory or optional (according to potential). The central government retained a policy-making, standard-setting role. Meeting these new obligation would be a tall order for the newly empowered local governments.

IPAC appreciated that our role would have to be different in Indonesia but still needed a way to measure results. The results were not always immediate. Exposure to Canadian one-stop shops and ways to improve local government enterprise management provided ideas and practices that took time to implement. As time went on and more Indonesians got involved, specific examples of improvements made by local governments as a result of missions to Canada grew. Yusharto referred to some of them, like municipal cooperation on providing waste and water services and the introduction of a one-call number service, in his presentation at a future IPAC conference. In the meantime, Ann and IPAC stressed the need for measurable short-term results while I took the longer view. We continued to measure inputs such as number of participants at seminars and study missions that focused on one-stop shops, local government enterprise management and issues related to decentralization. We also reported on expected medium- and long-term results that would be achieved through these inputs.

Soon after IPAC received CIDA's approval for the five-year Public-Sector Capacity Building for Governance and Social Development program (MSOP) Ann Masson asked me to join her on the February 2002 inception mission to Southeast Asia. We met with Siti Nurbaya and Home Affairs staff in Jakarta and confirmed the main areas of our cooperation for 2002-2005: local government enterprise management, public sector governance, and local councillor training. We agreed to continue exploring a partnership arrangement between Nova Scotia and the newly created Banten province, which borders Jakarta. Agung joined Ann and me for dinner at the Borobudur Hotel when we were in Jakarta. Ann enjoyed listening to him talk about our program and things he found useful from his missions to Canada like the visits to the one-stop shops in Montreal and Nova Scotia and the seminars on one-stop shops and revenue generation.

The inception mission included meeting with IPAC's other southeast Asian partners. We met colleagues from the Local Government Academy and the University of the Philippines in Manila, and local government officials in Panay (province of Cadiz). Alex Brillantes and Dante Bermejo, two of the people we met with in the Philippines, were participants in the May 1994 visit to Canada. They also participated in the annual missions to Canada under the IPAC Manitoba-Philippines partnership, and Alex was the lead on the 1996 International Conference on decentralization held in Manila. When we arrived at the Panay Presidencia, Ann and I were surprised to see a large banner welcoming its honoured guests from the Institute of Public Administration of Canada with our names in bright red letters.

Later in the year (September) Yuswandi led a twelve person Indonesian mission to Canada. At the time he was head of overseas cooperation at the Ministry of Home Affairs. For as long as I've known him, Yuswandi has retained his slim build. His roots are in Sumatra and he has a twin brother named Yuswanda who also worked in the public service. Our Indonesian colleagues found the similarity in their names amusing and accented the last syllable when comparing them.

He and Agung are close in age. Yuswandi also studied overseas (Cornell University) and has a good command of the English language. I've always had great respect for Yuswandi as he takes his work seriously and is thorough, a quality that sometimes frustrated us as it delayed decisions needed to finalize mission agendas during the last years of our cooperation when he was secretary general. He would later become rector at the IPDN campus in Jatinangor.

The program for the September 2002 mission followed the now established sequence of events of seminars followed by field visits and courtesy calls. The theme in 2002 was managing service delivery through local government enterprises (LGEs) and government departments. We arranged tours of water and solid-waste facilities. There were familiar faces in the group. Pak Marwan and Timbal Pudjianto had participated in earlier missions. Eko Subowo was the Indonesian lead on our local government enterprise project and had come to work with Blaine Rooney who was part of the 1999 mission to Indonesia. We had met Renny (who replaced Lies as coordinator for the mission) and Yuswandi in Jakarta when Ann Masson and I were there earlier in the year.

Participants in the September 2002 study mission to Canada attend a workshop at Dalhousie University in Halifax on managing service delivery through local government enterprises.

That fall I was teaching a university evening class in Canadian local government and invited Yuswandi as a guest speaker. He spoke about local government structure and reform in Indonesia. Using a white board, he made a professional presentation that was logical, methodical, and easy to follow. I was pleased he accepted the invitation and hoped his presentation would broaden student interest in Southeast Asia and Nova Scotia links with Indonesia.

The vice-governor of the newly created province of Banten and a few of her staff were among the self-funded mission participants. During our 2001 mission to Indonesia Nova Scotia Deputy Minister Patricia Ripley and I had met with officials in Banten province for a general discussion on the possibility of a sister province arrangement. Our colleagues at Home Affairs had suggested the newly formed province (previously part of West Java) would be a good match for Nova Scotia. The vice-governor was young, fashionably dressed and accustomed to being catered to. When we went to our meeting with the Nova Scotia Department of Intergovernmental Affairs her high-heeled shoes weren't suitable for walking from the parking spot to the office so she had to be steadied as she moved along the sidewalk. I lost patience and kept on walking at my normal pace. This distinguished me from the vice-governor's colleagues who were accommodating her every wish. As it turned out the province of Nova Scotia was cooling toward the idea of a sister province agreement. A large provincial debt had accumulated throughout the twelve years of government under a previous premier. Fiscal restraint was now the Nova Scotia government's priority and even small expenditures on a non-core function would be a problem. When I explained the situation to my Indonesian colleagues after the meeting, they asked if the premier who had overseen the activities that led to the financial crises had lost face with the public for his poor management of public funds. I responded that he had been appointed to the Canadian Parliament's upper house, the Senate, where a generous salary was provided until age seventy-five. The mismanagement of public funds was an ongoing issue in Indonesia as evidenced by its unfavourable score in the Transparency International Corruption Perception Index but Indonesians assumed it wouldn't be tolerated in Canada.

Planning for the Future: Local Government Enterprise Workshop Comes to Jakarta

The Jakarta workshop was a milestone event in our cooperation. Until then, all the seminars and workshops had been held in Canada. In Indonesia we had met with municipalities and local government enterprises but the discussions and presentations were limited to our respective systems of governance and service provision. The "Managing Local Government Enterprises" workshop marked a major shift in how IPAC participated in decentralization reform in Indonesian and was our largest collaborative effort to date. It took place over two days at the Hotel Borobudur in Jakarta in March 2003. Cathie MacDonald had started planning this workshop with Eko Subowo in 1998 but it was delayed because of the Asian financial crisis and changes in Indonesia's leadership. Cathie and Eko resumed workshop planning in 2001.

Cathie MacDonald and Eko Subowo (both wearing badges) were the main organizers of the LGE workshop in Jakarta, March 2003

The purpose of the workshop was to select and recommend a management structure that separates policy making, operations and regulations for Indonesian local government enterprises. Home Affairs took care of the local arrangements and reached out to contacts in the Indonesian donor community for recommendations for speakers from other countries. Cathie recruited the Canadian presenters and worked with Eko on program content and structure. Our Canadian team appreciated the effort our Indonesian colleagues had put into both the program agenda and the local arrangements and took this as a sign of their commitment to our present and future cooperation.

Jeffrey Ong (left) and Yuswandi at our first MOHA-IPAC international workshop held at the Borobudur Intercontinental Hotel in Jakarta in March 2003.

Blaine Rooney of Halifax Water presenting at the Local Government Enterprises workshop in Jakarta March 2003.

There were over one hundred delegates who were welcomed by the minister of Home Affairs and the Canadian ambassador to Indonesia. The six Canadian speakers were all practitioners with local government enterprise experience. There were several Indonesian speakers as well as presenters from Australia and Europe. Siti Nurbaya and Yuswandi participated in the workshop along with others (Timbul, Ramelan, Arlen Pakpahan) from the 2002 mission to Canada. Agung was there too. The feedback from the evaluation meetings that followed was positive and included in the detailed IPAC report of the workshop. We hadn't reached the stage where Home Affairs followed up with workshop participants on specific changes that resulted from workshop participation. Later on, when Pak Saut became the Indonesian project leader, he organized the first mission follow-up session. He asked participants to explain how they had applied the information from the Canadian study mission to their work in Indonesia and invited the IPAC team to attend.

We spent the remaining days of the mission working with Home Affairs on workplan goals and activities for 2003-2006. Home Affairs identified four needs related to public sector governance where IPAC could play a role. They were (1) to strengthen the governance and financial capacity of local government; (2) to define and implement the relationship, roles and responsibilities of the central and local levels of government in a decentralized environment; (3) to improve the governance and operations of state and local enterprises; and (4) to ensure that clean government policies and practices are followed.

Our three main areas of focus would be municipal governance (councillor training), developing local government resource manuals (for both administrators and elected officials) and governance and management of water systems, which were often set up as local government enterprises. Tasks and expected results were identified. Blaine Rooney was one of the workshop presenters and he and Eko Subowo set objectives for the water systems initiative. Blaine got the project off the ground by providing a package of sample information on the legislative framework, structure, governance, rules and regulations for a Canadian municipal water enterprise. There were several water LGEs in Indonesia that provided potable water, but the infrastructure required improvement and many parts of the urban communities were not serviced.

Planning began for another workshop, this time on local government fiscal decentralization (which took place in 2006), and we discussed dealing with accountability and transparency in local government through conflict-of-interest guidelines. A number of laws related to decentralization in Indonesia were coming into effect in 2004 and our projects would contribute to their implementation.

I stopped for a day in Manila on the way home to meet with Alex Brillantes at the University of the Philippines along with the executive director, Julian Payne, and a governance specialist, Jak Jabes, of the Asian Development Bank. IPAC was interested in strengthening the links between its Indonesia and Philippine programs. It also wanted to develop working relationships with other donors (like ADB) that would complement existing IPAC projects. It was St Patrick's Day and I saw a sign in the window on an Irish pub advertising green beer and a dinner with green potatoes. I couldn't resist an opportunity to celebrate St Patrick's Day in Manila.

A Tsunami, a Hurricane, and a New Chapter in South Africa (2003-2005)

In September 2003, as mentioned earlier, I took a two-year break from my work in Nova Scotia and my wife Lise and I moved to South Africa. My involvement in the Indonesia project led to a growing interest for me in international development work so when an opportunity arose to live and work in South Africa, I applied. IPAC had partnered with Ottawa-based Cowater International in a successful bid to provide technical and financial assistance to local governments in South Africa. The post-apartheid reforms had started at the national level, then moved to the provincial level and were now ready to be implemented in the country's local governments. I was one of the ten international advisors being recruited that year. Lise works as a cardiac sonographer and we both arranged two-year leaves of absence from our work and moved to Mangaung Local Municipality (Bloemfontein), located on the high veld in the middle of the country. My contract was with Cowater, which would be compensated by the South African National Treasury through access to loans provided by the African Development Bank and the World Bank.

Prior to leaving I had arranged with IPAC to have Stephen Feist manage the Nova Scotia side of the cooperation with Indonesia while I was away. Stephen worked at the Nova Scotia government's municipal affairs department and had expressed an interest in becoming more involved. Stephen is a big burly man who is a few years younger than me. He developed a good relationship with Renny (who replaced Lies) during the September 2002 mission to Canada and was a welcome addition to the IPAC team during the March 2003 mission to Jakarta.

Not much happened with the Indonesia—Nova Scotia —IPAC partnership while I was in South Africa. This was not due to lack of interest; the cooperation was sidelined by more pressing issues. There was only one mission to Canada and none to Indonesia. An Indonesian mission to Canada scheduled for the fall of 2003 was cancelled when Nova Scotia went into recovery mode to deal with the destruction caused by Hurricane Juan. It was the strongest hurricane to hit Nova Scotia in over a hundred years. When it reached landfall near Halifax, it was a Category 2 hurricane with winds of 160 km/hr. Uprooted trees fell on powerlines and buildings. Roofs were damaged and structures destroyed. One third of homes were damaged and boardwalks and parking lots were covered in storm debris.

The rescheduled mission to showcase councillor training in Nova Scotia took place five months later in February 2004 but the program was cut short by a hurricane-strength Nor'easter blizzard referred to as White Juan. It brought extreme sustained winds of 124 km/hr and over three feet (95.5 cm) of snow to the Halifax area. The combination of snow and wind reduced visibility to one metre. Nova Scotia imposed a state of emergency and Halifax imposed a 10 p.m. curfew to facilitate snow removal.[40] Our Indonesian colleagues arrived a few days before

---

40 Summary of information retrieved from the Weather Network December 26, 2022.

the storm. Arif, one of the Indonesian participants, told me that "it was a very exciting experience and an unforgettable memory."

Hurricane Juan and White Juan were not the last natural disasters to impact our cooperation. On Sunday morning December 26, 2004, a massive earthquake measuring 9.1 on the Richter scale struck off the west coast of Sumatra, Indonesia. The epicentre was thirty kilometres under the seabed and approximately 250 kilometres south to south-west of Banda Aceh. The earthquake generated a series of towering waves which could travel at 80 km/hr in shallow water, with the largest impact felt in Indonesia and Sri Lanka. Within fifteen minutes of the earthquake, waves began striking the coasts of northern Sumatra and the Nicobar Islands. Waves of up to thirty metres were recorded as the tsunami swept through Aceh, the hardest hit region of Indonesia. Around two hours after the earthquake struck, waves reached Sri Lanka, India, and Thailand.

The tsunami waves caused widespread death and injuries, displaced thousands, destroyed towns, homes, livelihoods, infrastructure, and wrecked coastal areas. Due to the scale of destruction estimates for total lives lost vary. According to the United Nations approximately 227,000 people were killed in fourteen countries. Data published by the Tsunami Evaluation Coalition indicated at least 275,000 people lost their lives. Across the region there are still people believed to have been swept away who have never been accounted for. Measured in lives lost, this makes it one of the ten worst earthquakes in recorded history, as well as the single worst tsunami in history. The worst affected countries were India, Indonesia, Malaysia, Maldives, Myanmar, Sri Lanka, Seychelles, Thailand, and Somalia. Indonesia suffered $4.5 billion in economic losses, representing the entire GDP of the Aceh province. The overall financial impact on the Indonesian economy lowered the projected growth by approximately 0.2 per cent in 2005.[41]

The Indonesian government and donor agencies focused their efforts on relief and rebuilding. There was little communication with our Indonesian colleagues that year.

---

41 Summary of data related to Indonesia retrieved from Australian Disaster Reliance Knowledge Hub on Indian Ocean Tsunami 2004 on December 26, 2022.

Because of these natural disasters occurring from 2003-2005, there wasn't much movement on our projects, so it was easy for me to pick up where I left off when I returned to Canada.

International Exposure Changes World View

The South Africa experience gave me an opportunity to think about my worldview as a Canadian living next door to the world's most powerful country, in terms of both economic and military might. Bloemfontein is similar in size to Halifax and is also a provincial capital and university town. It's the centre of Mangaung Metropolitan Municipality and during the apartheid era most residents were White Afrikaners, and the Black population lived in nearby townships. Fortunately for me, English was the common language used in the municipal workplace and most of the local population were fluent in English as well as Afrikaans, Sesotho and other Indigenous languages. The Afrikaner customs, values and way of thinking reminded me of my childhood years in Canada. The locals often used English words and expressions I hadn't heard in years. Religion was still a dominant factor in most peoples' lives, and they attended church every Sunday. There was a conservative community morality that caused people to keep any views sympathetic to the more controversial lifestyle issues to themselves. Drivers exhibited a sense of entitlement and had little respect for pedestrians or cyclists and did not observe no passing zones or speed limits. On the other hand, people were welcoming, helpful, generous and had a strong sense of community. By the second year my wife and I had settled in and were taking it all in stride. We also adapted our driving habits.

Born in Canada during the post-World War II era, I was part of a generation that grew up in conservative rural communities and small towns, then moved to the city for education and work, and adopted more liberal views along the way. I had also experienced the cultural shift from an attachment to things English in the post-war era to things American from the 1970s onward. It was only a matter of time before the trends and value shifts taking place on the American West Coast reached urban Canada and then trickled into Nova Scotia.

I realized that the South African and Indonesian lifestyles and values weren't as influenced by American and Western values as mine were in Canada. The Western emphasis on individualism and self-actualization differs from a focus on family and community well-being. In both South Africa and Indonesia, adherence to religious practices and conservative community values were still important, as was the focus on family. Families of four children were common in South Africa. Sue had told me that Indonesians sympathized with people who had no children. It was different in Canada. Among our circle of Canadian friends and acquaintances, families with one or two children, or no children at all, was more common. This marked a generational shift as several of them came from large families.

Another difference I observed between Canada and these two countries related to certain aspects of concern for the environment in daily life. In Nova Scotia, we spent a lot of time sorting our household waste for reuse and recycling, and littering had become for the most part socially unacceptable. At our rental house in South Africa all waste went into one bag and the city sidewalks and surrounding fields were covered in litter. Litter was also a problem in Indonesia and during the rainy season in Jakarta, plastic waste blocked canals and drains. When this happened, water had nowhere to go and flooded city streets and homes. However, because of a high standard of living, more Canadians own vehicles and our long winters drive up energy needs, as do our scattered populations, resulting in Canadians having an overall larger environmental footprint per person.

One of the things I learned from my two years in South Africa that I transferred to our cooperation in Indonesia was that I needed to be more open to understanding the reality and validity of different perspectives and situations. I had assumed that by adopting Western public sector governance and management practices Indonesian society would eventually transition to Western society values in other ways, like growing more secular. I now appreciated that Indonesia was not heavily influenced by Western trends (with the exception of pop music and shopping malls) and would find made-in-Indonesia solutions to issues. This realization validated the approach I was advocating for our cooperation, which was to share ideas and approaches in key areas and let Indonesians use what is workable for them.

On a more personal note, after completing my contract in South Africa I was glad to be back in Halifax. Two years earlier I felt my life there had become stagnant and repetitious. I couldn't wait to get away, live somewhere else, and do something different. Halifax had been my community for all of my adult life, a place where I had a lot of history and a sense of belonging. In South Africa people knew me as a professional man in his mid-fifties who was with them for a few years to contribute to post-apartheid reforms—a single, short chapter in my life story.

I hadn't appreciated how important it was to me to have a long history with a community. In Halifax, I was constantly meeting people I had known from my university years and studies, from thirty-plus years of working at various jobs, taking courses, part-time teaching and through sports and recreation, community organizations and the neighbourhoods where I lived. My interest in long-term international consulting was now satisfied. From now on short-term assignments and international vacations would be enough. This realization would later cause mixed feelings about building on our current work in Indonesia. It would be gratifying to see it evolve into something larger with a greater impact, but I would not be offering to be a permanent part of any long-term initiative that required a full-time presence there.

PART 4

Back on Track:
Our partnership grows (2006-2009)

"Indonesia's diversity is formidable: some thirteen and a half thousand islands, two hundred and fifty million people, around three hundred and sixty ethnic groups, and more than seven hundred languages."

– Pankaj Mishra (Indian essayist and novelist)

"We have it all. We have great diversity of people, we have a wonderful land, and we have great possibilities. So all these things combined, there's nowhere else I'd rather be."

– Bob Rae (former premier of Ontario and current Canadian ambassador to the United Nations)

Agung and I are sitting in the back seat of a borrowed luxury car with the driver heading east. We're on our way to the IPDN campus in Jatinangor. Our Good Governance Program (GGP) will be ending soon and we not only want to extend it, we want to expand it. Agung has arranged a meeting with the rector to discuss adding an academic component to our next program. My thoughts turn to coffee, which has linked our countries and played a part in our cooperation. Indonesia accounts for 6 percent of world coffee production and although no coffee is grown in Canada, Canadians are the third biggest consumers. When it comes to coffee, Indonesia is the provider and Canada is the beneficiary.

My first office coffee in Indonesia was at our initial meeting at Home Affairs in 1994. It was served with two spoonfuls of sugar. During the early years I brought home small bags of Tana Toraja coffee grown in the highlands of South Sulawesi. Before proceeding to the one-stop shop in Kentville, Nova Scotia, during the 1996 study mission I took the Indonesians to the local Tim Hortons for a sit-down cup of coffee. It was a sunny autumn day, and the experience was so relaxing we would have liked to stay longer.

My coffee reminiscences moved on to a less pleasant memory I shared earlier that happened during the 1999 study mission to Canada, when Ibu Ngadisah had reprimanded me for the way I handled a coffee-shop stop on the rainy, windy drive back from an arranged tour of the Confederation Bridge. Even though that was ten years prior, I'm a bit apprehensive about meeting her again. I hope she won't think me too uncouth / unmannerly for an academic partner and jeopardize our plans for future cooperation.

Promoting Good Governance

Lise and I returned to Canada and our work in Halifax in September 2005, and I resumed my responsibilities as IPAC—Indonesia—Nova Scotia project lead. The following month I went to Toronto and met with Ann Masson. The current CIDA-funded program, which included the Nova Scotia—Indonesian cooperation, was coming to an end in early 2006. Ann informed me that IPAC had applied for a renewal. It had been over a year since the tsunami had hit Indonesia and although there was still a lot of post-tsunami work to be done, Home Affairs was eager to resume its decentralization initiatives. So were we.

The laws on decentralization prepared in 2003 and 2004 were more specific in the areas of budgets, grants, auditing, accounting, and the Indonesian approach to development and planning. Indonesian regulations were issued to provide for minimum service standards, their implementation, and local government cooperation.

In 2006, a third Canadian government-funded program, with the Institute of Public Administration of Canada as the implementing agency, received approval. The same six partner countries and one professional association were included as were the Canadian provinces leading each partnership. The Indonesia—Nova Scotia partnership was one of them. The updated CIDA partnerships branch-funded program, called the Good Governance Program, (GGP)[42] ran until 2009. The three partnership objectives related to reforms in Indonesia were (1) enhance good governance in a decentralized environment, (2) build capacity for elected and appointed local government officials, and (3) develop sound policies on governance and decentralization. It linked Indonesia's 2008 national development priorities (economic growth, poverty reduction, infrastructure development, and increased access to

---

42 GGP's goal was to foster responsive, democratic governance and an enabling environment for sustainable social, economic and environmental development. There are six country—provincial partnerships (Indonesia—Nova Scotia was one) and three association partnerships.

health and education) to the program goals. GGP was the last program to be approved under that federal Liberal government.

During GGP (2006-2009) we renewed our cooperation and set the stage for the accelerated pace it would take in its final years. There were two bookend workshops in Jakarta—on fiscal decentralization in 2006 and decentralization and public services in 2009. In between there were missions to both Canada and Indonesia dealing with councillor training—the highest Indonesian priority for our cooperation at the time. Blaine Rooney and Eko Subowo continued their work on improving LGE water company management. A partnership arrangement signed by IPAC, Indonesia, and Nova Scotia formally recognized the role and contribution of the parties involved. The program renewal included funding for our international colleagues to attend the annual IPAC international workshop and conference.

A change in Canadian leadership was also on the horizon. A sponsorship scandal in Canada in 2004 damaged our credibility with Indonesian colleagues who were looking to us for advice on good governance. It related to a federal government sponsorship program in the province of Quebec that ran from 1996-2004. The program's purpose was to raise awareness of the Government of Canada's contribution to Quebec industries and other activities to counter the actions of the separatist provincial government. An audit in 2004 by the auditor general's office discovered broad corruption involving the misuse and misdirection of public funds. Money was awarded for work that was never done and several rules in the Financial Administration Act were broken. The governing Liberal party was defeated in the 2006 federal election.

Each time a new CIDA-funded program was approved an inception mission to lay out a plan that linked to the program and country priorities was undertaken. In February 2006 Ann Masson, Cathie MacDonald and I went to Jakarta and had several meetings with Home Affairs to firm up our program and activities. One of them was a Jakarta roundtable later in the year. Siti Nurbaya was still secretary general and, with assistance from Lies and Renny, arranged our program schedule, which included an update from Jeffrey Ong at the Canadian embassy.

Debriefing at the end of a workday with Ann Masson at an outdoor Jakarta café.
February 2006.

Ann and I met with Marco Domaschio, a counsellor with the Embassy of Canada
in Indonesia during one of our missions in February 2006.

Susilo Bambang Yudhoyono, a former general widely referred to SBY, had been elected president in 2004. Like Megawati, he was a member of the Democratic party (PDI-P). One of the challenges his government would face was dealing with local level opportunities for corruption and poor decisions related to the environment now that, under the decentralization laws, the regions had more responsibilities and autonomy. Jeffrey Ong told us things were stable on the political front. Decentralization reforms were moving forward, the implementation of several related laws was underway, and the post-tsunami economy was doing well.

One of my informal measures of the health of the Indonesian economy is the amount of activity at the Hotel Borobudur. In addition to its Indonesian clientele the hotel is popular with overseas industry (mining, agriculture) executives and aid agency staff living in other parts of Indonesia. It was a busy place in February 2006 and I spoke with a number of Australians working with NGOs on health-related projects.

During the mission Agung joined me for coffee at the hotel late one afternoon. I hadn't seen him in almost three years. He was relaxed and he hadn't changed a bit. We caught up on the news and he was interested in hearing about governance issues in South Africa. Our children were growing up and we were both enjoying our work. When he left, he surprised me with a hug[43], most likely due to a long absence. We normally shook hands. I knew in that moment that we had become close friends. I developed friendships with many other Indonesian colleagues, including Arif who acted as Indonesian coordinator for the second decade of our cooperation, but it was Agung who I knew the longest.

Muhammad "Arif" Hidayat took part in our 2006 inception mission program. Arif was the third (after Agung and Lies) and final Indonesian coordinator to become a regular contact with me between

---

43 A hug between Indonesian men or an arm around the shoulder is not unusual in Indonesian and is common in other Muslim majority countries.

missions. Like Agung, he is Sundanese, and he comes from Bandung. He was born in 1967 (Canada's centennial year) though he looks much younger than his age and was often mistaken for a young professional at IPAC conferences in Canada. Arif is slim, of medium height and has a ready and disarming smile. His graduate studies in the Netherlands and Japan were government sponsored and he is fluent in English. He has a wonderful singing voice and enjoys entertaining colleagues with romantic songs at Home Affairs social gatherings. Other Indonesians have told me that Hidayat is not really a surname but more of a religious term referring to guidance or instruction. Many Indonesians do not use surnames but will often select one to conform when studying or working overseas.

Arif's love of singing and performing would provide future opportunities for us to socialize and get to know our Indonesian counterparts better. He never seemed to have a full night's sleep as he responded quickly to messages and emails no matter what time of day or night they reached him. Arif proved to be good at working behind the scenes to keep activities and relationships moving forward. We eventually reached a point where we could be open with each other about the internal project challenges we were each facing. For Arif it was navigating the mission travel approval process; for me it was short-term measurable results.

After confirming everything was on track for the roundtable being held in Jakarta later in the year, the IPAC team flew home via Manila. In Manila, Ann, Cathie, and I met with two IPAC partners (the Local Government Academy and University of the Philippines), the Asian Development Bank and other non-government organizations. As director of international programs Ann was responsible for IPAC's decentralization program in the Philippines. Plans were made for future cooperation initiatives such as Philippine speakers at future Home Affairs / IPAC roundtables in Jakarta and linking common themes of the two Southeast Asian decentralization projects during international partnership sessions at IPAC annual conferences.

A Second Jakarta Roundtable

In November I participated in my second 2006 mission to Indonesia. On the way over I made a stop in the United Kingdom. Don Ross, a Canadian friend of mine who taught at an Australian university, was attending a conference at Cambridge University. Don and I had both done our PhDs under the supervision of Richard Pike at the University of Bradford (West Yorkshire). It was a rare opportunity for us to pay a joint visit to Dr. Pike, take him out to dinner, and assure him that the time he had invested in us had not been in vain. In a small but important way it was my Bradford studies that led to my involvement with Indonesia. When I attended the IPAC Board of Directors meeting in December 1993 I had mentioned my UK studies to Marie Fortier-Balog, IPAC director of international programs. Marie said, "If you are studying oversees you must like international activities—why don't you speak to Jim Beaulieu about an international team he's putting together to explore opportunities in Southeast Asia." I did and Jim invited me to join the team a few weeks later.

Arif came to the Hotel Borobudur with our program schedule on the weekend we arrived in Jakarta. On Monday the IPAC team met with Home Affairs to finalize plans for our second Jakarta roundtable and I spoke with Jeffrey Ong. An afternoon walk with the IPAC team to Pasar Baru helped us acclimatize. In the evening a pre-roundtable dinner was held at the hotel's poolside restaurant with a Home Affairs minister's advisor as guest speaker. It was a hot and humid evening and my shirt stuck to my back when I went to get up. Alcohol was never served at these dinners and unless there was singing afterwards they were usually brief.

One hundred participants came to the Hotel Borobudur for the "Roundtable on Local Government Fiscal Decentralization." Our Indonesian colleagues chose this topic in order to raise awareness of the changes in central / local fiscal arrangements under the "Big Bang" decentralized reforms. A related concern was the proliferation of requests for the creation of additional local governments[44]. The Canadian ambassador made opening remarks and later that morning he met with the IPAC team for coffee in a private meeting room. He was appreciative of the work we were doing as it strengthened Canada—Indonesia ties. The room for the roundtable was set up in a conference room format with a head table for speakers and rows of chairs for the audience. The original plan was to use a hollow square [45]setup for twenty participants, and the Indonesian participants would be selected on the basis of their knowledge of the reforms and for the contribution they could make to the discussion. Instead, we ended up with one hundred participants, many of whom were there to learn rather than contribute to the discussion[46]. Knowing there would be no point in objecting to these changes, our Canadian team quietly adapted to them. The agenda topics and presentations remained the same.

The Indonesian presenters spoke about the challenges they faced in implementing the new decentralized system and identified five major issues: functional assignment, regional expenditures, regional revenues, financial management, and capacity development. The Canadian speakers explained how these issues were dealt with in Canada, a country where subnational governments have been responsible for the delivery of most public services for over a century. The change in format and number of participants turned out well. Useful and relevant information was presented and discussed. The larger audience resulted in a greater variety of questions and sharing of regional realities. The Canadian embassy staff was pleased with the roundtable and suggested we organize more of them. The agenda

---

44 In 1995 Indonesia had 305 local governments level 2 (cities and districts). The number increased to 341 in 2000, 440 in 2005, 497 in 2010, and 511 in 2013. Source ADB Institute Government Decentralization Program in Indonesia Anwar Nasution No 601 October 2016.

45 A configuration of multiple tables placed together to form a rectangle with open space in the middle.

46 I later learned that part of the compensation package for civil servants was receiving a stipend when attending workshops and seminars.

called for a meeting the following day to discuss ways to put the information gained through the workshop into practice. The turnout for this meeting was low and we were disappointed that the enthusiasm generated during the workshop hadn't resulted in greater interest in its application.

Unlike Blaine Rooney, Cathie MacDonald and me, the other two Canadian roundtable speakers were seeing Indonesia for the first time. It's a long way to travel and the first timers were interested in seeing some of Jakarta. After the workshop we went to the former Dutch administrative centre of the city for a celebratory meal at a restaurant favoured by expats when in the old city. The menu featured both Indonesian and international cuisine, along with signature drinks and specialty coffees. The mood was upbeat and afterwards the waiter brought separate bills as requested. The atmosphere took a U-turn when one of our speakers, a senior municipal administrator, asked for a receipt so he could be reimbursed. When Cathie quietly informed him that he would have to cover any extra cost of his meal that was beyond our per diem allowance he became visibly upset and asked why she hadn't told him this when she recruited him. She deescalated the situation by saying she was sorry. Later in the week I mentioned to Blaine that I was bothered by the incident. Blaine has a more practical view of life than I do and said it was not worth getting upset about. As team leader I wanted every aspect of the mission to go well and no doubt set a higher expectation than was needed. From past experience I appreciated the importance of a good attitude among Canadian team members. The missions were typically for one or two weeks and after a long flight and time zone changes people were always tired and sometimes wired from the adrenaline. I knew that often the simplest slight could de-rail an otherwise amicable relationship. Fortunately, Cathie was especially good at staying cool, maintaining a sense of humour and coming up with ways to keep things moving forward.

The rest of the week was spent discussing a program for training elected local government councillors and officials, meeting with Home Affairs colleagues (Yuswandi, Yusharto), and attending a workshop on special status for Aceh[47]. After the others left, Blaine, Eko Subowo and I attended a meeting in Tangerang, Banten province, to discuss providing technical assistance to the city's water company as part of the local government enterprise cooperation project. On the drive back through Jakarta we saw several construction cranes in the downtown business district where new apartment buildings were being built. The economy had recovered from the post-Asian crisis period that saw idle cranes and partially built high-rise buildings abandoned all over the city.

At the end of the mission, I met Agung, Lili and their three children, Arief, Adimas and Anissa, for dinner at a Chinese restaurant in Menteng (a neighbourhood in central Jakarta). There were lots of laughs and conversation. The boys were both at university and had stories to share. Adimas took photos with his smartphone.

Communicating in Jakarta—Changing Technology

In 2006, we were near the midpoint of our cooperation and at a good point to mention the changes in communication technology during the missions to Indonesia. From 1994 to 2003 I didn't bring a phone with me as I mainly used landlines in Canada and seldom used my flip phone. It was difficult to have a landline installed in Indonesia[48] so Home Affairs staff skipped that technology and adopted cellphones (which Indonesians often call handphones) much earlier than we did in Canada. They enjoyed putting novel ring tones, like lines or motifs from popular songs, on their phones, which were rarely put in silent mode. Up until 2003, I relied on my hotel room phone and the business centre for communications. When I went to Jakarta in 2006 I brought

---

47 Special status discussions for provinces and regions were of mutual interest. Aceh and Papua were two Indonesian provinces demanding more autonomy; the former for more latitude to introduce Islamic law and the latter to receive more benefit from the extraction of its natural resources. In Canada the predominantly Inuit region in the north had been granted territorial status in 1999 and a 1995 Quebec referendum proposing the province separate from the rest of Canada was narrowly defeated.

48 During the IPAC 1995 mission I read a letter Agung wrote to the editor of the Jakarta Post documenting his long wait time experience when trying to have a phone line installed at his home.

the Nokia handphone I had used when living in South Africa, bought an Indonesian SIM card, and used it for making local calls and text messaging with Home Affairs colleagues. By this time, I was using a smartphone (Blackberry) in Canada but it was prohibitively expensive to use in Indonesia because of roaming charges, so I left it home. In 2010, Wi-Fi became more accessible and affordable at the Hotel Borobudur (first only in the lobby and later in the rooms), other hotels and airports, so I relied more on my smartphone. This meant less time spent at the hotel business centre dealing with email correspondence as I could do that on my Blackberry, which I also used for taking photos. There was a period when Blackberrys were popular in Indonesia and I could use BBM (a Blackberry message application) to correspond with Home Affairs colleagues. When technologies evolved Indonesians switched to other phones (Samsung and Apple products). I did too.

Communication between missions was a challenge in the mid-1990s. It was all done by fax and telephone. I'd call Agung or Lies from Halifax early in the morning, which with the eleven-hour time difference would be evening there, to plan our upcoming missions. We shared draft agendas by sending faxes. Once we were able to communicate using email it became much easier, but I missed hearing the enthusiasm for our work in Agung's voice. Now I keep in touch with Agung, Arif, Jeffrey, Yusharto, Yuswandi, Nurdin, Kuswanto, and other colleagues through social media and the occasional email.

Local Government 101–Training Councillors

IPAC increased the size of its international program staff to manage the Good Governance Program (GGP). In addition to Ann Masson, director of international programs, there were a manager, two program officers, and administrative support personnel. IPAC staff was now more involved in the project details and having the last word on what we were doing. I welcomed this change because it moved a lot of the project's official communication and reporting off my desk. During GGP I took an early retirement from my work at a provincial government Crown corporation and accepted a faculty position at the Dalhousie School of Public Administration. The extra IPAC support was timely. Instead of writing reports I was asked to contribute to workplans and complete activity and result forms. Another form I completed on a quarterly basis related to the amount of time I spent on the project, which was later monetized as an in-kind contribution.

The first Indonesian mission to Canada under GGP was in August 2007. It started with our colleagues arriving in Winnipeg for the IPAC annual conference. More than three years had passed since the last Indonesian mission to Canada. Muh Marwan, who was secretary of the training and education agency at Home Affairs, led the group that included Arif. Canadians had elected a Conservative government under Prime Minister Stephen Harper since the last Indonesian mission. It had no immediate impact on our cooperation. Jim Beaulieu was still living in Winnipeg and as a former IPAC president he attended the opening reception. I hadn't seen or spoken with him for nearly a decade. Jim had reluctantly left the Indonesia program when the demands of his consulting business prevented him from actively participating in the project. We embraced as old friends when we arrived at the conference. I introduced him to our Indonesian colleagues and he asked them about the status of the one-stop shops initiative that came about as a result of the 1995 mission meeting at Access Montreal. It was Jim who had suggested we include Access Montreal on the mission program. They were able to fill him in on all the positive developments that had taken place since his involvement.

After the conference ended the Indonesians and I flew to Toronto and then Nova Scotia to work on the councillor training initiative and make plans for other projects. Six activities (the IPAC conference being the first one) were agreed on prior to the mission. I documented the progress on each one and it was included in the mission report. Training for newly elected councillors was now the Indonesian priority. One of the decentralization laws dealt with local governance. Prior to the "Big Bang" local governments acted as implementers for national policies and programs, often with the help of central government staff. Now they were responsible for approving budgets, delivering most public services and planning and promoting economic development. We agreed to have elected Canadian local government (municipal) councillors participate in the next mission in early 2008 to Indonesia to share their insights and experiences.

As planned, the spring 2008 mission to Indonesia was built around training for newly elected local government councillors. Stephen Feist, who had managed the Nova Scotia side of the cooperation when I was in South Africa, led the four-person mission. Two of the participants had education and training experience in local government and the other two were experienced elected officials from Nova Scotia municipalities. I had recently returned from my work on the government reform support project in Indonesia and was unable to join them. It was the only one of the twenty IPAC missions to Indonesia between 1994 and 2014 I didn't make. When the group members returned to Halifax, they reported that the workshops had gone well. So well in fact that one of the Indonesian participants asked them to come and talk with their local council. Without contacting IPAC, they adjusted the schedule to accommodate the request and travelled there anticipating the costs would be covered by the IPAC program budget. This was not in line with the way the program was now being administered.

During the earlier years of our cooperation (1994-2000) Home Affairs prepared an agenda for our missions to Indonesia. The Indonesian government took care of all of our in-country travel costs. IPAC covered our overseas flights and expenses in Jakarta using program funds provided by the Canadian government. From 2001-2006 our activities were focused on Jakarta-based international workshops. The day trips to Tangerang and Banten province to discuss the local government enterprise and other projects were organized by Home Affairs. Staff arranged the travel using a government vehicle and accompanied us to the meetings.

By 2006, the cooperation had moved well into project implementation and both IPAC and CIDA were taking a greater interest in mission planning and deliverables. As its international program activity grew, so did IPAC's resources. It now had staff dedicated to working with the IPAC volunteers and our partner country counterparts like Yuswandi and Arif in Indonesia. The IPAC staff booked all our flights (before, we booked our own using IPAC's travel agent) and hotels in Jakarta, made local arrangements for the Indonesian missions to Canada, and approved all program agendas and travel in advance. The IPAC staff was professional and supported our goals and initiatives.

This misunderstanding about the process for making program changes that had financial consequences for IPAC took some time to resolve. The discussions over who should pay the extra travel costs arising from Stephen's decision strained his relationship with IPAC. In the meantime, Stephen was making a positive contribution to the councillor training initiative and I appreciated his commitment to the partnership. It was another example of why it was important that mission team members are knowledgeable about IPAC program administration requirements.

Nova Scotia Puts Pen to Paper: A Formal Partnership Arrangement

In November 2008, Pak Nuryanto, the head of the Centre for Management of Overseas Cooperation at Home Affairs, led a five-member mission to Nova Scotia. Local governments in Nova Scotia had recently held elections for mayors and councillors, and an orientation session for elected officials coincided with the mission. Indonesian law 32 / 2004 on decentralization and regional autonomy required local governments to take more responsibilities and, to do this, councillors needed to understand their responsibilities, powers and limitations. Our Indonesian colleagues were designing policies for educating and training local government councillors and coordinating the relative activities between governments. They had come to see how orientations for local government councillors were done in Nova Scotia. The program we prepared for them included attendance at an orientation event in Truro for all newly elected councillors organized by municipal stakeholders, and two smaller orientation sessions designed for single municipal councils.

The cooperation between Indonesia and Nova Scotia was formalized during the mission, through the signing of a six-page partnership arrangement by IPAC, Home Affairs and the province of Nova Scotia. Up until then the memorandums of understanding and workplans included only IPAC and Indonesia (Home Affairs) as signatories. Nova Scotia was added for two reasons. The first was to recognize the contribution Nova Scotia was making to the partnership. The second was to formalize the commitment and support of each participant. Indonesian ambassador Djoko Hardono flew in from Ottawa and formally witnessed the signing of the agreement by Nova Scotia Minister of Service Nova Scotia and Municipal Relations at the time, Jamie Muir, team lead Pak Nuryanto on behalf of the government of Indonesia, and IPAC President William Greenlaw. The reason it was called an arrangement instead of an agreement was that the Indonesian government only signed agreements with other national governments and not with subnational governments such as provinces.

There was one section on Canadian participant commitments that was unusual and potentially open to interpretation. In addition to each party's commitment to develop, approve, implement and report on annual plans, the partnership arrangement contained nine items specific to the behavior of IPAC and Nova Scotia participants. They included clauses on refraining from a number of activities (such as intelligence / clandestine activities, political and commercial activities, religious propagation), respecting local customs and traditions, refraining from supporting separatist movements, and complying with the laws, regulations and policies of the government of Indonesia. Indonesia's last authoritarian president had resigned a decade ago and the current president was the first to be directly elected by the Indonesian people. It's hard to know if these formal restrictions were a holdover from a previous era or if there were other reasons for including them. There were no similar clauses related to Indonesian activity in Canada.

IPAC invited our international partners to the annual conferences it held in August. Part of the program was a workshop for international participants and IPAC members involved in international programs. It was both a learning experience and a reunion. I looked forward to meeting many of the same people each year, following the progress of their provincially partnered IPAC projects and comparing it with ours. In addition to the one in Winnipeg there were three others during GGP. Our Indonesian colleagues were active participants at the workshops and dutifully attended the conference sessions on public administration geared mostly to a Canadian audience. There are a few conference-related activities lodged in my memory.

During the IPAC annual conference in Quebec City, Arif and I were asked to meet with Diana Ivancic-Skinner, IPAC manager of the Good Governance Program (GGP), and program officer Regan Mancini to discuss the workplan and project deliverables. The separate meetings with the GGP country teams were held in a hotel conference room. Diana and Regan were formally seated at the head of a large table with notepads and pens in hand. When Arif and I entered we felt like school-boys being called to account for our actions. In a way we were as the focus of the meeting was on measuring and reporting our short-term and medium-term results.

Kartiko Purnomo, Home Affair's director of capacity building and evaluation of local government performance, led the Indonesian delegation, which included Arif, at the conference in Fredericton. On the evening before we drove to Halifax the group told me they were tired of conference food and would like a meal with rice and spice. There was a small Caribbean restaurant near the conference centre operated by a recent university graduate and his food was a hit with our Indonesian delegates. They became more animated as the meal progressed. Kartiko has an outgoing personality and he started joking with the owner. Soon they were carrying on like long-lost friends and I was taken by how easily they related to one another. The owner had come to Fredericton to study business administration at the University of New Brunswick. He told us that he found it hard to find restaurant meals that suited his Caribbean tastes, so he opened one after completing his studies. One of his professors told him Fredericton wasn't ready for this kind of restaurant but the owner could see that the provincial capital was becoming more cosmopolitan and he went ahead. When Kartiko asked how it had worked out he replied, "Business is good."

IPAC program manager Regan Mancini had met Arif and other Indonesian colleagues at the IPAC conferences in Quebec City and Fredericton. One of her responsibilities was to organize the travel schedules of Indonesians attending the conferences. The earlier the flights were booked, the lower the prices, and IPAC had a limited budget. This was no easy task as Indonesia had a lengthy bureaucratic approval process. The travel also required the approval of the Canadian embassy in Jakarta where Jeffrey Ong was our go-to person. This process did not mesh well with IPAC timelines for booking flights and hotels. The lead-up to the Ottawa conference was especially stressful for the Institute of Public Administration of Canada staff as we waited for Home Affairs to select and approve participants. It finally happened and IPAC arranged for next day-departures. The IPAC annual conference starts with a Sunday evening reception. We were well into the evening when the Indonesians arrived. I was standing near Regan when I saw Arif enter the room. He was wearing a *batik* shirt and smiling. Ria was behind him and carried a bag filled with small gifts. Their smiles and energy spread, and any frustrations Regan and the other staff had quickly evaporated as the gifts were presented to them with apologies for any trouble the booking delays may have caused.

The 2010 IPAC annual conference was held in Ottawa. IPAC program officer Regan Mancini, Arif, Ria and I met to discuss our cooperation.

There were no Indonesian participants at the IPAC conference again until the one in Montreal in 2013. The rules had changed and conference participation had to be linked to a larger mission with the provincial partner. Autumn was usually a better time to schedule our Indonesian missions to Nova Scotia as civil servants and academics are back from summer holidays and the Nova Scotia weather is at its best.

The Big Durian: Jakarta (2007-2008)

In 2007 I had an opportunity to live and work in Jakarta for a few months. Hickling Corporation was a consulting company with Canadian roots based in Jakarta and led by David Deziel. The IPAC team had met with Hickling managers on previous missions to talk about ways we could work together and also to gain a better understanding of current events in Indonesia. Hickling showed particular interest in the format for our Indonesian study missions to Canada. When Ann Masson and I met with David in 2006 he expressed an interest in working with IPAC to recruit consultants for the second phase of a large CIDA-funded project called Government Reform Support Project (GRS2). IPAC had a recruitment system in place for other projects it was managing, so Ann agreed.

IPAC advertised a short-term consulting opportunity with Hickling for a local government enterprise expert in Indonesia during the summer of 2007. I expressed interest, IPAC forwarded my application to Hickling, and I was accepted. My contract was with IPAC and covered three months of work starting in October 2007.

I needed a work visa from the Indonesian government. Agung was a friend of Djoko Hardono, Indonesia's ambassador to Canada. Earlier that year, Agung asked him to meet with me when his duties took him to Halifax and his excellency had made a courtesy call to my office a few months later. He was accompanied by Yul Edison, an Indonesian working at the embassy. I called Yul for advice on submitting the work visa application and it was processed quickly.

The work involved preparing an academic paper (called a *naskah akademis*) to provide an opinion on the proposed local government

enterprise legislation. In addition to the research, there was a requirement to consult with stakeholders. This involved meeting with local
government enterprise (which Indonesians call by the acronym BUMD)
officials involved in water and banking services (the most common
Indonesian LGEs) to obtain their input. I was teamed up with Made, a
local consultant around my age. He was originally from Bali, had a good
sense of humour, and years of public sector experience.

The Hickling offices occupied a two-storey building in central
Jakarta close to three large shopping centres. I rented a furnished
apartment at the Ascott within walking distance of the office. I had
spent too much time stuck in Jakarta traffic to even consider a location
where I would be dependent on driving to and from work. Another
positive feature of the four-star Ascott was that it was considered to
be a safe hotel as it had a lower profile than some of Jakarta's five-star
hotels. A few years earlier a bomb was detonated at the JW Marriott
Hotel in Jakarta, killing twelve people and injuring over one hundred
more[49]. I was more focused on settling into the work and adjusting
to life in Jakarta, so I didn't give much thought to my personal safety.
Arif helped me take inventory at the one-bedroom apartment before
I signed off. The apartment hotel had a gym, small outdoor pool,
breakfast included in the room rate, and a restaurant / bar. A few years
earlier there had been a well-known chain restaurant in the building
and when I told people where I was staying, they said, "Oh, the TGI
Friday's building." I met other consultants who also used the gym
while staying there—a Chinese man in the financial sector who later
relocated to a Borobudur Hotel apartment with his wife, and a White
New Zealander who worked in communications and was married to
a Māori woman. A number of the US embassy staff lived at the hotel.
One of them was a young woman from California, accompanied by
her Mexican husband. He told me Indonesians were constantly speaking to him in Indonesian as they mistook him for a local. I fell into a
routine of breakfast at the hotel, weekday lunches at the Starbucks

---

49 The JW Marriott hotel in Jakarta experienced another suicide bomber attack in 2009
    during a breakfast meeting of members of Jakarta's expatriate business community.

in Plaza Indonesia, and dinner either at a casual restaurant at Plaza Indonesia or at my apartment.

My walk to work in the mornings took me through the narrow lanes of a *kampung*, the name given to Jakarta's poorer inner-city villages. I usually had no time to spare so I'd pick up my pace as I walked through the narrow lanes. Then I'd feel the morning heat and stop rushing as I didn't want to be dripping with sweat when I arrived at work. I didn't attract local attention the way I had on my first time in Jakarta over a decade ago, and no one asked me questions or said, "Hello mister." Like everyone else, I stepped aside to make room for the food carts, vans, and motorbikes that travel the laneways. I got distracted by the high-volume noise of household televisions, but I couldn't see many of the screens. Cats moved about lazily while enjoying the sun and chickens pecked away looking for food. Potted plants and flowers adorned the mostly concrete buildings. In the evenings I took a longer route along the main streets that were teeming with young people returning from their daily activities or out socializing. On one of these walks home I had gone through the Grand Indonesia, a large, upscale shopping mall in central Jakarta, and found it was raining heavily when I reached the exit. A young boy with an umbrella offered to escort me to my nearby hotel. I accepted the offer (which involved a small fee) from this umbrella boy who stretched his arms high to protect me from the rain. Indonesians call them *tukang payung* (which translates as umbrella man, but they are also known as the heroes of the hour) and although they keep their customers dry, they are often wet themselves.

Two evenings a week I took Indonesian language lessons from a local who went by the name of Rita. She was an ambitious and conscientious young woman who had a day job in administration and taught Indonesian to foreigners (or *bule*—pronounced boo-leh) as a sideline. Her enthusiasm was often at odds with my post-workday fatigue and as the only student I always had to be "on." Indonesian is not as difficult to learn as some other languages and I did learn quite a bit during the lessons with Rita. If I did it again, I would pick a better time of day with other students in the class.

There were security personnel at the gated entrance to the Hickling offices, which was welcome even though security in Indonesia was never a major concern for me. The meeting rooms and managers / administration offices were on the ground level of the building. Upstairs on the second storey there were two adjoining rooms for the consultants. The first room had ten desks and a doorway opening to a second room with six desks. Mine was in the second office and faced the end wall. To reach my desk I had to navigate an obstacle course of plugs, power chords, and chairs. I was accustomed to having a private office and found this arrangement distracting. The man at the desk beside mine printed everything he saw on the internet related to his project. The man beside him had a teenage daughter who often telephoned for advice or to complain. A woman on the other side of the room wore hard heels that clattered loudly on the tiled floor and constantly talked on her cell phone. Impromptu meetings were held in our small room along with casual conversations. I often stayed late to work after the others had gone home. Fortunately, most of us did some fieldwork and attended outside meetings. Some days the office was quiet but I never knew what to expect.

Made and I met with stakeholders at their offices, or in hotel lobbies, or meeting rooms if they had travelled to Jakarta. Once we went to Surabaya, a city Made knew well from his earlier work there with East Java province. Before leaving the City of Heroes, Made took me to see a house a previous governor had given him as a reward for good service. It was a three-bedroom bungalow in a good neighbourhood and we met with the young man who was the caretaker.

Made had been trying unsuccessfully for weeks to make an appointment to see a Home Affairs official named Fauzi who was responsible for implementing the local government enterprise (BUMD) law once it was passed. He wasn't interested in meeting with us for reasons that were never clear to me. Some Home Affairs officials were known to deliberately delay the implementation of the decentralization reforms and the transfers of power from the central government they were part of, and he could have been one of them. Made persisted in a good-natured way and some days we would go to Fauzi's office on the off chance he would be there. One day we were sitting in an empty Home Affairs office when a man in his fifties came in, sat down and started talking with Made in Indonesian. I couldn't follow what was being said but I could tell by his belligerent tone and his ranting that he was upset. He left abruptly. When I asked Made, "Who was that man?" he smiled and said, "It was Pak Fauzi." I was glad not to have been part of the discussion. It would have been difficult to sit through this lecture and criticism of our project if I had known what was happening. Updating the BUMD laws to bring them in line with decentralization policy may have been a government priority but it didn't appear to be Fauzi's. Our Indonesian colleagues had always treated the IPAC volunteers with courtesy and respect. I was learning that while consultants may be paid for their work, they have a lower status than peer-to-peer IPAC volunteers who were always treated as equals.

There were both long- and short-term consultants on the project and many were expats who made a career out of consulting. I enjoyed talking with them and learning about the work they had done. A common theme was a marriage to an Indonesian and then taking the best local work available. There were weekly meetings of Hickling staff and consultants. The Hickling CEO enjoyed confrontation so the Monday morning meetings could get the week off to a lively start. International projects like ours normally encounter obstacles and challenges and people had different ways of dealing with them. While I was there, Gabe Ferrazzi (the Canadian whom I'd met when he worked in Indonesia for GTZ) undertook an evaluation of the Government Reform Support Project (GRS2) on behalf of the Canadian government. He presented his initial findings at one of our Monday morning meetings. I was impressed that the evaluation criteria not only considered whether Hickling had done its part with respect to reports, consultations, advice and recommendations, etc., but that the evaluation also focused on the successful implementation of the work.

When my wife and I lived in South Africa I observed that the advisors accompanied by their spouses had fuller lives outside of work. This time I was alone and lonely, especially on weekends. However, there were three weekends when I found interesting diversions.

I'd been in Jakarta for a month when I flew to Singapore for the weekend. I joined Don Ross (the friend and colleague I'd travelled with in 2006 to the University of Bradford to visit our thesis supervisor) who was teaching an executive MBA weekend course there. We went out in the evenings and I explored the city-state on foot during the day. I hadn't realized how much the Jakarta crowds, traffic and pollution were wearing me down until I arrived in clean, orderly Singapore. During the two-week IPAC missions, I was never in Jakarta long enough to settle into the environment so it hadn't been something I had fully experienced before.

Friends from Vancouver, a couple who had both worked as advisors in South Africa with me, spent a few days on holiday in Jakarta. I took them to places not on regular city tour agendas that I thought they would enjoy—Café Batavia in the old city, Pasar Baru, the market I walked to when staying at the Borobudur, and Pasar Ria market, a favourite of Sue MacLennan's during our missions in the mid-1990s. On Sunday we hired a car and driver and explored Banten province (located on the western end of Java). A highlight was going to Merak to view the Sunda Strait and watch the ferries and cargo ships navigate the twenty-four-kilometre crossing between Indonesia's two most populous islands (Java and Sumatra). On an earlier mission, colleagues had told us about Indonesia's decades-long interest in building a bridge across the strait that joins the Java Sea and Indian Ocean and during the 1999 mission we had taken a group of Indonesians on a tour of the 12.9 km Confederation Bridge linking Prince Edward Island to the Canadian mainland. Now just a few months earlier (October 2007) the Indonesian government had given the go ahead for a suspension bridge to be built across the strait[50]. We were glad to be here to witness the "before the bridge" view. Our driver didn't speak English so I had an opportunity to practice the limited Indonesian I had learned from Rita. We gave the driver a large tip as I knew drivers didn't earn much. When I had looked into car rental rates in Jakarta the cost per month was US$1,000 without a driver and US$1,100 with one.

---

50 The project was shelved in November 2014 by President Widodo due to its high cost and a view that it would benefit only the middle class. Other options like more ferries will be considered.

One weekend in early December I went to my first Indonesian wedding. Pak Marwan, who led the 2000 and 2007 Indonesian missions to Canada, invited me to his daughter's wedding. Arif met me at my apartment and we took a taxi to the special events facility where the wedding and reception were taking place. It was a grand affair with beautiful traditional costumes and was by far the largest wedding I had attended. The women (guests included) wore heavy layers of makeup on their faces and looked beautiful. Both the bride's and groom's families dressed in their traditional costumes. There were dance and mock-combat performances and an endless supply of food. I saw a lot of familiar faces from Home Affairs there but no one else from Hickling.

I made an effort to see Home Affairs colleagues involved in our IPAC cooperation while working on GRS2. One evening I took Yuswandi and Eko out for dinner at a business district restaurant with a revolving rooftop restaurant. Another time I invited Arif, Renny and other Home Affairs colleagues out for a meal at one of the restaurants at Plaza Indonesia. Arif and I stayed in touch by texting but only got together a few times as he usually went to Bandung on weekends to visit his mother and siblings. The Hickling office was within walking distance of the Canadian embassy and Jeffrey Ong and I would meet for coffee to catch up on our news. It was always nice to see a familiar face.

Agung was now working with the government ministry responsible for international border issues. Indonesia's land borders are located on three shared islands: Papua, (shared with Papua New Guinea), Kalimantan (shared with Malaysian Borneo), and Timor (shared with East Timor), and he spent a lot of time in remote areas. I didn't see much of him for the first two months I worked with Hickling. One mid-December day he called me and asked if he could bring his tailor to my office to take my measurements. The result was a gift of a beautiful long sleeve *batik* shirt decorated with shapes and figures that represented features of Agung's ancestral Sundanese village in West Java. A pair of black slacks were added to the gift. I was touched by his thoughtfulness and generosity.

I spent Christmas in Canada and returned to Jakarta in late January 2008. Toward the end of the project Made and I held a workshop in

Malang, East Java. A number of academics at the Brawijaya University (located in Malang) were also involved in the research. Made and I both made presentations. Few of the workshop participants spoke English and there was no simultaneous translation. Each slide I presented in English was repeated in Indonesian. I knew everyone was waiting for the translation so I spoke quickly. Afterwards Made asked, "Mark, was there a train chasing you?"

There were still a few loose ends to tie up when I returned to Canada and Made took care of them. I saw him again the following year when Ann Masson and I visited the Hickling offices to meet with David Deziel during an IPAC mission.

My wife, Lise, joined me toward the end of the assignment and got reacquainted with Jakarta. Yuswandi, Eko and their wives took us out to an al fresco dinner at Ancol in North Jakarta one evening. The Indonesian wives referred to each other as Mrs. (Husband's Name), a formal practice that is no longer common in Canada. Before returning home we took a trip to Yogyakarta with Agung and Lili and visited many of the same places I had seen in 1997. Lili had lived in Yogyakarta when her father was governor there and she was proud to show us around. It was fun to be together. Lili and Agung decided not to climb the Borobudur Temple steps. I went up them again with Lise as she hadn't had the experience of climbing the steps of the largest Buddhist monument in the world to reach a rooftop terrace covered in stupas. There was an incident with a hopeful photographer who took unsolicited photos of us and then got upset when we didn't want to buy them. Agung resolved it but I don't remember the details. Lili later told us that when we were climbing the temple steps she and Agung spoke with a man selling post cards. He had lost his regular job and was destitute. They gave him money.

Before visiting the Buddhist Borobudur temple, we spent time at the nearby Hindu Prambanan temple complex. Indonesia's largest Hindu temple was built in the ninth century and abandoned within one hundred years when the centre of political power shifted. Both Borobudur and Prambanan were restored in the nineteenth and twentieth centuries and are now UNESCO World Heritage Sites. The time we spent at these historic locations led me to ask myself who was learning and benefiting most from the Indonesia—Nova Scotia project. The program existed so that Indonesians could benefit from the Canadian public sector / decentralized local government expertise. The IPAC volunteers took this responsibility seriously and did it well enough that our cooperation eventually made the Home Affairs minister's "top three" list of international donor projects. The Canadians were benefiting in another way—learning about the rich history and culture of a civilization much older and more religiously diverse than ours.

After spending three months in Indonesia, I was more familiar with the country. I'd always felt comfortable in Indonesia but now it was becoming a second home. Only my lack of speaking Indonesian kept me from becoming more immersed in the culture.

Because of the contrast between Indonesia and Canada I also had a greater appreciation of my Canadian environment and lifestyle. In Canada I lived in a mid-size city with good public infrastructure, a temperate climate, varying amounts of daylight throughout the year, and easy access to nature and clean air. In Indonesia I liked the abundance of pungent and fragrant smells that heat and humidity keep close to the earth, and the energy of densely populated Jakarta where people move with ease through crowds and traffic jams and take time to laugh and joke. There was a certain comfort in the formality and traditions celebrated in places like Yogyakarta, a respect for the elderly, and the importance of family. I was grateful to have a place in both of these worlds.

Roundtable on Decentralization and a Move to Academia

The third Home Affairs—IPAC roundtable discussion was on decentralization and public services and held at the Hotel Lumire in Jakarta in June 2009. There were ten speakers plus session facilitators and over one hundred participants. Home Affairs organized the event and prepared a background paper outlining the recent decentralization reforms and the challenges involved in meeting the legal requirement to ensure equal access for all citizens to basic services. Roundtable objectives (exchange perspectives and best practices, develop recommendations, strengthen our cooperation) were identified. Discussion topics were provided and the expectations of speakers explained. IPAC provided four speakers (Judy Rogers, a former Vancouver city manager, Alex Brillantes from the University of the Philippines, me, and another Canadian). Ann Masson, IPAC's director of international programs, shared her observations at the end of the day wrap-up session. The Indonesian speakers were from central government ministries and local governments. Program speaker number six is identified as Mr. Joko Widodo, mayor of Surakarta, on the first program draft shared with IPAC. His name wasn't on the final roundtable program but the Home Affairs organizers must have recognized the valuable contribution he could bring to the workshop. Jokowi, as he was known, was elected president of Indonesia in 2014 and again in 2019. Canadian ambassador John Holmes joined Home Affair's secretary general, Diah Anggraeni, in opening the roundtable. A lively question and answer period followed each of the two sessions and Home Affairs deemed it a success. The remainder of the mission was spent working with colleagues on the councillor training and local government enterprise initiatives, program planning, and making courtesy calls.

Before we left for Indonesia one of the Canadian participants told me he wanted to take a side trip within Indonesia to meet with a group he and a Canadian colleague had been corresponding with about working on a project together. IPAC's procedures and policies guide (s3.1) covers missions to Canada and abroad. It refers to five working day missions and an expectation that participants will participate in all partnership activities for the duration of the mission. I advised him to wait and go after our mission was over and also to discuss it with IPAC beforehand. He didn't take my advice and made arrangements to leave Jakarta on a Thursday evening, saying Friday was only really a half day of work because of Friday prayers. The day after the roundtable he changed his flight to Wednesday. Ann Masson did not take this news well and had no hesitation in confronting him. His burly build did not intimidate her at all. She met with him for an early breakfast on Wednesday morning and

Ann reminded him that we had all committed to a minimum five-day mission. She informed him if he left early he would have to pay 50 percent of all his travel costs. The venture he was pursuing had no budget so he reluctantly cancelled his side trip. IPAC didn't have an issue with Canadian organizations leveraging IPAC—Home Affairs cooperation to strengthen public and private sector ties between Indonesia and Canada. The issue here was fulfilling an obligation to IPAC and the program. Ann was annoyed with me as team lead for not intervening sooner. I always made sure our Canadian volunteers knew what was expected of them on missions and as we were all professionals I felt that compliance would not become as issue.

In 2008, as mentioned earlier, I took an early retirement from the province of Nova Scotia and accepted a faculty position at Dalhousie University's School of Public Administration. I was brought in to add a local government stream of courses to the master's degree in public administration program. Before leaving my government job, I arranged to continue leading the Indonesia program until the current phase of the cooperation ended in 2009. IPAC suggested we consider adding an academic component in our renewal proposal. Agung knew we were interested in including an academic partnership in the next renewal of our CIDA-funded program and thought that the Institute Pemerintahan Dalam Negeri (IPDN) would be a logical counterpart. It was not only a degree granting institution but also part of Home Affairs. After the other Canadian participants in the 2009 mission left Indonesia, Agung and I drove to the IPDN campus in Jatinangor (near Bandung). Lili loaned us her company car and driver so Agung and I were able to talk comfortably in the backseat of the air-conditioned vehicle. Ibu Ngadisah, who participated in the 1999 mission to Canada and had been critical of the casual approach I'd taken at a Tim Hortons café in Nova Scotia, had recently been appointed IPDN rector. She was formally dressed and wore a headscarf when she gave us a warm greeting upon arrival and then invited us for coffee. With Agung's help I expressed my interest in learning more about IPDN and a possible academic partnership. Agung had already explained all of this when he set up the meeting so I wasn't surprised when afterwards she arranged for us to view a forty-eight-slide presentation about IPDN.[51] Once again Agung had moved our cooperation forward. As a result of his initiative, I was able to remain involved and the cooperation was expanded to include an academic and research component.

The funding application for the next phase of the project included the achievements to date for the IPAC—Indonesia—Nova Scotia project. It also provided a detailed project-planning sheet linking program purpose, goals, activities, outputs, immediate and intermediate outcomes, and ultimate impacts. It required a multitude of performance indicators as well as risks and assumptions. It was a mammoth undertaking. Planning, accountability, and documenting results are important, but for a project to be effective it's the time spent doing the work that is the most important.

---

51 I have a copy in English.

PART 5

Doubling the Effort: Project Leaders Ask for More Canadian Input in Implementing Reforms (2010-2015)

"The perfect ending to any day, race, or project is to finish strong."

– Gary Ryan Blair, American entrepreneur and author.

Saut braves an early winter storm as we walk along University Avenue in Halifax during the November 2011 study mission.

An early season snowstorm has thrown a curveball at the November 2011 mission to Canada program. Pak Saut and I are leaning into the wind as we walk along University Avenue on the way to a Dalhousie campus meeting. Snow is blowing all around us, the sidewalk is slippery, and our shoes are wet. Pak Saut is not one to bow to adversity of any kind and moves forward in this unfamiliar and unforgiving weather. I relive this scene a few days later when Mel Sweetnam, a new IPAC program officer, sends me a black and white photo she took of us that day. Saut looks elfin, bent forward with a parka hood over his cap and a winter coat buckle showing. One ear is exposed, and he looks to be concentrating on something—a thought, a plan—or wishing the cold away.

Peer-to-peer Initiatives—Practitioner and Academic

The next phase (2010-2015) of our Canadian government-funded cooperation was called the Democratic Governance Program (DGP). The DGP years of the Indonesia—Nova Scotia cooperation were our most productive. They also brought a return to extensive travel within Indonesia but on a much larger scale than the IPAC team experienced in the early years of the cooperation. Senior staff from Home Affairs and IPDN were now accompanying us on the in-country travel. They collaborated with their local government colleagues to show us public facilities (hospitals, schools, enterprises) and local attractions. As I got to know our Home Affairs colleagues better, I was able to organize extracurricular activities that matched their interests when they were in Canada.

During this time the politics and quality of democracy in our two countries were on different paths. It stalled in Canada as the government of the day continued the historic practice of manipulating the system to its own advantage. Canada became the first country to withdraw from the Kyoto Accord (2011), Parliament was prorogued to avoid a vote of non-confidence in the government, omnibus bills were introduced, and restrictions were placed on government scientists sharing their research findings. These events, which some Canadians viewed with concern, were problematic from the perspective of sharing of good governance practices. Canada continued to follow the Westminster model of government that does not permit voters to directly elect the leader of the country; the selection is left to the members of the political party that forms the government. Indonesia on the other hand was moving forward with policies that enabled local governments to become more democratic and decentralized. Its score on Transparency International's corruption index had improved to 32 compared with 17 during the Suharto era, although it still lagged behind Canada's score of 77. A peaceful presidential transition took place following the 2014 election when Joko Widodo (Jokowi) was elected president, directly by the people, with 53 percent of the votes.

Indonesia experienced a number of natural and manmade disasters during the DGP years. The Mentawai earthquake / tsunami of 2010 in West Sumatra caused over 450 deaths and the wall of water following the quake levelled villages. Mount Merapi, Indonesia's most active volcano (located in Central Java), erupted three times in October 2010. There were over 350 deaths, and thousands were evacuated from their homes. Heavy monsoon rains and an inadequate colonial-era drainage system caused massive flooding in Jakarta in January 2013. Blocked roads and high water levels caused people to abandon their homes and closed government offices and businesses. Fifteen deaths were reported. In 2014 a volcanic eruption at Mount Sinabung, North Sumatra, displaced 20,000 people and resulted in fourteen deaths. It had been 400 years since its last eruption. Smoke and haze from fires set by farmers using slash-and-burn techniques to clear vegetation in Sumatra and Kalimantan in 2015 is estimated to have caused 100,000 premature deaths. While none of these disasters had a direct impact on our cooperation, they provided context for the work we were doing on service delivery and service standards, especially those related to health and emergency services.

Religious tolerance received a setback when Ahmadi Muslims were persecuted and killed in Banten province for their lack of adherence to the religious practices of Indonesia's Sunni majority. One Indonesian colleague I discussed this with said he was not bothered by it and held the majority view that the Ahmadis (Ahmadi Muslims) were apostates (those with non-mainstream beliefs) and therefore not to be accepted in the Muslim community. Shiite cleric Tajul Muluk was imprisoned for blasphemy in 2012 and six drug traffickers were executed by firing squad in 2015. Although the quality of our democracies was moving closer in areas like democratic elections and the provision of basic public services, Canada and Indonesia differed on tolerance of minority rights, freedom of speech on religious matters, and capital punishment.

Looking back at an earlier time in Canadian history when there was capital punishment, less protection for minorities, and religious discrimination and intolerance, I was curious about whether Indonesia was on the same path forward but at a slower pace.

An academic component was included in the new Indonesia—Nova Scotia program. There were now two Nova Scotia team leads. IPAC's executive director asked Kevin Malloy, the deputy minister responsible for local government in Nova Scotia, to assume the lead of the practitioner stream and he agreed. I was asked to take responsibility for the Dalhousie / IPDN academic segment. As I was familiar with the practitioner stream I often filled in for Kevin in organizing the practitioner side of study missions and communicating with IPAC on project-related issues.

The Democratic Governance Program included the current seven partners (Mali / New Brunswick, Malawi / New Brunswick, Uganda / Ontario, Namibia / Saskatchewan, Indonesia / Nova Scotia, Philippines / Manitoba, and the African Association for Public Administration and Management / IPAC) and added three new ones (Ghana / Alberta, Vietnam / Toronto, and Tanzania / Canada School of Public Service). The program added new features and requirements that reflected the Canadian government's official development assistance priorities (economic development, food security, youth and children), and included case studies and publications. IPAC's contribution agreement with the Canadian partnership branch contained new requirements on gender mainstreaming (such as making gender-specific issues like maternal care and participation in the workforce a budget priority) and partnership agreements. This was the first program renewal since the Conservative government led by Stephen Harper was elected in 2006 and the wording reflected government priorities. In reality the core activities related to supporting decentralization in Indonesia remained the same as they had been under programs approved by the previous Liberal government.

The goal of DGP was to enhance the well-being of citizens in developing countries by contributing to socio-economic recovery and growth of up to 5 percent.[52] The project document included the Indonesia—Nova Scotia cooperation's achievements to date under the headings of training, education and certification, fiscal management, and service delivery.

The knowledge sharing and technical assistance provided to IPAC partner countries under DGP varied widely but were always based on country priorities that aligned with Canada's development assistance goals. In Indonesia it related to decentralization and local governance (which fit with the Canadian government's economic development priority). It was health care in Mali, early childhood development in Namibia, human resource management and communications policy in Uganda, education in Tanzania, management development in Vietnam, gender mainstreaming in Malawi, internal audit in Ghana, and local governance and interregional collaboration in the Philippines. CIDA agreed to contribute $5.8 million and the IPAC / Canadian partners' in-kind volunteer contribution would add an additional $2 million. All monies would be managed directly by the Institute of Public Administration of Canada. IPAC's international program division was fully staffed to handle the Democratic Governance Program planning, documentation, reporting and results monitoring that were more comprehensive and detailed than before. There were two reasons the budget was relatively small for the scope of the work in all these countries. The participating Canadians (or their employers) were volunteering their time and there were no Canadian overhead costs in the project countries as there were no offices to maintain. These were important factors to consider when managing project impact expectations.

---

52 The objective was to enhance the individual and institutional capacity of selected public sector ministries, departments, agencies and associations to contribute to socio-economic priorities, such as economic growth and food security, and enable women, youth and children to reach their full potential. The Indonesia—Nova Scotia partnership includes knowledge sharing and technical assistance activities and will meet the listed objectives by increasing the pace of public administration reform and ensuring the successful implementation of decentralization policy.

Partnership Priorities and Fewer Prohibitions

The November 2010 inception mission was our most carefully planned and documented mission to date. This was due to the inclusion of IPAC support staff who also prepared the mission report that linked the results to our objectives. IPAC were now using a logic model[53] framework to measure results. I was familiar with this framework as South Africa's National Treasury had used it to monitor progress on the municipal financial management technical assistance program in South Africa. The six female and eighteen male mission participants are listed, in keeping with Canada's interest in reporting on gender issues.

The mission's packed program schedule reflected the momentum our cooperation generated during this phase. We had good working relationships, the decentralization reforms were moving forward, and there was a need that Canadian knowledge and experience could fill. The week began with a meeting with Jeffrey Ong at the Canadian embassy followed by meetings with a number of colleagues at Home Affairs, IPDN, UNDP, and other international donors. During the later part of the week, we met with ministerial advisor Dr. Suwandi at Home Affairs for further input into how the IPAC programs could complement those of other donors, and Indonesia's foreign affairs policy planning and development agency (BPPK) to discuss IPAC's Deployment for Democratic Development initiative.[54] Arif and Ria (Dameria) accompanied us to all the meetings, each of which had a specific written objective that was provided in our program schedule.

The Indonesian—Nova Scotia partnership priorities areas were established. Yuswandi, the acting secretary general, wanted the partnership to have a clear agenda, specific outputs and clear results focused

---

53 The logic model is a tool used in project management. It has five parts: impact / objectives, inputs, activities, outputs and outcomes. The outcomes are divided into short-term, medium-term and long-term.

54 This initiative was also CIDA funded and involved providing a specialist to work on a specific issue / project in Indonesia (and other countries) for a period of twelve to eighteen months.

on Indonesian government priorities linking bureaucratic reform and revised law 32 / 2004 concerning regional autonomy. He identified four specific areas of the reform agenda: function, structure, human resources, and finance. Yuswandi told us more about Indonesia's "grand design." Home Affairs would lead bureaucratic reform at the regional level and provide direction to local governments. IPAC was advised to support the reforms through technical assistance and knowledge sharing. Yuswandi said he expected it would take ten to fifteen years to complete the bureaucratic reform initiatives. Law 32 / 2007 on regional autonomy was under revision. The law emphasized subsidiarity; an organizing principle that recommends services should be offered by the level of government closest to the people served (local government in this case). Yuswandi suggested that MOHA and IPAC cooperate on projects that were both interesting and relevant and keep a clear agenda linked to current reforms. IPDN were undertaking policy work that would be used to advise the minister and he suggested our comparative study initiative could be helpful in identifying areas where changes in policy were needed.

Harunata (who replaced Nuryanto as team lead) suggested a focus on local government training in areas such as licencing, identity cards, one-stop shop services, and permits. Jeffrey Ong identified areas where Home Affairs required assistance: improved ministry coordination, human resource capacity building (an item on the president's national agenda) and expenditure management. We used this input to select the areas of focus for our cooperation. They were: sound fiscal management, service provision, capacity development of elected and appointed local government officials, and collaboration / accountability relationships between local and national governments.

Four priorities were identified for the newly created IPDN—Dalhousie University partnership: 1) joint research and publications; 2) joint lectures; 3) faculty exchanges; 4) training of trainers, so IPDN lecturers could train students and local government employees.

The addition of an academic stream to our cooperation with Indonesia provided me with an opportunity to stay connected and undertake international academic research. Dalhousie University had been involved in Indonesia-based projects in the past and welcomed an opportunity to continue. Dalhousie's School of Public Administration faculty, the university's international research and development group, and the centre for advanced management education were all active participants in the campus portions of the missions. My Indonesian lead counterpart was the rector of the Institute of Local Government / Institut Pemerintahan Dalam Negeri (IPDN), Dr. Nyoman Sumaryadi (who had replaced Ibu Ngadisah). The province of Nova Scotia component was a continuation of what we had been doing since the program began, i.e. study missions, joint seminars, knowledge sharing, technical assistance, and roundtables. In addition to councillor and staff training there was a high level of interest in service standards, public service delivery options, and strengthening local government fiscal capacity. At my first meeting with IPDN in November 2010 we agreed on six areas where we would work together. The first and most interesting one was an Indonesian—Canadian comparative study of local government public service standards and delivery. The others were development of course material, joint lectures, joint research and publications, adding an academic component to the roundtable discussions, and spreading knowledge through short courses and faculty exchanges.

The expansion of the program enabled greater engagement and buy-in from both the public and academic sectors in Nova Scotia. The number of Nova Scotia public servants and academics taking part in the missions grew and we added health, education and fire services to the list of service areas we would include in our program.

One event that was not included in the inception mission program schedule took place on our last evening in Jakarta. Agung and his family invited our Canadian team for dinner at a trendy central Jakarta restaurant we had been hearing about all week. IPAC staff were delighted at the opportunity to spend an evening with an Indonesian family. The conversation was lively. Arief, the eldest of Agung's three children, told us about his university experience in Queensland, Australia. He said he had lost weight there, but not because he couldn't find rice and enough to eat. We all nodded, remembering from past experiences with our Indonesian colleagues how important rice was for their diet. Arief explained the reason he lost weight was that he took a paper delivery route for extra spending money and got more exercise.

*IPAC staff share a meal with Agung, Lili and their family
during the 2010 Inception Mission.*

Although he no longer had direct responsibilities related to our program, Agung was always interested in learning about our workplans and activities. Before leaving we discussed them and some of the broader governance topics. These informal discussions with Agung gave me a better perspective of what was going on in Indonesia and where our efforts were apt to be the most meaningful and have the biggest impact at the community level. Our team had come a long way from our first mission when Louis and I were promoting local government amalgamations in Sulawesi at a time when there was a desire for more, not fewer, local governments in Indonesia.

During this time in our mission, Indonesian President Yudhoyono (SBY) was in his second term and the decentralization initiatives were gaining momentum. Indonesian challenges to be faced over the next five years related to service delivery, accountability of local government, strengthening regional processes and measuring and monitoring results. I reviewed the "USAID 2009 Report: Stock Taking on Indonesia's Recent Decentralization Reforms," which recommended enhanced local government revenue generation, greater transparency and accountability in service delivery, improved skills in working with civil society, and other initiatives.

A new memorandum of understanding / partnership arrangement for the Indonesia project was prepared. The logos of the five Democratic Governance Program (DGP) partners[55] dominated the first page. In addition to specifying the numerous commitments of the parties, it included a clause respecting the ongoing needs of governing by acknowledging that the timing and duration of activities will depend on partner capacity. There were no clauses related specifically to the behaviour of IPAC and Nova Scotia participants as there had been in the 2008 partnership arrangement. Those remnants of the Suharto era were gone.

High Profile Jakarta Workshop–One-stop Shops

Interest in one-stop shops for service delivery was a constant in our cooperation so I wasn't surprised when I received a letter of invitation from Secretary General Diah Anggraeni to speak at the roundtable discussion in June 2011 on building local competitiveness through one-stop service provisions. Kevin Malloy also received an invitation. He wasn't available that week so proposed that one of his middle management staff go instead. IPAC replied that the criteria for selecting volunteers had changed and Kevin was asked to appoint someone holding a more senior position. By this time, it was too late to find a replacement.

While IPAC and Kevin were in discussions about a replacement, staff in Kevin's department prepared a slide presentation and forwarded it to IPAC and Home Affairs. Mel Sweetnam, the new IPAC program officer, was handling the administrative and organizing arrangements for the IPAC team. She was also participating in the mission and we had corresponded amicably through phone calls and emails. However, the tone of her exchanges with the province of Nova Scotia on a suitable

---

55 IPAC, Indonesian Ministry of Home Affairs, province of Nova Scotia, IPDN and Dalhousie University.

replacement for Kevin caused me to think my mission colleague might be inflexible. I needn't have worried. She was just doing her job. We met for the first time in the departure lounge at the Toronto airport. Mel was pleasant and reserved but opened up as we waited for our flight. I learned she had a lot of experience working with international NGOs. We talked about the program for the mission before boarding the plane and taking our assigned economy class seats in different rows.

Arif met us at the airport and took us to the Sari Pan Pacific hotel where the roundtable would be held. He led us through the detailed program he and his colleagues had prepared for the mission. The program structure included two sessions with multiple speakers, one in the morning and one in the afternoon, with a Canadian presenter at each of them. When we told them I was the only Canadian speaker on the mission, our Indonesian colleagues came the closest I've seen to being visibly upset, in a non-Javanese way, that I had experienced in our nearly twenty years of working together. They said, "This is a high profile, carefully planned event and IPAC must honour its two-speaker commitment." The only other Canadian present was Mel, who was there in an IPAC administrative role. After much coaxing from the Indonesians Mel agreed to read the information on the slides at the second session. The roundtable was well organized and the seven Indonesian speakers included senior people from central, provincial and local government. To raise the profile of the roundtable, facilitators from the Harvard Kennedy School Indonesia Program and UNDP were included in the program. The Canadian ambassador attended the opening session and we joined him for coffee at the morning break. The morning sessions covered one-stop shop policies in Indonesia and Canada and how they could be used to promote local investments and deal with regional problems. The afternoon presenters discussed best practices. It all went smoothly, and our colleagues were pleased with this high-profile event as they thought it would accelerate the adoption of One-stop Shops by Indonesian local governments as well as the use of best practices in existing ones.

In the days that followed we held project planning meetings with Home Affairs and went to the main IPDN campus in Jatinangor,

West Java, to meet with students and faculty. In her role as IPAC program officer, Mel provided staff support during the 2011 mission to Indonesia. She was an advocate for gender equality, which was one of the DGP goals. Mel was also impulsive. When the taxi we were taking to the airport stopped in traffic beside a woman with an outstretched palm carrying a child, Mel told the driver to wait. She dug through her purse for a 100,000-rupiah bill (C$14 at the time). She found one (her last), rolled down the window, and passed it to the woman. The average monthly earnings for an Indonesian in 2011 was US$100 so Mel had just given the woman the equivalent of three days wages. We had been reminded when leaving the hotel that we each needed 150,000 rupiah in cash for the departure tax levied at the airport and Mel no longer had that amount. I had extra rupiah and offered her some but she found an airport ATM that would accept her card. I was impressed that her need to help this woman and child was more important to her than the risk of not being able to board the flight home.

Academic Cooperation and Research

Our work with IPDN gained momentum after the 2010 inception mission. The following year the IPAC team spent two days at the IPDN Jatinangor campus. On the first day I participated in a series of lectures on public service provision through one-stop service, the term Home Affairs preferred for what we had called one-stop shops. The 100-plus participants consisted of IPDN students and lecturers, lecturers from other private and state universities in the region, and practitioners from cities and regencies in West Java. It was well organized and a lively question period followed each presentation. There were a couple of Indonesians in the audience with prior Canadian knowledge or experience who added to the discussion. The following day we discussed joint research and curriculum development and made plans to move them forward.

The IPDN campuses became the venue for seminars, workshops and roundtables for the remainder of our program. There was an

IPDN campus in every region in Indonesia and they specialized in different aspects of government administration. The main campus was in Jatinangor, West Java, and the Cilandak campus in Jakarta offered master's-level degrees.

In November 2011, the Home Affairs and IPDN participants spent time on the Dalhousie campus in discussions with faculty members about curriculum, course integration, internships, professional development, and joint research. They attended a faculty meeting and gave presentations on local government reform in Indonesia to two graduate classes; one in strategic management and one in city government.

The following year (2012) the Home Affairs / IPDN group spent two days on the Dalhousie University campus at meetings related to curriculum development, joint research and our comparative study. They sat in on a policy workshop and made a presentation to my city government class.

Nurdin was the Indonesian Home Affairs lead for overseas collaboration on education and training for civil servants. IPDN educated future civil servants, while the Education and Training Agency (ETA) that Nurdin represented was tasked with providing training and education for current civil servants. Dalhousie University did both. Nurdin is an energetic man with a thin mustache that highlights a ready smile and, most importantly, he is dedicated to his work. This was his second mission to Canada and he was interested in offering new programs to Indonesian civil servants. Nurdin was impressed with the blended learning method that was used in the Dalhousie's Master of Public Administration program (MPA Management). It was developed for mid-career public servants who wanted to keep working while earning an MPA.

Nurdin asked me to have Dalhousie prepare a proposal to create a specialized academic education program using a blended learning format for administrators working in Indonesian local government. I spoke with Martine Durier-Copp at the Dalhousie Centre for Advanced Education and Management and we prepared a proposal to strengthen local government in Indonesia. It included three training level offerings: a blended delivery model MPA program for managers, a one-semester certificate program, and a specialized three-week study term. IPAC was included as a partner and the proposal included participation at the IPAC annual conference and an option to contribute to IPAC case studies as part of the MPA program. We did not receive a response from the Indonesian government. It was disappointing but not surprising. I felt it was still worth the effort as in the long run any information gathered and shared can be usefully repurposed.

The IPAC program officers report had this to say about our academic collaboration during the 2012 mission: "Academic collaboration. The sharing of Master of Public Administration (MPA) curriculum and course information from Dalhousie University and faculty exchange lectures has established a good platform for IPDN to update and improve the curriculum and course content in its bachelor and master degree programs. The comparative study of Indonesian and Canadian decentralized governance models is close to completion and will help further effective collaboration between Indonesia and Nova Scotia in the delivery of decentralized public services."

Kuswanto helped coordinate the IPAC team's April 2013 mission to Indonesia. He was a young family man who had already studied abroad and now had Indonesian government approval for overseas doctoral studies. He had prepared a PhD research proposal on decentralization and governance and was looking for a university that would accept him. The Indonesian government had made some funding available for his studies and he asked if I would make inquiries at Dalhousie University on his behalf. I approached colleagues at Dalhousie and inquired about the application process for an interdisciplinary PhD and their interest in being one of the three required thesis supervisors. It looked promising. In the fall of 2013, Kuswanto sent me an email saying, "After considering my wife's health heart condition and discussing the PhD time frame with my sponsor it is very hard for me to go to Dalhousie University." The sponsor was allowing him 3.5 years to complete the degree. He had been admitted to the University of Groningen, Netherlands, and enrolled there. I saw him again in Jakarta in 2018. He had completed his doctorate and was back working for the Indonesian government. I was pleased to learn he had completed his studies.

When the Home Affairs / IPDN participants came to the Dalhousie University campus in December 2013, we established a framework for presenting and analyzing the data collected for our comparative study. The four service areas that would form the basis of the study were chosen. They were water, education, infrastructure, and regulations for licences and permits. IPDN was represented by Dr. Untung Subagio who was now the Indonesian research lead on our comparative study. Professor Untung Subagio is a small man with an impish grin and, not unlike most of my Indonesian colleagues, a ready smile. His hair was grey and he sported a goatee, which some studies link with a capable, dependable, commitment-keeping personality. He was born in the mid-1950s and was lecturing at the IPDN campus in Jatinangor when we first met. During our meetings on the Dalhousie University campus, we agreed to provide the relevant context and background information for our countries and gather the information needed for the comparison and analysis. We set timelines for completing a written report. IPAC had budgeted funds for us to present our findings at the October 2014 EROPA conference in Hanoi.

Nurdin (far right) at a meeting on the Dalhousie campus, December 2013. Nurdin was responsible for the education and training for Indonesian civil servants.

There were also three mission participants (including Nurdin) from Home Affair's education and training agency and I arranged meetings with Dalhousie faculty and staff to discuss adult training and education programs. Indonesia was engaged in a donor-funded public sector leadership training program with Harvard University and Nurdin expressed interest in having a similar program with Dalhousie University. He asked Dalhousie to prepare a proposal and I worked with the Centre for Advanced Education and Management to prepare another proposal for the Indonesian government. Like the one submitted through Nurdin in 2012, it didn't receive the approval of the Indonesian government, or in this case the donor agency funding the project. At Dalhousie we were learning the key to a successful solicited proposal was that the person requesting the proposal have the authority or influence to approve it.

A few months later in February 2014 Professor Untung and I met at our hotel after the international seminar on the Jayapura IPDN campus in Papua province. We confirmed the public service areas agreed to in Halifax and set timelines for the completion of the comparative study. Prior to the next mission, we exchanged country and service information for the cooperative study. In May 2014 we spent a few days in Halifax with Yusharto (Indonesian team lead), Marvin MacDonald (Kevin Malloy's designate) and others selecting the data needed to analyze each of the four services being compared. We discussed the standards used for each component of each service in each country. Indonesia leaned toward standards set to reflect basic needs and Canada to standards set by professional bodies. We then looked at how areas with low standards could be improved. Affordability, regulation, and enforcement were factors that had to be considered.

Although we had collected and analyzed all the data for each comparative service during the May 2014 mission, there was still a lot of work to be done to provide additional context and background information for the study. Professor Untung had already provided some but a lot more was needed. Back in May, Untung had told me that he had recently been appointed rector at the IPDN campus in Pontianak, West Kalimantan. As rector, he said he had several responsibilities, including campus maintenance, that he had to carry out himself because he lacked the staff. He said that he would do his best to provide the information we needed to complete our study. After he left Canada, I didn't hear from him again. I completed the Indonesian context section of the study as best I could and included Professor Untung as one of the authors of the study. Afterwards I applied and was invited to present the research at the 2014 EROPA conference.

Indonesian Team Leads New Priority– Financial Management

On the practitioner side of the cooperation, the information sharing priority shifted from training for elected local government councillors to improvements in local government service standards / delivery and financial management. The information sharing / technical assistance approach included seminars in Canada and Indonesia, field and site visits during the study missions to Canada, assessments by Canadian experts, and teams dedicated to working together in selected service areas. The priority services identified by Home Affairs were health, education, infrastructure, and fire. In Canada some of these services were a provincial responsibility and I was glad our work had the support of the province of Nova Scotia. In Indonesia, provinces were tasked with a coordination role but not service delivery responsibilities. The alternative service delivery (ASD)[56] methods were also a priority and I had recently conducted research using primary data on the use of ASD by local governments in Canada. We were also asked to share information on other decentralization topics[57] at IPDN campuses that specialized in those areas.

Six months later, in November 2011, we met Saut Situmorang, the new Indonesian DGP team leader, in Halifax. There had been a high turnover in Indonesian team leads since Nuryanto had signed the GGP partnership arrangement in 2008, and I relied on Arif as coordinator to keep things on track.

---

56 In this context it refers to any service not provided directly by a government department.

57 The topics were integrated development plans, democratization and local politics and elections, capacity development for local government officials, and central-local government relations.

Saut Situmorang was advisor to the minister of Home Affairs in government fields when he led the first DGP mission to Canada. He brought a great sense of urgency to our cooperation that ramped up both our activities and our profile. Pak Saut used our cooperation to foster the implementation of local government reforms in the areas of service delivery, service standards, financial planning and budgeting, and one-stop shops. He was a small, fifty-something man with tired eyes, when he became involved in our program. I found him to be intense and task oriented. He was more assertive in his manner and approach than any of the Indonesian leads we had worked with before. He was serious and gruff, and seldom exhibited the harmonious and fun-loving qualities I had experienced with other Indonesian colleagues. The Indonesian team members always prefaced his name with the word "Pak" (Mr.) when they referred to him, something they didn't do with the other project leads. Pak Saut remained the Indonesian lead on our program until he was appointed to a provincial governorship in mid-2013.

Pak Saut's first priority was financial management in local governments. The November 2011 mission to Canada was dedicated to financial planning for local governments. There were multiple representatives from cities and regencies in six Indonesian provinces (Aceh, Riau, Lampung, DKI Jakarta, West Java, and South Kalimantan) and the others (including Arif and Nurdin) were from Home Affairs and IPDN.

The program started with a series of presentations on provincial—municipal government relations and financial responsibilities in Canada. IPDN Professor Sadu spoke about issues facing Indonesian provinces in a decentralizing unitary state. He expressed interest in strengthening the role of provincial governors as representatives of the central government. He told us that at the present time there were no instruments for supervision or mechanisms for involving stakeholders in determining minimum service standards, no penalties for failure to meet minimum service standards, and money had not followed function (unfunded mandates). Local governments often misused allocated funds through poor priority choices or a lack of knowledge about their responsibilities. He informed us that the current Indonesian priorities were providing proper public services, meeting minimum service standard targets, and strengthening capacity. Mechanisms were needed to ensure they were achieved and he was looking to Nova Scotia for examples and best practices.

The group was divided into two streams for the next two days. The city and regency (county) participants visited municipalities in Nova Scotia to view examples of the information provided in the seminar. On Thursday evening a dinner was held at Cha Baa Thai on Queen Street and the left-over rice was packed and taken to nearby Cambridge Suites where the group was staying. This restaurant was the preferred evening eating spot for the group and at one point I overheard Arif telling Mel that "Cha Baa Thai saved my life." Having rice and spice on the menu was just as important in 2011 as it had been during the initial mission in 1994, and having some on hand for a midnight snack for jet-lagged travellers was appreciated.

On Friday morning all the participants met on the Dalhousie University campus to share experiences and discuss the link between policy (theory) and implementation (practice), complete the mission evaluation forms, and finalize plans for our ongoing cooperation. Mel prepared the mission report, which confirmed that most mission objectives were achieved and some were exceeded as fourteen self-financed delegates leveraged and augmented IPAC—Home Affairs partnership priorities. She also reported under gender statistics that one hundred males and twenty-five females participated in mission activities.

An early snowstorm prevented one objective from being met as some visits to municipalities outside of Halifax had to be cancelled. A couple of the participants were overwhelmed by the stormy weather and refused to leave the hotel that day. The others enjoyed the winter experience, bought warm clothing at a campus store, and learned how to make snowballs.

The last activity of the week was a guided tour of the Dalhousie campus that included picture taking. Afterwards the men[58] attended Friday prayers in the Student Union Building.

---

58 Muslim women are not obliged to attend Friday prayers.

I didn't get to know Pak Saut outside the work environment—his moods were hard to read and he was most comfortable when working and directing the work of others. He told us he often discussed our cooperation with the minister and actively promoted it as a way to achieve the ministry's decentralization objectives.

Participant Feedback

A few months later, in April 2012, Kevin Malloy and Betty MacDonald[59] joined me on an IPAC mission to Indonesia to work with Pak Saut on improving financial management practices. On the first day (and for the first time) there was a feedback session on the recent Indonesian mission to Canada and several of the Indonesian participants joined us. Pak Saut opened the meeting by saying, "I have both met with and written to the minister of Home Affairs to recommend reforms to the organization structure between Indonesian provinces and municipalities along the lines used in Canada." At the time, all 491 municipal local governments in Indonesia were allocated the same powers and Pak Saut recommended differentiating them based on their capacity. At the provincial level he recommended changes to the way governors were appointed and empowered by the national government, as they did not have the capacity to finance and exercise the duties that had been delegated to them. Pak Saut said the minister had informed him that he was pleased with our work and considered our cooperation to be one of the ministry's top three international partnerships. I was pleased to hear that our hard work was being recognized but it wasn't without ongoing challenges.

One of the obstacles to implementing reforms in Indonesia is the lack of fiscal capacity at the provincial level. Professor Sadu Wasistiono told us he was using information gained from the 2011 mission to Canada relating to categorizing local governments by size, the use of

---

59 Betty MacDonald was the executive director of the Nova Scotia Federation of Municipalities.

the chief administrative officer[60] governance structure, and budget processes in preparing the *naskah akademis* (academic paper) to accompany the recommended legislative changes. Rohan Julu, the Gorontalo
local government CFO, said he was interested in providing Indonesian
local government with direct access to Canadian-style property tax
revenues.[61] He predicted a higher collection rate if taxes were collected
locally as they are in Nova Scotia. A representative from the DKI Jakarta
planning bureau was interested in using Canada as a benchmark for legislative—executive communication and transparency.

At the end of the session Secretary General Ibu Diah presented a
list of our areas of achievement to date. They were one-stop service,
councillor training, improved local government management (including local government enterprises), capacity development of local government officials, central-local government relations, a comparative
study in progress, roundtables, public service delivery, joint lectures,
and joint research.

Regional Seminars and Workshops

In 2012, a seminar on local asset management[62] was organized by
DIKLAT (the education and training agency) and held at the Acacia
Hotel. A number of the attendees had participated in the 2011 mission
to Canada. Nurdin planned to integrate the seminar material in the asset
management training courses his division prepared. Pak Saut said this
demonstrated the benefits obtained through our cooperation.

The IPDN campus in Bukittinggi, West Sumatra, had a concentra-

---

60   A chief administrative officer is the administrative head of a local government and all staff
report to council through the CAO and not through committees or department heads. The
CAO is responsible for making policy recommendations to council, implementing council
decisions and policies, and supervising staff.

61   The law authorizing the collection of land and building taxes by subnational governments
had been passed but not yet implemented. Previously, the central government collected
the taxes and made grants to local governments, depriving local governments of own-
source revenues.

62   Asset management was part of the fiscal balance law 33 / 2004 and regulations.

tion in financial management and Home Affairs arranged for IPAC and IPDN faculty to hold a seminar there. In April 2012, Professor Sadu Wasistiono, Nurdin and Arif accompanied Kevin Malloy and me to Bukittinggi. Our flight from Jakarta took us to Padang, the provincial capital, and we drove from there. Along the route we made several stops—a waterfall next to the highway, a retreat for artists located on a hilltop with a spectacular view, and a museum featuring a traditional Sumatran house designed to withstand earthquakes. The museum also displayed photos of Mohammad Hatta, Indonesia's first vice-president, who was from the area. A 7.6-magnitude earthquake had a devastating impact on the region in 2009 and I saw places where the railway line had been damaged and a number of homes that were being reconstructed. During the colonial period, Bukittinggi was referred to as Fort de Koch and Kevin and I had time to check out the old fort and clock tower before the seminar.

Professor Sadu, Kevin and I made presentations to an audience of 400[63] on local government finance, budgeting, and taxation. Local governments were running deficits and the central government wanted to improve budget practices. The topics that came up most frequently during the question period related to auditing, budget planning, revenue generation, and dealing with infrastructure deficits. One participant asked if Canadian law permits greater cooperation among levels of government to deal with the infrastructure deficit. I wasn't sure if it was a general interest question or if she had prior knowledge about Canadian provincial government practices of discouraging direct federal—municipal interaction. I explained that local governments come under the list of powers allocated to Canadian provinces, and the provinces prefer to be gatekeepers when federal money is made available for municipal infrastructure and services. She seemed to accept my explanation.

While Kevin and I were in West Sumatra, Betty MacDonald went to the IPDN campus in Makassar with Professor Wirman Syafri and Ria to

---

63 We had 300 in person and another 100 using video conferencing at other IPDN campuses. This was the first time we had used video conferencing in Indonesia.

present at the 200-person seminar on integrated development planning. This function had been delegated to local government as part of the decentralization reforms.

I stayed in Indonesia a few days longer to participate in the seminar at the IPDN Mataram, Lombok, campus (80 participants) on democratization, local politics, and elections. Factors such as lack of qualified staff, corruption and nepotism, plus poor central government oversight were causing service provision problems for some local governments. Professor Sadu and Cecep Efendi were the other presenters. Dr. Efendi is an Indonesian activist and academic and was about to start a four-year term as director general at the Centre on Integrated Rural Development for Asia and the Pacific (CIRDAP[64]). He was the panel's most passionate speaker. He challenged the mostly student audience to take an active role in implementing decentralization to improve education services, infrastructure, and economic development. He talked about how these changes would improve the quality of life for Indonesians and help them keep up with other countries in the region. Cecep Efendi was a hard act of follow but I was prepared and delivered my PowerPoint presentation on local governance in Canada. The two areas that generated the most interest, reflected by the number of questions, were the role of the chief administrative officer (CAO) and the components of good governance.[65]

After the seminar, it was time to explore and relax. Arif, his colleague Omar, and I went to Gili Trawangan (Gili T), one of the three Gili islands off the northwest coast of Lombok. We took a speedboat (outboard motor) piloted by a young man. There was one life jacket on board and we skimmed the water at top speed. The crossing took less than an hour and we arrived early in the afternoon. There were no cars to impede our short walk from the waterfront to our villa as cars are not allowed on Gili T—only bicycles and horse-drawn carriages. The Indonesian small island (Gili T is six square kilometres) experience was

---

64 CIRDAP is affiliated with SOCEAN, the organization Agung moved to in 1999.

65 These included good policies, best practices, establishing indicators for service delivery, accountability, transparency, financial reporting, performance measurement, and long-term planning that reflects financial capacity and community priorities.

a new one for me and it didn't fit the popular image of the deserted tropical island. This one was densely packed with hotels, restaurants, and Westerners, and is one of Indonesia's most popular tourist destinations. We ate our dinner that night at one of the many crowded open air eating establishments near the beach. The Lombok Mountains were visible on the other side of the strait.

In the morning, I took a saltwater shower before joining Arif and Omar for a drive around the island on rented bicycles, stopping for coffee and exploring the beaches along the way. The number of tourists and the mix of accommodations, combined with the dive shops and advertisements, gave the place an international destination atmosphere. We returned to Lombok in the afternoon and stayed overnight at a Senggigi Beach hotel. The next morning, we walked along the shore to a market area where (with Arif's help) I bought Lombok pearls. There were huge trees on the resort property and Omar took a photo of Arif and I standing at the base of a tree. We are standing tall, each with an outreached arm, and still don't fill enough space to cover the width of the tree.

Fast-Paced Reform Implementation Agenda— Better Service for Indonesians

The next Indonesian priority with IPAC / Nova Scotia was finding ways to improve service standards and service delivery. Pak Saut led his second mission to Nova Scotia in November 2012. This time the weather was typical for the time of year—skies are often grey, temperatures are cool but not cold, and cloud formations come to life in the light of late afternoon sunsets. There were twenty-four participants, seven from Home Affairs / IPDN and seventeen elected and administrative officials from seven Indonesian local governments.[66]

Arif, Ria, and Nurdin were part of the MOHA group and Wirman

---

66 The seven local governments were Banyuwangi Regency, Kutai Kartanegera Regency, Mamuju Regency, Palangkaraya City, PakPak Bharat Regency, Solok Regency, and South Tangerang City.

Syafri represented IPDN. The local government participants made their own funding arrangements.

Kevin Malloy and I organized a program with help from IPAC program officers[67] Joseph Taylor and Laurent Tyers. The mission focused on two areas. The first was minimum service standards for public services. Indonesia had passed laws and regulations but needed to work out the details for each service and wanted to learn about the Canadian experience. The second area was academic collaboration between IPDN and Dalhousie that included a comparative study of public services in Indonesia and Canada.

We started with a two-day seminar that included presentations from both Nova Scotians and Indonesians. Nova Scotia's municipal affairs minister, John MacDonell, gave opening remarks. At the request of the Indonesians the service areas our presenters emphasized were health, education, and infrastructure (water, wastewater, solid waste). The group split in two for the next two days. The local government group made visits to municipalities, hospitals, and schools in Halifax and other parts of the province.

At the end of the week, after our final session, our Muslim colleagues attended Friday prayer and we later met for a farewell dinner where certificates of participation were awarded. The local government participants left Halifax on the weekend. The Home Affairs / IPDN group stayed behind and joined us for an IPAC-sponsored workshop on gender mainstreaming and results-based management.

The IPAC program officers prepared a DGP mission report. It concluded the mission objectives were achieved and identified the activities completed. Preliminary objectives for the next mission and a timetable for key action items were included. Pak Saut used them to develop the program for our next mission. The achievements reported by IPAC staff for the practitioner / minimum service standards segment of the missions were as follows: "Minimum service standards and alternative service delivery. The 2012 mission to Halifax provided an excellent learning environment for the Indonesian local government officials.

---

67 Mel had left IPAC and bought an old farmhouse on Cape Breton Island.

Theoretical components of the mission relating to MSS / ASD issues in health, education and waste management sectors were followed up with practical site visits. The access to Canadian experts and exposure to field-level implementation has supported seven senior local government officials who are primary decision makers (mayors and regents) to improve medium-term development plans (strategic plans) that comply with minimum service standards established in the 2005 government decree. The mission also increased the capacity of ten senior local government officials (heads of education and health department level and support staff) to deliver public services in order to meet MSS."

Part way through the November 2012 mission to Canada, I invited Arif to have Sunday brunch with me at a downtown restaurant. Our program was so full that we hadn't had an opportunity to talk and he was the only one in the group I knew well. Arif welcomed the invitation but didn't want to have the other Indonesian participants think he was getting special treatment. I met him by the city library, a block away from his hotel, and we drove from there. Our meeting was mainly a social one and we talked about music and our families. Arif did confirm that Pak Saut was interested in expanding our cooperation and increasing Indonesia local government's exposure to Canadian policies and practices.

Pak Saut wanted to accelerate the dissemination of information about the Canadian experience with developing minimum service standards and evaluating alternative service delivery options. He asked us to bring a larger delegation and hold more international seminars on our next mission to Indonesia in April 2013. Travel money was available, and I was able to recruit additional volunteers. We arrived in two groups, which Home Affairs called Team A and Team B. Team A were the generalists[68] and Team B the specialists (health, education, solid waste)[69]. The team schedules overlapped by one day. On that day (a

---

68 Team A members were Dan MacDougall (Nova Scotia Department of Municipal Affairs), Rob Taylor (IPAC CEO), Mark Gilbert.

69 Team B members were Sandra Christie (Nova Scotia Department of Health) , Brian Smith (retired Kings County CAO), Allan Lowe (Nova Scotia Department of Education) accompanied by Laurent Tyers from IPAC.

Sunday), Pak Saut invited us all to a luncheon in a private room at a central Jakarta restaurant to tell us once again that our project was one of the minster's top three international partnerships and that Indonesian local governments were benefiting from our work. I was already aware of the minister's top three comments and pleased that Pak Saut had mentioned it in front of the Canadian volunteers who were on their first mission to Indonesia.

The IPAC teams were made up mainly of current and retired senior civil servants and municipal administrators from Nova Scotia. I represented the academic sector and I'd also invited IPAC's chief executive officer. Rob Taylor had recently been appointed as the Institute of Public Administration of Canada's CEO following a long career in provincial and local government in the province of Ontario. He is about my age and an experienced public speaker. When I served on the IPAC Board of Directors and later became more involved in the Indonesia project, Joe Galimberti was IPAC's CEO. Joe was dedicated and devoted to IPAC for his entire career and we developed a close working relationship. Joe was warm, patient, and willingly shared his knowledge. I considered him a mentor. Rob, like me, was in a late career transition. He had dual priorities—meeting his IPAC responsibilities and seeking out career opportunities. We had a lot in common (age, public sector careers, mid-career doctoral studies), which made it easy for us to work together. Rob was interested in measurable results from our IPAC—Indonesia—Nova Scotia cooperation (which IPAC was getting on its projects in small African and Caribbean countries) and I wanted him to see the broader benefits we were achieving in Indonesia first hand. His municipal / provincial background made it easy to include him as an IPAC team presenter at the international seminars.

Prior to Rob's arrival, I met with the Canadian ambassador, Jeffrey Ong, and Home Affairs colleagues to discuss the detailed program MOHA had arranged. A welcome dinner held at a Jakarta hotel was followed by an evening of singing. Arif sang some Frank Sinatra songs and Indonesian romantic ballads. Secretary General Ibu Diah Anggraeni sang "Mother" (a song made popular by Barbara Streisand) in English with intense emotion. She was Javanese, didn't speak English and was normally reserved with us. Her performance was unexpected but welcome as I got to see another side of her. I was still too reserved and unprepared to sing at these events, which made me appreciate her performance all the more. Lies Kurniawati attended the welcome dinner and when we greeted one another I noticed she didn't look well and wasn't her usual lively self. It was the last time I saw her. A few years later Agung informed me Lies had passed away from an illness. I don't think she reached sixty. Although Lies was no longer active in our cooperation her earlier involvement was key in keeping it moving forward during the early, tentative years of our work together. I was sad when I heard she had passed away and grateful for her contribution both to our work and our knowledge of Indonesia.

After our high energy, entertaining welcome dinner, we were ready to get down to the serious work ahead, which included round table discussions with our two teams. Team A's round table discussion was titled, "Alternative Service Delivery: Opportunities and Challenges." Team B's presentations explained how health, education and solid waste services were financed, provided and measured by governments in Canada. Team A international seminars were held at a hotel in Jakarta and on IPDN regional campuses. Over one hundred faculty, students, and representatives from local governments and universities in the region participated in each seminar.

Home Affairs prepared a background paper for the Jakarta workshop, which included six roundtable goals and the names of the nine speakers. Pak Saut and Rita Widyasari (then head of Kutai Kartanegara Regency) were two of the presenters. Secretary General Diah Anggraeni, the Canadian ambassador, and the minister of Home Affairs provided opening remarks. Jeffrey Ong was a session facilitator. Pak Saut made a comprehensive seven-topic presentation that ended with identifying challenges and future directions. The challenges included accelerating the implementation of MSS (minimum service standards) for basic services, measuring performance, financing infrastructure, and how to treat regions with different financial and resource capacities. Future directions pointed to revising laws to link funding sources to service responsibilities, more revenue sources for local government, categorizing local governments based on capacity, encouraging public participation, and exploring ways to use alternative service delivery to achieve MSS. Two other future directions he laid out were related to the workshops and seminars IPAC was participating in on this mission. One was the need to familiarize MSS implementation through regional facilitation in order to accelerate its adoption (Team A). The second was to focus on finance, measurement, and standards for a few selected basic services such as education, health, and infrastructure (Team B).

Dan, Rob, and I used our same presentations for the international seminars that followed. There were different (local) Indonesian presenters at these seminars. The workshops and seminars started south of the equator in Jakarta, moved to the equator in Pontianak (West Kalimantan), and then north of the equator in Manado (North Sulawesi). The last seminar of Team A's mission took place in Manado on a Friday, and the schedule included a free day there on Saturday. Our colleagues organized a boat trip to Bunaken (Island) National Marine Park and snorkelling on one of its coral reefs. The water was clear and warm (high 20s Celsius). The reef where we snorkelled was in shallow water and had only a few fish. My eyebrows raised in surprise behind my mask when the guide broke off a piece of coral from the reef and offered it to me as a souvenir. I shook my head and said I didn't want it. I learned later most, but not all, of the tour operators took coral reef protection seriously.

The Jakarta airport had only two runways at that time and was limited to 52 aircraft movements per hour.[70] As a result several flights were scheduled for less convenient times—we left our Jakarta hotel at 3:30 a.m. the day we flew to Pontianak. Arif, Kuswanto, and Yusharto went with us.

Team B's program started after Team A's ended. They presented at workshops in Palangkaraya (Central Kalimantan), Kutai Kartanegara (East Kalimantan), and Banyuwangi (East Java). In addition to discussing how health, education, and solid waste services were provided by governments in Canada, they also circulated materials relating to minimum service standards and measurement criteria for each

---

70 Retrieved from *Jakarta Post* article dated July 27, 2017.

service. Between the two teams we reached more than one thousand Indonesians through our six seminars and workshops.

New Leadership—Different Style

Whenever there were program leadership changes on the Indonesian side I was concerned about continuity and commitment to our cooperation. When I joined the IPAC team I naively thought that because we (IPAC) were bringing what I believed to be "superior" Western knowledge on governance and decentralization, Indonesian civil servants would be lining up to work with us. I soon realized that incentives were just as important to our Indonesian colleagues as they were to us. I had gone for the adventure and to learn, then quickly became invested in the project. Some of our Indonesian colleagues were more committed to the decentralization reforms than others and IPAC was one of many international donors competing for the attention of those who supported change. The missions to Canada were not only important because of the educational and travel opportunities they provided. They reinforced the peer-to-peer nature of our work—a feature our Indonesian colleagues said they valued most.

A few weeks before the arrival date for the 2013 Indonesian mission to Canada, I received an email from Arif informing me that Pak Saut would no longer be leading the Home Affairs side of our cooperation. Saut Situmorang had been appointed governor of the Maluku province. Maluku takes in the Banda Spice Islands, coveted for centuries by Europeans seeking to profit from the nutmeg and cloves grown there. Pak Saut had done a great deal in a short time to raise the profile and intensity of our cooperation. He made sure our projects were relevant to the government's decentralization priorities. The local government leaders he included in the cooperation were committed to applying the information gained from study missions to Canada and IPAC workshops in Indonesia to improve public services in their cities and regencies. I was concerned that without Pak Saut's leadership our project momentum would be lost. As it turned out, there was no need to worry.

Yusharto Huntoyungo led the 2013 thirty-five-person mission and replaced Saut as the Indonesian lead on our cooperation. I first met Yusharto during the November 2006 IPAC missions to Indonesia when he worked with the ministry's Education and Training Agency and joined us in meetings on training for local councillors. He was born in the same year as Arif (1967) but, unlike Arif, this Sulawesi-born man with a solid build and square face wasn't mistaken for a young professional, although he retained the energy and enthusiasm of a young man. At the time of the 2013 mission, he was the head of the Centre for the Management of Overseas Cooperation at Home Affairs.

Our cooperation had flourished under Pak Saut's leadership. He was serious about implementing decentralization reforms and willing to use IPAC resources to achieve his goal. He had a no-nonsense, authoritarian manner and was all business. Yusharto was outgoing, had an infectious laugh, was easy to talk with, and valued social and family time. To our relief, his personality and leadership style accelerated the momentum established by Pak Saut. To use a management analogy, earlier colleagues built the product, Saut improved the product, and Yusharto promoted it. Agung got the program off to a good start and along with Siti Nurbaya, Yuswandi and others laid the groundwork and selected projects like one-stop shops and councillor training as areas for our cooperation. Pak Saut was task oriented and through his influence with the minister was able to expand and accelerate IPAC involvement in the decentralization reforms. Yusharto inherited the leadership of a well-functioning, high profile program. Yusharto had the energy and personality to keep the momentum going and to communicate it successfully to larger audiences in both Indonesia and at IPAC conferences. There weren't leadership parallels on the Canadian side. It was the qualification and experience of Canadian mission volunteers for workshops and specific projects that adapted to the changing needs.

IPAC program manager Regan Mancini worked with us on planning the 2013 mission, participated in program activities, and prepared the mission report. Home Affairs provided us with a terms of reference that outlined what they wanted to achieve. They requested training on building local government capacity to strengthen the implementation of minimum service standards in public service delivery. The terms of reference provided a list of relevant laws and regulations, highlighted the things they still needed to achieve, and identified problem areas such as mismanagement, human resources capacity, accountability, and a lack of clear standards. Home Affairs set out short-, medium- and long-term expectations for the mission. It was Pak Saut-style terms of reference and showed that our cooperation played a key role in the implementation of local government reforms.

As we worked with Home Affairs to improve local government service standards and delivery, the seminars and field work in Canada became less general and more focused on individual services. At the request of our Indonesian colleagues, we focused on health, education, fire services, water, and solid waste. We also talked about governance structure in order to provide context for the way service responsibilities were established. Some of the local government service responsibilities in Indonesia were provincial ones in Canada.

The twenty-eight Indonesian local government participants (a mixture of elected officials and heads of decentralized municipal services) visited schools, hospitals, firefighting facilities, and ambulance service providers. We would see some of these Indonesians again in a few months. The regents of South Minahasa and Muna would go out of their way to develop an equally good field-visit program and a much fuller social program for us.

The Dream Team Travels by Air, Land, and Sea

The IPAC team's penultimate DGP mission in early 2014 was a highlight of our cooperation. Our Home Affairs colleagues repeatedly told us that what they liked best about our program, which differentiated it from other donor programs, was that it was peer-to-peer and they had flexibility in setting the priority areas for our work. When we met in Halifax a few months earlier, Home Affairs requested that IPAC conduct seminars on minimum service standards and alternative service delivery in six Indonesian regions. Home Affairs also asked that we form

Canadian—Indonesian teams for each of the service areas where we had experts available, and that team members work together during the mission. The main focus of the Dalhousie—IPDN cooperation would be the comparative study. It was coming along well, and we wanted to complete it before IPAC's Democratic Governance Program ended. An added incentive was the Eastern Regional Organization for Public Administration (EROPA) conference scheduled for Hanoi in October. If the study was finished before the submission deadline, we would apply to have it included in the conference presentations.

There were five Canadians in the February / March 2014 mission, each with a different area of specialization: Marvin MacDonald (infrastructure and shared services), Judith Sullivan-Corney (education), Pat Lee (health), John Cunningham (fire), and me (ASD, team lead). Rob Taylor of IPAC joined us for the first few days of the mission. Of the nineteen missions I took part in under the IPAC—Indonesia—Nova Scotia program, this was the one I found the most enjoyable and rewarding. Home Affairs prepared a comprehensive program that included over one thousand Indonesian participants. It involved six locations: two in Sulawesi, two in Kalimantan, one off the east coast of Sumatra, and one in Papua, in addition to meetings in Jakarta. There were international seminars and field visits to schools, training institutes, hospitals, and local attractions. Governors, mayor / regents, local government staff, academics, and students all participated. The tight two-week travel schedule meant we were often together with our Home Affairs and IPDN colleagues, which gave us an opportunity to get to know them better. The other Canadian members of the IPAC team, all mature first timers to Indonesia and experts in their fields, came with good attitudes and were flexible when it came to both business and social activities.

My two-stop, twenty-nine-hour route to Jakarta involved flight changes in London and Dubai. Arif met me at the Jakarta airport. There were no clouds in the sky and it wasn't too hot or humid—pleasant weather for Jakarta. The Wi-Fi was working at the Borobudur Hotel. The mission was off to a good start. On Saturday when I was waiting for other team members to arrive, Agung and his three children (Arief,

Adimas, and Anissa) joined me for an evening dinner at the hotel. On Sunday the IPAC team was invited to a lunch meeting with Home Affairs in a former colonial administration building in Menteng that had been converted into a restaurant and art gallery. Pak Saut was there along with Yusharto, Arif, and Nurdin. In the afternoon, I took the IPAC team on a high-humidity walk to Pasar Baru where, in addition to the usual market attractions, we listened to a blind man with a beautiful voice singing and a donation box beside him.

The theme selected for the seminars and workshops was concepts, strategies, and experience in the implementation of alternative service delivery and minimum service standards in Indonesia and Canada in general. We were also asked to share Nova Scotia and Canadian experiences in education, health, water systems, and firefighting. The seminars were held on IPDN campuses or in regions represented on the December 2013 study mission to Nova Scotia.

Home Affairs divided us again into two groups for the first week of the mission. Marvin, Judith, and I (accompanied by Yusharto and Professor Sadu) were on Team A, and Pat, John, and Rob (accompanied by Arif) were on Team B. Having Yusharto, the head of the centre for managing overseas cooperation, and IPDN Professor Sadu, with us raised the profile of our work and confirmed the value Home Affairs placed on our cooperation. We had moved beyond night-train travel with junior staff.

Judith is an energetic former deputy minister. She was inclusive and warm in her interactions with Indonesians, flexible when it came to our schedule and an active participant in all parts of the program. At the time Marvin, whose background is in engineering and public infrastructure, was an executive director with Nova Scotia's municipal affairs ministry. He comes across as easy going and is well liked by his colleagues. He was in his late fifties and fully embraced all aspects of the mission. Our Indonesian colleagues found him jovial and approachable, and he provided (often unintentionally but most welcome) comic relief—which Judith referred to as "Marvin stories."

Team A was scheduled to spend the first week in Jayapura (Papua) and Muna (Southeast Sulawesi).[71] It began with a 2 a.m. wakeup call to catch a 4:50 a.m. flight to Jayapura with a stop in Makassar. We arrived at 2 p.m. local time (Indonesia has three time zones). Jayapura is the capital and largest city in the Indonesian province of Papua on the Indonesian (west) side of the island of New Guinea. This region is rich in resources like gold, nickel, and petroleum and was the last of the former Dutch colonial territories to join Indonesia (1962). Papua has different Indigenous ethnic groups (Papuan, Melanesian) that set it apart from the rest of Indonesia, and Christianity is the dominant religion. The rector of the IPDN campus, Dr. Sunajar Djantoro (Marguerite), met us at the airport and we had tea before driving to the new IPDN Jayapura campus that was under construction. The new campus was isolated from the city by design as a remote campus has fewer outside distractions. Several of the city streets were still flooded from the heavy rains that had led to a mudslide with eleven casualties the previous day. We checked in at the Swiss Bell Hotel located on the waterfront. It was a classic tropical paradise setting—a harbour dotted with islands in front, imposing mountains covered in tropical vegetation in the back, and tall palm trees off to the side. The evening was less glamorous as the sombre atmosphere after the tragic flood made for a quiet dinner followed by an early night.

There were over 200 participants at the international seminar the next day. It began with singing the Indonesian and Canadian national anthems and opening remarks from the Papua governor and IPDN rector. Following the presentations there was a cultural program featuring Indonesian dancers in costumes with headbands and feathers. Then a uniformed student choir standing three rows deep moved their feet side to side to keep time with their patriotic songs. The band director moved with energetic military precision and her every move was followed by the front row singers. Some of the students in the back were just going through the motions. I found the songs moving even though I couldn't follow the words.

---

71 Team B spent week one at international seminars in Central Bangka (Belitung Islands province) and Landak (West Kalimantan).

Jayapura, Indonesia, February 2014.

A few of the male students approached me afterwards to ask about university studies in Canada and for my business card. Back in Canada, I received an email from Amos, who expressed an interest in studying in Canada and was looking for sponsorship. His tone was casual and, unlike my Canadian students, he addressed me by my first name. IPDN operates in a quasi-military fashion where students wear uniforms, live in dorms and follow strict rules. Amos's degree of familiarity in his email to me was surprising but likely a reflection of his perception of the Western way of doing things.

In the evening, we joined Ibu Rector and her staff for dinner at a waterfront seafood restaurant. She is a lively, intelligent, personable Papuan woman with a strong missionary influence in her life. I ate cassava for the first time. The cooked yucca root vegetable is said to be more nutritious than potatoes but I found its paste consistency in the soup starchy, sticky, and hard to eat. I smiled and nodded anyway, as I've learned to do when things don't go quite right, whether in formal meetings or casual dinners.

Something that happened during our stay at the Swiss Bell Hotel speaks to the perceptions people have about places they have never been. At breakfast after our first night there Marvin told us about his frightening nighttime experience. His wife had told him to check for spiders and scorpions each night before he got into bed. He'd done that in Jakarta but after our long day of travel and a late dinner Marvin was too exhausted to check the bed. During the night he woke and saw a large insect-like shape on the bed sheet. He leapt out of bed thinking he was in danger. Marvin is a heavy guy and the image of him frightened and bounding out of bed stays with you. Once the lights were on he saw the sheets had patterned grey designs. For the record, none of the IPAC team members ever reported having an issue with insects in hotel beds.

It was the first funny "Marvin Story" putting us in good humour for the long day ahead as Team A left the hotel at five the following morning. The drive to the Jayapura airport took us over steep hills and past early morning joggers. We flew to Makassar (South Sulawesi) and then to Kendari (Southeast Sulawesi). Our final destination was Raha, the capital city of Muna. Muna Regency is located on an island bearing the same name in Southeast Sulawesi. Dr. Baharuddin, the regent, joined the Indonesian mission to Canada in late 2013 and requested the IPAC team include Muna in the February 2014 mission program. Raha is 100 kilometres to the south of the port city of Kendari as the crow flies. The region's irregular coastline and terrain make it a much longer distance by road and sea. The original plan had been to drive for less than an hour to catch a ferry to Muna. That changed. Now we were taking a three-hour drive to a spot where we would board the Muna Regent's power boat. It was docked at the far end of a long wooden wharf with some of the planks missing and others rotted or broken. To complicate matters, we were carrying heavy suitcases. It seemed to take forever to reach the end of the wharf but, eventually, picking our way around the debris and over gaps, we made it unscathed. Two hours later the boat docked in Raha, where a large welcoming party was waiting to greet us. We were taken to a local hotel and then to dinner.

Our Indonesian colleagues wanted to make the most of our mission so every morning was an early one and sometimes it was more like the middle of the night.

The IPAC team is greeted by the children and teachers during a visit to a school in Muna Regency, Southeast Sulawesi, February 2014.

Before the seminar opened at 10 a.m. we visited five Muna Regency schools and one clinic where in addition to regular clinical services they performed dental extractions. Two-hundred and thirty-five people attended the seminar. Our presentations were well received and there was a lot of discussion about ASD options that ranged from informal cooperation to transfer of functions and restructurings. Local government enterprises (referred to by the anacronym BUMD in Indonesia) were widely used to deliver water services and we discussed the trade-offs between flexibility / efficiency and accountability when using them. Some interesting comparisons were made during the discussion that followed Judith's presentation on education. Indonesian governments are mandated to spend 20 percent of their budgets on education (it's an unmandated 12 percent in Nova Scotia), Indonesian children attend school six days a week (five in Nova Scotia), and competition is more highly valued in Indonesia than in Nova Scotia. One of the reasons that Nova Scotia scores higher than Indonesia on the program for international student assessment is because it moved away from rote pedagogy (still used in Indonesian schools) to inquiry-based learning relying on problem solving.

After the site visits and seminar were completed a few hours of daylight remained. There was one more municipal site to see. Yusharto accompanied us to a municipal coastal park at the Napabale Lagoon. A traditional wooden boat was waiting to transport us from the emerald waters of a lagoon surrounded by steep coral walls out into the bay. The boat was long and narrow and the local helmsman sat at the stern on a rickety bench. The rest of us sat in single file on cushions and gripped the gunwales for support. In the photos, Yusharto is the only one who lifted his hands to wave. That evening the regent hosted a dinner. It was followed by speeches and performances by traditional dancers and musicians. Afterwards, we all accepted the invitation to join our hosts on the dance floor and move to DJ selections of Western and Indonesian songs.

The next morning, we left for Tampo to take the three-hour ferry to Kendari. Muna doesn't have a large population so I was surprised by the size and density of the crowd waiting at the wharf. There was no queuing when it was time to board—everyone moved toward the gangplank at once. Marvin, Judith and I formed a tight line behind Yusharto, hoisted our luggage and followed him through the crowd. He found below-deck seats for us. The passengers entertained themselves with their smartphones. After docking we flew back to Jakarta via Makassar and checked in at the Mandarin Oriental Hotel located in the city centre.

Pat Lee and John Cunningham (Team B) returned from Central Bangka and Landak and spent the weekend with us in Jakarta. Rob wasn't with them but asked Pat to tell me that he wouldn't be joining us for the rest of the mission. Pat Lee, the team's health expert, held a senior position with the Nova Scotia health ministry. He was fit, close to my age, and quick witted. One preceptive observation that Pat included in his mission report that was shared with our Indonesian colleagues was, "Indonesia seems uniquely positioned to make the tough decisions concerning scope and quality of public service now in the 'good times' while enjoying a 5 percent rate of economic growth rather than what we are experiencing in Canada, making tough decisions in 'bad times' with stagnant economic growth, high public entitlement expectations, and unaffordable social programs."

John Cunningham was our firefighting expert and the youngest member of our team. He was an experienced traveller, good with technology and both affable and professional. John and Pat interacted well, delivered excellent workshop presentations, and prepared useful follow up reports. John was able to make a number of site visits on a second mission later in the year where his interest, enthusiasm, and willingness to assist endeared him to Indonesian firefighters.

Weekend in Jakarta

The recently reopened Mandarin Hotel was a convenient spot to spend the weekend. It was within easy walking distance of shopping malls, local craft markets, restaurants, and Medan Merdeka (Freedom Square), the home of Monas, the name Indonesians give to the National Monument. Bluebird taxis were readily available for longer distances.

Over the weekend, I learned that not all Canadians working in Indonesia were as relaxed as our group when it came to personal safety. I made arrangements to have Saturday lunch in Jakarta with a former Dalhousie University student who was on a business trip to Indonesia. He lived in Calgary and worked in the oil business. His company was doing exploratory work in Sulawesi and he was in Jakarta to expedite the application process for Indonesian government exploration and operation permits. That evening he was going to an industry dinner but for security reasons would not be given the location until an hour before the event. In stark contrast, our IPAC team had been given a detailed two-week schedule before our team arrived. Not surprisingly, our Indonesia experiences and perspectives were quite different.

While my Canadian friend and I were having lunch, Marvin and Judith went shopping at the Plaza Indonesia located near the hotel. To avoid crossing the non-pedestrian friendly roundabout, they took the above-street pedway over Jalan M.H. Thamrin. On their way back to the hotel they were making their way down the pedway exit stairs when a young man pointed to an object on the landing. He asked Marvin if he had dropped it. While Marvin was engaged in the discussion, another young man removed Marvin's Blackberry smartphone from his belt holster. Judith saw it happen and grabbed the phone out of the robber's hand. Marvin and Judith walked away. The perpetrators stayed put. Later Judith said, "If I'd had the time to think about it I wouldn't have risked taking the phone back because of the confrontation that might have followed." It was a reminder to always be aware of our surroundings and keep valuables concealed.

Another one of Marvin's experiences in Jakarta later that afternoon led me to think about Canadian culture and the worldview for people in my generation. It's the story of "Marvin and the Pink Purse." By way of background, Indonesia is a socially conservative nation that promotes traditional family values and discourages any behaviour that does not support them. However, Jakarta is a big city and in 2014 there was some tolerance for individual expression. Undaunted by the pedway pickpocket incident, Marvin and Judith went shopping again later in the afternoon—this time accompanied by two Indonesian colleagues. Home Affairs had contracted out the simultaneous translation service for our workshops to two men named Sebastian and Gee. They worked and lived together and were competent professionals and a pleasure to work with. They were also flamboyant. Sebastian hailed a taxi that took them to a mall some distance from the hotel. Marvin and I were of the same generation and, like me, had grown up in rural Nova Scotia where, in our younger years, there were clear lines between what men and women wore. Pink was not a suitable colour for men and only women carried purses. Sebastian didn't follow that dress code and when shopping he sported a bright pink purse with a single shoulder strap. Marvin became self-conscious when the four of them decided to split up for a while and Sebastian offered to accompany Marvin to a shop that sold a gift he was looking for. The looks from other shoppers sent Marvin out of his comfort zone. He laughed about it later when he told the story but I doubt he would feel differently if it were to happen again.

Work and Travel with the Dream Team—Part 2

On Monday the five Canadians accompanied by Yusharto, Arif, Nurdin, and other Indonesian colleagues flew to Manado, North Sulawesi. We arrived in time to attend a dinner hosted by Christiany Paruntu, regent of South Minahasa, who had participated in the 2013 mission to Canada. The dinner was followed by a presentation by the regent and then karaoke and dancing. Arif and a woman from the Home Affairs staff were the best and most sought-after singers. They were happy to oblige.

The next day the international workshop on the implementation of minimum service standards and alternative service delivery in Canada and Indonesia, opportunities and challenges, was held at the Sintesa Peninsula Hotel. There were 250 participants and a CD of the event with the regent's picture on the cover was made available the next day. The workshop opened again with the singing of our national anthems. Yusharto made opening remarks on behalf of Home Affairs, and Regent Christiany provided the opening speech. Arif and Nurdin were the moderators for the two three-person speaker panels (five Canadians, one Indonesian) on minimum service standards and alternative service delivery.

In the late afternoon we boarded a bus for South Minahasa. Heavy traffic delayed our progress and the Indonesians took turns singing to pass the time. The first planned stop was a visit to a school. We were running behind schedule and the students stayed late to meet us. As our bus approached the school we saw banners welcoming IPAC with photos from the 2013 mission to Canada. The schoolyard was jammed with students and teachers standing shoulder to shoulder and a large band (using what appeared to be homemade instruments—some resembling a tuba, others a flute—used to play traditional bamboo music, plus sets of drums that would normally be seen in rock bands), provided a welcome. The elementary school students wore uniforms, took us on a tour of the school and, along with the teachers, asked to have their photos taken with us. We also toured a hospital where we were greeted by a group of warriors in traditional costumes who performed a vigorous war dance as a welcome (or perhaps a warning). There was a minor operation about to be performed and Pat, our health expert, asked if he could observe it and was given permission. The regent organized a late dinner for us when we got back to Manado. We sat at a long table, bowed our heads and listened to a long prayer before the meal was served. The area was predominately Christian.

At four-thirty the following morning we carried our suitcases to the Manado hotel lobby. The flight was on schedule and our group arrived in Balikpapan, East Kalimantan, in time for the international workshop being held at our hotel. The opening ceremony followed the same format as the one in South Minahasa except that this time the governor's speech lasted an hour and twenty minutes. Rita Widyasari, the regent of Kutai Kartanegara, who had participated in the 2013 study mission to Canada, joined the five Canadian speakers at the head table. Rita's presentation showed how she had implemented service improvements in her regency based on what she called lessons from the study mission to Canada. The list was long. It included improved technology for office communication, streetlights, and a procurement policy. Efforts to improve the quality-of-service delivery included adopting minimum service standards, an ombudsman agency, and a call centre. Efforts were being made to develop partnerships for water and wastewater services, recruitment based on qualifications, and long-term planning (development and financial). In the area of education, the district was working toward the adoption of internationally recognized minimum standards, collaboration among stakeholders, and included art and gymnasiums in all schools. It covered health and infrastructure services too. It was such an informative presentation that Yusharto used some of the slides in his DGP workshop presentation at the end of the program to highlight the benefits of our cooperation.

Students and teachers in South Minahasa Regency, North Sulawesi were standing shoulder to shoulder when our bus arrived. March 2014.

The local band provided us with a tremendous welcome.

International seminar participants in Balikpapan, East Kalimantan, March 2014.

Jeffrey Ong (left) represented the Canadian Embassy at the Balikpapan seminar.

Jeffrey Ong attended on behalf of the Canadian embassy. During the seminar we sat for photographs and one of them was featured in a 2014 IPAC *Public Sector Management* article about the IPAC—Indonesia—Nova Scotia DGP cooperation.

The day didn't end when the workshop was over. The province of East Kalimantan wanted to enter into a sister province arrangement with Nova Scotia to cooperate in a number of areas related to public services and governance. It was another testament to the perceived value of our cooperation that one of Indonesia's most prosperous provinces with a population of 3.5 million would initiate a partnership. Marvin was asked to sign a letter of intent, a first step toward a memorandum of understanding and formal agreement. He had no time to clear this with anyone in the Nova Scotia government but knowing how governments worked he felt comfortable in making this non-binding initial step. He knew the government attitude toward investing in international initiatives had changed since the 2002 meeting with Banten province, and there was renewed interest in promoting Nova Scotia abroad. The signing ceremony (photo included) made the local Balikpapan newspaper the next day. Neither province followed up on the partnership initiative afterwards but probably would have if our cooperation had continued moving in the same direction.

To celebrate a successful series of seminars our Balikpapan colleagues hosted an evening dinner at the rooftop restaurant of the conference hotel. I wasn't surprised when our hosts announced the dinner would be followed by karaoke and line dancing. Our Indonesian colleagues coaxed us to join in the singing. We were all reluctant until Judith said, "Why don't we sing as a group?" There were two microphones to share among the five of us and we sang two pieces we all knew: *Country Roads* and *Hey Jude*. Our Indonesian colleagues joined in on the choruses and we ended to great applause—not because of the quality of our singing but because we had been good sports and joined in, solidifying our collaboration on yet another level.

The next day our provincial / regency hosts organized field visits for us. We started with a Balikpapan hospital and clinic. The next stop was a factory that employed advanced technology and provided learning opportunities for students in technical programs. Its success was attributed to the support of a German company and a forward-looking local government. Afterwards, we went to the Samboja Lestari Lodge (a venture of the Borneo Orangutan Survival Foundation) at a park for orangutan and sun bears located in a restored tropical rain forest. The bears were viewed from a narrow sky bridge, with a low handrail on only one side, and the bridge swung when others walked on it. I was halfway along the bridge when Marvin and John got on and it started moving like a boat on a rough sea. I struggled to keep my balance and avoid joining the bears below.

The orangutans were on islands and viewed from the opposite side of a wide stream. This was considered safe for visitors as orangutans don't wade or swim across bodies of water. We watched reddish-brown adults and infants eating and moving gracefully through the forest. I found it peaceful to stand quietly and observe them in their natural habitat. *Orang* is the word for people or man in Indonesian and *hutan* is the word for forest. After I connected with Ed Stoddard in Jakarta in 1998 he had gone to Kalimantan (Banjarmasin) to see orangutans and write an article about them. Sixteen years later I was seeing them for the first time. During lunch at the lodge, we scanned the brochures about their temporary orangutan adoption program. For an amount ranging from C$35 for three months to C$200 for one year, donors would receive an adoption certificate, the history, and photo of one of the park's orangutans. After a lunch at the lodge, we drove to the Balikpapan airport and flew back to Jakarta.

The Canadian team with Yusharto at the Samboja Lestari Lodge, East Kalimantan, March 2014. From right to left: John Cunningham, Pat Lee, Judith Sullivan-Corney, Mark Gilbert, Marvin MacDonald, Yusharto Huntoyungo.

Another Marvin story illustrates how easy it is to become disoriented when travelling in a foreign country for the first time. The IPAC team had stopped to shop at the Balikpapan fair market on the way to the airport. Balikpapan was the last stop on the international seminar tour and Marvin was running out of space for gifts in his big suitcase.

This was his first trip to Indonesia and he wanted to buy presents for people back home. Pat Lee suggested Marvin buy a small suitcase similar to the reasonably priced one Pat had just bought. Marvin left to purchase the suitcase at one of the airport shops while we were waiting in the lounge for our flight to Jakarta. Our shopping and gift bags were on and around the lounge chairs. It was getting close to boarding time when Marvin returned with his new suitcase. Unaware that the flight had been delayed another twenty minutes, he hurriedly started stuffing bags in his new suitcase. Marvin not only packed his own things but grabbed other people's shopping bags as well. The rest of us watched and exchanged surprised and questioning looks. Marvin stopped only when John alerted him to what he was doing. It took a few minutes to sort things out. Marvin took a ribbing about that for the rest of the day.

A Bright Bilateral Future?

The next morning Marvin and I met with Jeffrey Ong and senior staff at the Canadian embassy at their offices in Jakarta's World Trade Centre 1. They encouraged us (IPAC, Dalhousie, and Nova Scotia) to develop a multi-year proposal between Canada and Indonesia with a focus on sustainable economic growth. This would be achieved by creating an enabling environment through the provision of high-quality government services. It was suggested the program operate in East Kalimantan (which had economic partnerships with resource sector industries), South East Sulawesi (mining and agriculture), and East Java (which had a reputation for being well administered). Five local governments in each of the three provinces would be selected as project participants. The province of Nova Scotia could be an enabler, and we should include the private sector (industry) and Dalhousie University (education) as partners. The program proposal would build on the existing momentum our program had developed and the Canadian government would accelerate the approval process in keeping with its mandate to grow Indonesia—Canada cooperation. A request for a $15 million bilateral agreement over six years, averaging two to three million per year and heavier in the earlier years, would be appropriate. The budget components should include a responsive component and technical assistance, a mechanism to share recommended practices with others, monitoring and evaluation, and a role for the national government ministries such as Home Affairs. The focus should be on impacts and development partners. We were reminded that the Institute of Public Administration of Canada / Dalhousie University relationship with Ottawa was key. It was recommended that we meet with the Department of Foreign Affairs and International Trade / Global Affairs Canada before submitting an unsolicited bilateral proposal as there is no opportunity for discussion afterwards—it is only accepted or rejected.

It was gratifying to receive such a strong endorsement of a program our IPAC and Nova Scotia teams had been involved with for twenty years. A bilateral proposal of this magnitude would enable us to have a full-time presence in Indonesia and help accelerate local government improvement in governance, management, budgeting, financial planning, revenue generation, service standards, and delivery. The first thing I would do when I got back to my office was to call IPAC with the news. IPAC had been the contract partner and link with the Canadian government during our twenty-year cooperation with Indonesia and were in the best position to submit a bilateral proposal.

Yusharto hosted a farewell dinner at a Chinese restaurant in a central Jakarta hotel. The success of our workshops and field visits left him brimming with optimism about all the things we could achieve in the future. He spoke of our cooperation in three time periods. The first was the past where we focused on Java. The second was the present with the focus on Manado and Balikpapan. The future would be more Sulawesi, Papua, and eastern Indonesia. Small gifts were exchanged. We each received an imitation silver replica of either the Borobudur Temple or a horse-drawn carriage (common in the Manado / Gorontalo region). Our gifts to them were useful items with logos from IPAC, Dalhousie, and Nova Scotia (clocks, business card holders, picture frames), as well as IPAC publications. The Home Affairs wrap-up notes and future expectations provided both a ten-point summary of mission accomplishments and five proposed areas of future cooperation (see appendix 7).

Transition and Disappointment

The bilateral balloon burst when I got back to Canada. IPAC was in the process of winding down most of its international activities as its funded projects were nearing their end dates. It's common to hear that a successful person or initiative was at the right place at the right time. Our cooperation with Indonesia was at the right place for expansion but, unfortunately for us, it was the wrong time. The federal government's foreign development aid strategy was moving in a different direction. Under the rules that came into place after our Democratic Governance Program was approved, NGOs could not apply for partnership branch funding for new projects or renewals; they could only respond to government calls for proposals. Our current program would not be renewed and there would be no Canadian government funding to continue our peer-to-peer cooperation with Indonesia. CIDA had recently been folded into the Department of Foreign Affairs and International Trade, which created uncertainty for NGOs like IPAC. The experienced IPAC international project staff realized they would be out of work when the project ended, so they applied for jobs elsewhere and left. They were replaced through short-term offers to individuals who were between jobs.

IPAC was lukewarm on the idea of submitting the $15 million bilateral proposal that the Canadian embassy in Indonesia had promoted. They had two reasons. The first was limited staff capacity and the second was based on a past experience of rejection with similar Canadian embassy recommendations in other foreign countries. This was a situation similar to our Dalhousie University experience with Nurdin's requests. The Canadian embassy in Jakarta was in a good position to identify and promote needed and useful initiatives that would be supported by the Indonesian government, but not able to approve them.

This was a double whammy situation. In addition to not being able to build on our twenty-year cooperation by taking it to the next level through a bilateral proposal, it appeared we'd not even be able to continue it in its present form. I wasn't ready to accept the latter and kept hoping an eleventh-hour solution would be found.

Yusharto Presents at IPAC's International Forum—Outlines Future Plans

The first Indonesian mission to Canada was in the spring of 1994, but after that the subsequent annual missions had typically been between late August and December. There were good reasons for this. The IPAC missions to Indonesia were usually in the winter or early spring and a later mission to Canada provided time for project work between visits. Some missions were tied to the IPAC annual conference and international workshop, which was usually held in late August. The academic cooperation benefited from holding the missions during the fall semester when students and faculty were on campus.

The last Indonesian mission to Canada would also be in the spring. It was Edmonton, Alberta's turn, to host the IPAC annual conference. The IPAC regional group there wanted to try something different by holding the conference before schools closed for the summer, instead of in August before they reopened. The plan was to have the Indonesians come to Halifax in late May to participate in a workshop dedicated to revenue generation and public services, complete our comparative study, and develop training modules on service delivery and monitoring. They would also work on service standard initiatives with assigned Nova Scotia partners from priority sectors. The initial proposal was to have twenty-seven participants and follow the established program format of a two-day workshop for everyone, followed by site visits for local government participants, and academic and planning work at Dalhousie for Home Affairs / IPDN delegates. After this was completed Marvin MacDonald and I would accompany the Indonesians to the Edmonton conference. IPAC staff were involved in the mission planning and there was a three-way communication stream through email between IPAC, Arif, and me.

In April 2014, Yuswandi had been appointed secretary general at the ministry of Home Affairs. Known for his thoroughness, it was not surprising to learn he wanted to review the plans for the upcoming mission to Canada, as well as determine whether the Democratic Governance Program objectives were being achieved, before signing off. He gave his approval for the five Home Affairs / IPDN participants on May 20, 2014. Jeffrey Ong arranged for Canadian embassy approval the same day and the group arrived in Halifax on May 23. Yuswandi would not approve the travel for the twenty-two local government participants until the review was completed and they could not travel without it. We went ahead with our workshop, and the presentation topics covered local government revenues, health, education, and fire services programs. Improving service delivery and standards was still a top Indonesian priority.

During the Indonesian missions to Canada there were always site visits for the practitioner group and if an IPAC conference was held at the same time, opportunities to see other parts of Canada (Montreal in 2013 and Edmonton in 2014). There were more recreational / social activities than usual during the 2014 mission to Canada. We wanted to make all aspects of the mission memorable for Arif, Yusharto and the others, as it was looking more and more like it would be the final one to Canada.

Arif was always looking for an opportunity to sing so I sought a local venue we could go to in the spring. I also wanted to take a more active role in these social events. In April, I contacted the Maritime Conservatory of Performing Arts in Halifax and arranged to take singing lessons. It was my good fortune that an experienced voice teacher had recently relocated to Halifax and was accepting new students. We worked well together and through her I gained an appreciation of the range of my voice, confirmed I could carry a tune, and became aware of all the things I had yet to learn. The week before the Indonesians arrived, we worked on "Farewell to Nova Scotia," a traditional folk song / sea shanty. If called upon to sing I would be prepared. There are two Saturday morning farmers markets on the Halifax waterfront and the Big Life Café operates a booth at one of them. The owner John Dalton is a musician who writes and records his own music. He also held Wednesday evening open mic sessions at his café in downtown Dartmouth. I asked him if I could bring five Indonesians.

On the last Wednesday in May, the six of us boarded the ferry to Dartmouth, ate a rice and seafood meal at a ferry terminal food court, and walked three blocks to the Big Life Café. The café is on a street of two- and three-storey commercial buildings that gives it more of a Main Street town atmosphere than a city one. Outside the café, three long-haired men with tattoos who came of age in the 1970s were standing around a motorcycle smoking. They ignored us.

John greeted us warmly when we walked in and led us down the corridor to the seating area; an aisle separated the booths on either side. My initial impression was we were joining a rougher, less well-groomed crowd than we saw every day in our white-collar offices. There were a few free spaces but they weren't together. When John announced the group from Indonesian had arrived, the crowd made space for us at two of the front booths near the improvised stage. They brought us tea and coffee and we settled in. The local performers played guitars and sang rock and folk songs. One was a poet who recited two of his poems that were lively and entertaining—one an exercise in alliteration and the other a more thoughtful piece. Arif had brought piano music but there was no keyboard so I asked if someone could accompany him on the guitar. Arif prefers romantic songs and likes performing Frank Sinatra's music. This was not a Sinatra crowd and most of the guitarists didn't read keyboard music.

The crowd was coming and going (the going was mostly outside for a smoke). Some people brought children with them and coming from a family-oriented society this helped put the Indonesians at ease. Eventually we found a guitarist to accompany Arif while he sang Elvis Presley's "Love Me Tender." He sang very well and with lots of emotion. The audience cheered and asked for more—something Indonesian. He sang a patriotic Indonesian song, a cappella, which was followed by great applause.

Afterwards, we listened to John Dalton sing a lively Nova Scotia song that he had written. He opened by saying, "I composed this piece because I was so tired of hearing 'Farewell to Nova Scotia.'" I decided not to do my rendition.

We left in time to catch the uncrowded 9 p.m. ferry back to Halifax and stood on the upper deck enjoying the fresh air and the scenery in what remained of the daylight (in tropical Jakarta the sun sets around 6 p.m. year-round). Yusharto said it was a very different ferry ride from the packed one we had taken from Muna to Kendari a few months earlier. When I told the group John Dalton's father had been one of my university professors they thought it funny and had a good laugh.

The next day we flew to Edmonton where the international program activities took place before and during the IPAC conference. Most of the fifty-eight individuals on the international delegates list were involved in one of the nine provincial—partner country Democratic Governance Program partnerships. There were also public administration association partners from Africa and America and other international guests.

The theme of the IPAC international forum was celebrating the Institute of Public Administration of Canada's international programing since its beginning in 1992. The Honourable Bob Rae gave the keynote address. He is a well-respected Canadian politician who had served as premier of Ontario and as interim leader of a federal party. At the time he was involved in First Nations and international development issues. As he was walking back to his seat, Yusharto stood up and intercepted him so he could congratulate him on his presentation and shake his hand. Yusharto was the only one to make such a spontaneous move. He did the same thing with other speakers as well. Later, in the forum when I provided Canadian partner insights, Yusharto stood up and shook my hand when I returned to our table. He was the most gregarious person in the room.

The Democratic Governance Program workshop was held on our last day in Edmonton. The twenty-year relationships IPAC developed with partner countries was coming to a close and partners were asked to share their stories—successes, challenges, lessons learned, and plans for the future. Yusharto delivered a sixty-five-slide presentation on our

Indonesian delegation at the IPAC International Forum in Edmonton, June 2014.

*Arif (pictured at the IPAC International Forum) was the Indonesian coordinator
during the second decade of our cooperation.*

Indonesia—Nova Scotia cooperation. Arif hadn't been able to join us
for the previous evening's conference event as he was putting the finish-
ing touches on the presentation. Before going to the podium Yusharto
was solemn and preoccupied, not his usual outgoing self. He covered
the history of our cooperation and all aspects of our achievements,

including the results of the comparative study, and included several photos, tables, and charts. One of the findings of the study was that Indonesia had adopted minimum standards for the four service areas under review, whereas Canadian local governments relied more on professional standards. Obstacles to bridging the gap and ways to overcome them were part of the study. Some of Yusharto's slides were about the application of lessons from the study mission to Canada by Indonesian local governments. They included the adoption of a one-call service, like 911 in Canada, for emergency situations, making psychology services available in schools, improvements in communicating with the public, and greater inclusion and transparency in planning and budgeting. He was also advocating for having both the private sector and the public authority involved in designing service standards. Study missions were a focal point of our cooperation and we averaged two a year. Yusharto presented the five benefits of these missions: sharing knowledge and good practice, capacity building, transfer of knowledge and information, global networking, and adopting and replicating.

Other achievements from our cooperation related to Indonesians advocating for reforms at home based on Canadian practices, such as having different categories of municipalities based on capacity and ability to provide services, adopting the municipal chief administrative officer model, and in-house (rather than central government) tax collection. These would all have practical applications on the ground that would positively impact the lives of Indonesians at the community level.

Yusharto's slide on future plans for programs with IPAC, Nova Scotia and Dalhousie University included five program activities[72] and four specific service categories.[73] We were all aware that the DGP program would end in nine months but remained optimistic that a way would be found to extend it. The combination of an abundance of

---

72 1) collaboration on analysis and research 2) exchange of best practices through round-tables, seminars, and training 3) work with a few local governments in three regions / provinces to promote sustainable economic growth by creating an enabling environment through the provision of high quality government services 4) annual missions to each country 5) peer to peer learning and field visits.

73 Health, education, environment (water and solid waste), and public safety (fire).

material about our work together and his enthusiasm in presenting it took Yusharto well beyond his allotted time. I was glad to see he was back to his gregarious self afterwards. Unfortunately, our program funding was coming to an end so we wouldn't be able to continue our work together and implement the plans he had outlined.

After lunch on the second day of the IPAC conference in Edmonton, Marvin and I rented a seven-passenger van at our own expense, and drove our Indonesian colleagues to Jasper so they could see and spend a few hours in the Rocky Mountains. When I suggested it to Marvin, he was game and we were glad to be able to reciprocate the wonderful hospitality we'd received in Indonesia earlier in the year. The drive took four-and-a-half hours each way. The Alberta oil industry was doing well (the price of oil wouldn't start to drop until later in the year) and we had a first-hand view of the business and industry spinoffs through the facilities and activities we observed along the route. A grey sky provided the backdrop for the photos of the snowcapped mountains taken when we stopped outside of Jasper.

Arif celebrates his first visit to the Canadian Rockies, near Jasper, June 2014.

On the way into town, three black bears foraging in a wooded area near the road happily ignored us. After a bit of Main Street shopping, soaking up the tourist town / holiday atmosphere and a meal, which included rice, it was dark and time to head back to Edmonton. Marvin and I took turns driving and, to stay alert, talked about work in Nova Scotia and people we knew. Our passengers quickly fell asleep except for Yusharto, who stayed awake and listed to our conversation. We returned the van at 2 a.m. and walked back to our hotel.

Indonesian–Canadian Teams' Training Collaboration

In October 2014 the IPAC team returned to Indonesia. Home Affairs prepared an agenda that concentrated on developing training material in the areas of health, education, and fire services, building institutional capacity, and supporting the development and implementation of minimum service standards. The team consisted of three returning Nova Scotians who were our leads on the three service areas, as well as me as team lead and liaison with IPDN on minimum service standard curriculum development. The capable IPAC program staff I had been working with had left to take other work before they found themselves out of a job when the program ended. A person hired on a short-term contract to fill the gap was assigned to provide IPAC support for the mission. I missed the experienced staff.

Yusharto, the Indonesian lead for our cooperation, was supported by Nurdin, Arif, and Ria. The mission activities organized by Home Affairs included meetings in the Jakarta area with senior ministry staff and site visits to locations where health, education, and fire services were provided. Working groups established for each service area reviewed current material used by the Indonesian training institute and discussed issues and challenges. Canadian case studies and other training materials used in Nova Scotia were showcased. The working groups spent most of the week discussing ways to develop and enhance the course curriculums.

Yusharto, the Indonesia lead for the final two years of our cooperation, outside a government office in Jakarta 2014. He presented his plan for our future cooperation at the June 2014 IPAC conference.

The working groups meet at the IPDN campus in Jatinangor, October 2014.

Jeffrey Ong joined me at the hotel for breakfast at the end of the mission. We discussed the bilateral proposal again and I shared with him the reasons for IPAC's reluctance to use its limited resources to make an unsolicited bilateral proposal application.

I was feeling gloomy after the meeting with Jeffrey and decided to cheer up by reading a few more chapters of *Indonesia, Etc*. Finding general-interest information about the world's fourth-most populous country written in English was always difficult so I was thrilled to learn that this insightful and humorous book by Elizabeth Pisani had recently been published. I bought a copy at a Halifax bookstore a few days before leaving for Jakarta. Pisani lived in Indonesia at various times over a twenty-five-year period, first as a foreign correspondent and later as an HIV epidemiologist. The *Economist* included *Indonesia, Etc.* in its books of the year list and described it as "a richly entertaining account of a year spent travelling around the archipelago. It takes on some big themes: democracy, decentralization, inequality, the failings of the educational system, and radical Islam, as well as the ghosts of hundreds of thousands slaughtered as Suharto took power in 1965."[74] I had told the others about it when we were making plans for the mission. When I walked through the hotel's poolside sitting area, I saw Judith and Sandra holding books on their laps and laughing and my spirits lifted. They were enjoying hard-cover copies of *Indonesia Etc.* John was reading the book on his tablet and my copy was tucked under my arm.

Sharing our observations and impressions made for a lively dinner discussion that evening. In her book, Pisani mentions that political decentralization was President Habibie's response to the East Timor referendum on independence. He was concerned that other resource-rich provinces might favour independence, so he bypassed them and gave power directly to the cities and districts. One consequence of this move that I was aware of was the intense lobbying to create more districts. We discussed how the abrupt ("Big Bang") transfer of the new responsibilities had left cities and districts unprepared and how we could help them fill the gaps through sharing ideas and best practices

---

74 The *Economist,* December 6, 2014, p. 95.

through the subject-area working groups Home Affairs had helped us set up. Pak Saut had often advocated for a stronger role for provinces in coordinating regional services and I now had a better understanding of why this may not have been a government policy priority.

A mission report was prepared in the required results-based management format and reported six mission deliverables.[75] It also tracked gender participation during our activities and reported it was near parity and in line with the Canadian government's gender mainstreaming requirement, a significant accomplishment. The mission evaluation forms showed a positive response to the mission and suggested future missions last longer so more work could be done. One respondent commented, "The most valuable element of the mission about firefighters is the explanation about the participation of volunteers." Another wrote, "The information given by the Nova Scotia team was very useful. They really helped us on giving lessons learned and best practices from Canada." Our joint plan was to have a final mission to Indonesia to achieve more progress in training and curriculum development for our service priority areas before the program ended in March 2015.

University Comparative Study Results Presented at EROPA

On what turned out to be the last IPAC mission to Indonesia in October 2014, we continued our work at the IPDN campus in Jatinangor, a three-hour drive from Jakarta. In addition to the comparative study we were working on course curriculum, further research on MSS implementation, and a joint degree program. I shared the results of our comparative study, which was being presented at the EROPA conference later that month.

---

75 1) baseline data collected for education, health, and fire safety, MSS and curriculum development; 2) MSS challenges tool developed to capture Canadian solutions and experience; 3) SWOT analysis performed in four areas; 4)draft curriculum developed for IPDN and DIKLAT to improve MSS implementation strategy for civil servants; 5) action plans for curriculum development and implementation established; 6) continued support from Home Affairs and DFATD.

I was surprised to see Professor Untung on the Jatinangor campus shortly after our bus arrived. When he saw me he grinned and pretended to hide his face behind his arms. I greeted him but was cool. I tried to keep my emotions under control and show the proper degree of self-control, balance, bearing, and grace that the Javanese would expect of themselves if not of most foreigners. I didn't want my Indonesian colleagues to see me being overly critical or rude to one of their own. Professor Untung asked me if he could attend the EROPA conference and take part in the presentation. The conference was three days away and the presentations had already been submitted. It was too late to obtain approvals for him to be sponsored by either IPAC or Home Affairs. I was still bothered by the fact that he hadn't completed his part of the research but mostly I was disappointed. A joint presentation by an Indonesian and a Canadian academic at the EROPA conference would have showcased the joint effort of our research and made the study more interesting for the Asian country audience.

The 2014 annual EROPA conference took place in Hanoi, Vietnam. EROPA is the acronym for the Eastern Regional Organization for Public Administration headquartered in Manila. The member countries are Asian. IPAC is also a member. As both IPAC and EROPA are NGOs dedicated to improving public administration, IPAC is invited to send a representative to the EROPA conference each year. In 2014, Maria David-Evans (a former IPAC president) was the IPAC delegate and a keynote panel presenter. IPAC had suggested the EROPA conference would be a good venue to present the research findings of the Indonesian—Canadian comparative study. The paper I'd submitted based on the one-hundred-page study had been accepted for presentation. There were also several conference presenters from Indonesia on the program. They were all academics from Indonesian universities, including IPDN.

The four hundred conference participants stayed at the Daewoo Hotel, a fifteen-minute drive by chartered bus from the conference centre, with no back-and-forth trips during the day. One of the challenges the conference organizers faced was the number of presenters not showing up for their panel presentations. Sometimes they moved whole sessions forward, at other times they lengthened (or shortened if combining sessions) presentation times. No one seemed to mind and this flexibility may have been a reason that no return transportation to the hotel was offered until the end of the day. My session was moved from late morning to an early morning slot after a number of early morning presenters failed to show up. My fellow panellists were from the Philippines and Vietnam. The presentations went smoothly and there were lots of questions afterwards. I was hoping one of the delegates would suggest a comparative study between Canada and their home country similar to the one we had done with Indonesia, but there were no offers.

I was also working on a formal agreement between Dalhousie University and IPDN / Home Affairs that would enable us to expand our work together in the future. It included joint degrees, faculty exchanges, curriculum development, and many of the nascent initiatives included in our current workplan. I brought a memorandum of understanding / letter of intent with me for IPDN approval and took it to the Jatinangor campus for the rector to sign. There were some procedural issues to be resolved before it could be signed, and I left with assurances that it would be delivered to my hotel in Jakarta before I left Indonesia. It arrived with an initial in the signature space on the morning I was due to leave. The university initiative lost its momentum when the Canadian government funding for our cooperation ended.

Last Mission Farewell

A visit with Agung was always an informal part of my mission schedule. We would meet for a meal and most of the time Lili and all or some of the children would accompany him. Lise would send small gifts to Lili and I would accept wrapped packages from Lili to Lise. We usually met at a hotel (often the Borobudur) restaurant but sometimes we would go to a trendy restaurant. I'd often add a day on either end of the mission so I could visit with him. Sometimes we'd get together during the mission and include other IPAC team members.

On my last evening of the last DGP mission, Agung, Lili, Arief, Adimas, and Anissa joined me for the buffet dinner at the Mandarin Oriental Hotel. Arief was now working with the World Bank in Jakarta, Adimas was preparing to go to Europe for graduate studies, and Anissa was near to completing high school. Lili was still managing her consulting business. Agung would be turning sixty (the mandatory retirement age) a year from now and was thinking of going into business. Through his work in border services, he had observed a lack of water and other goods in border communities. He had also observed ship-cargo unloading bottlenecks in Malacca Strait ports. He said he might pick up on meeting one of these needs or something in a related area when he retired. It was good to see him thinking positively about the future.

October 2014 dinner at the Sari Pan Pacific Hotel, Jakarta with Agung, Lili and their children (pictured here with me: Anissa, Arief, and Adimas).

We were all in good spirits and took lots of photos. The variations in our attire was reflective of how dress styles were evolving. Agung wore a plain blue short-sleeve dress shirt and black slacks. Lili was dressed in a *batik* blouse with a black scarf. Arief and Adimas both looked very Western in their dress, with long-sleeve dress shirt, open neck with slacks for Adimas, and jeans for Arief. Arief's shirt wasn't tucked in and his sleeves were rolled up. Anissa looked fashionable in an expensive looking Western-style dress. I wore a colourful *batik* shirt but not the one Agung gave me as I'd already worn it many times at our dinners.

I told Agung that our cooperation project was not going to be renewed and I didn't know when we would meet again. Arief, the elder son, said, "My dream is to bring my parents to Canada for a visit with you one day not far away."

I left hopeful that Arief would make that happen for all of us.

Reflections on a Twenty-year Cooperation

The IPAC team had been planning for a final IPAC mission in early 2015. The mission to Indonesia would enable us to continue our work on developing training material in the areas of health, education, fire services, and building institutional capacity. The evaluations from that October 2014 mission showed our Indonesian colleagues found the working group for each service approach worthwhile and they had asked that future missions last longer so more work could be done. The mission had to take place before DGP wound up at the end of March and we set tentative dates for it.

Indonesia had a new president. Susilo Bambang Yudhoyono had served two five-year terms, the maximum under the constitution. He was replaced by Joko Widodo (Jokowi) and one of the actions taken by the new government was a complete review and restructuring of Home Affairs. Our Home Affairs colleagues were fully engaged with the restructuring and not able to host an IPAC mission in early 2015. That meant the end of our missions.

I had mixed feelings about IPAC's lack of interest and capacity in pursuing the multi-million-dollar bilateral proposal Jeffrey Ong and his colleagues at the Canadian embassy in Jakarta had promoted. The proposal would have been a joint IPAC—Dalhousie University initiative with Nova Scotia support but IPAC would be the key to receiving bilateral approval. IPAC had applied for and administered all the programs funded by the Canadian government related to our twenty-year cooperation with Indonesia. I had recently retired from full-time work and my earlier interest in long-term international project work had been satisfied during my two-year posting in South Africa. If the bilateral project had gone ahead my involvement would have been limited. The leadership and implementation would be left to those with a full-time commitment to the project. It would be difficult for me to see the project go ahead and not be part of it. On the other hand, it would confirm the value of the work we had done to date that brought us to this point. Most importantly, it would accelerate the improvement in service standards and delivery at the local government level—and because of decentralization, local governments were now responsible for providing most of the public services accessed by Indonesians.

As I reflected on the twenty-year cooperation that had abruptly come to an end, I believed IPAC, Canadian provincial and local governments, Nova Scotia, and Dalhousie had played an important role in the reform process. We shared ideas and practices with our Indonesian colleagues that were useful to them. The peer-to-peer approach coupled with having project priorities set by our Indonesian colleagues were the two program features that gradually made our work so highly regarded by the minister of Home Affairs. Our mission program topics always reflected the changing priorities and needs of the day. We supported the "Big Bang" by responding to an urgent need for training resulting from the rapid changes to Indonesian laws. To support components of the "Grand Design" we took a slower, more thorough long-range approach to implement the accompanying reforms.

IPAC, the province of Nova Scotia, Dalhousie University, and other Canadian provinces and cities had contributed to implementing improvements in service delivery through decentralization. We worked with our Indonesian colleagues to improve access to services through one-stop shops and local government enterprise management, explored options for more own-source local government revenue generation, and helped to train local government officials so they would better understand their service and governance responsibilities. During our last five years we worked together on service standards, quality, and delivery. I observed first-hand how Indonesian leaders had implemented many of the service initiatives they learned about on study missions to Canada in their own local governments. The highlight of our academic cooperation was the Indonesia—Canada comparative study of service standards and service delivery. It provided a reference point for discussing Indonesian service needs and ways of achieving them. We had done what we could. The rest was up to our capable Indonesian colleagues and the political environment that sustained them.

The relationship with our Indonesian colleagues also changed over the life of our cooperation and in some ways this was the most personally satisfying part. There were many reasons for this change. On the Indonesian side an improved ability to communicate in English with Canadians who didn't speak Indonesian was a major factor. Another was the pressing need to reform democratic governance and service delivery practices after President Suharto resigned in 1998, and IPAC was well placed to accommodate Indonesia priorities. A third reason was having consistency in relationships. Agung remained engaged during the entire period, Lies and Arif provided stability in their role as coordinators, and Yuswandi, Siti Nurbaya, Saut, Sadu, Nuryanto, Yusharto, and others provided the leadership in moving our initiatives forward. Jeffrey Ong of the Canadian embassy in Jakarta worked with us during all phases of the program and provided valued advice and perspective as well as coordinating embassy participation at our seminars and expediting travel visas.

When asked what conditions are necessary for a successful peer-to-peer approach to work in international development, I use Indonesia as an example. It starts with the country's commitment to democratic reform and the involvement of committed Indonesian individuals for the duration of the project. Access to (Canadian) practitioners with the knowledge and skills needed is key. Participants in both countries need to be given opportunities for professional and life experience learning and be comfortable working together. Good coordination, a good relationship with the agencies providing the funding, and an adequate (low-cost) budget round off the list. Changes in the developing country team's leadership can be positive if reform priorities change or are at different stages as long as the coordinator remains in place.

On our introductory missions the IPAC team spent a lot of time waiting at the hotel for phone calls or seated on hard chairs in reception rooms. A few years later, we had fuller agendas but spent sleepless nights travelling by train or van around Java accompanied by junior officials. During the last five years, it was a heavy schedule that kept us from a full night's sleep as we took pre-dawn flights from region to region, this time accompanied by senior officials who had become more than just colleagues. The large number of Indonesians (including a few thousand seminar / workshop participants) and Canadians involved over the years also contributed to buy-in and project success.

There were a number of trends and changes I observed over the twenty years. When the Institute of Public Administration of Canada first started working with Home Affairs in the mid 1990s President Suharto had been in power for close to thirty years. Elections were not free and fair and senior civil servants had little incentive to promote reforms. The government was highly centralized. Administrative decentralization was seen as a way to improve the national economy by reducing requirements for central government approvals so that goods could move more quickly and freely. Five years later, in the wake of a financial crisis Indonesia had a new president with a reform agenda. The transfer of most service responsibilities to local governments became a priority and the focus of our work for the next decade and a half. Within this broader mandate there were many senior civil servants who were committed to designing and implementing the changes needed for decentralization. A related change was that in the later years of our cooperation, in addition to being fluent in English, more of the senior Indonesian officials we worked with already had exposure to other governance structures and practices through overseas studies at American, British, Dutch, Australian, and Japanese universities.

The number of subnational governments increased with decentralization. Between 1995 and 2013 the number of provinces grew from twenty-seven to thirty-four, local (city / regency) governments from 305 to 511, sub-districts from 3,844 to 9,982, and villages from 65,852 to 80,414.[76] Time will tell whether this proliferation of subnational governments will prove more responsive to public service needs or not. The trend in Canada during this period was to reduce the number of local governments.

The late 1990s transition to a more robust democracy also made our colleagues more open to sharing information or opinions with us about the needs of Indonesia. It provided an incentive for them to work more closely with IPAC as a partner in implementing the decentralization reforms the government had prioritized. Pak Saut and Pak Yusharto, the last two Indonesian leaders of our cooperation, were both active in expanding our activities and ensuring Indonesian participants used the program activities and information to the full advantage of their communities.

Jakarta became more cosmopolitan and commercial. Several high-rise residential towers and mega malls (large shopping complexes) were built or expanded. In preparation for the twenty-sixth Southeast Asian Games in 2011, the centre of the city became off limits to street venders and panhandlers. Twenty years after my first visit, Indonesians were no longer greeting me in the streets and wanting to befriend me. The streets were filled with motorbikes weaving in and out of the heavy traffic. They had become the most efficient way to get around the gridlocked city. Many of them were being used as taxis (*ojek*), replacing the less nimble three-wheeled (and black-fume belching) *bajajs*. During my earlier missions to Jakarta, I ventured out on foot to explore the areas near the hotel and felt safe. Regardless of whether it was an early morning run, a midday visit to Pasar Baru, or an evening walk, I never felt uneasy or in danger. In later years, a fuller program that often took us to other parts of Indonesia meant less time in Jakarta. That, combined with a lack of new places to explore within walking distance of the Hotel Borobudur, meant I didn't go out as much. I was still comfortable when I did. The most common crime I saw reported in the media was pickpocketing.

Our Indonesian colleagues were early adopters of cellphone

---

76 ADB Institute Working Paper Series Government Decentralization Program in Indonesia Anwar Nasution No 601, October 2016, Table 1 p.4.

technology, in part because of the difficulty of having a landline installed. They were also early adopters of smartphones and for a time the Blackberry was their smartphone of choice.

There were changes in the balance between secularism and religion. I observed more tolerance in Indonesian society in the early years of our cooperation. After Indonesia became more democratic, new laws were introduced to protect basic human rights and personal freedoms. A backlash to these progressive moves followed. In the 2010s a Shiite cleric was imprisoned for blasphemy and members of the Ahmadi Islam community, who hold some beliefs that differ from mainstream Sunni Muslims, were killed. Later in the decade, the governor of Jakarta was found guilty of blasphemy and laws enforcing a conservative view of morality were introduced. Recent changes to morality laws will not only restrict the sexual practices and freedom of speech for Indonesians, but may also have a negative impact on tourism.

Professor Untung referred to the "Ring of Fire" of volcanoes and the "earthquake belt" that surround Indonesia when providing context for Indonesian governance and service delivery issues for our comparative study. The 2004 Indian Ocean earthquake and tsunami interrupted our cooperation for a period of almost two years. There were several other volcanic eruptions, earthquakes, floods, mudslides, and fire-induced hazes during the years we worked together, and although they were devastating to people directly impacted by them, they didn't interrupt our work. There were floods and forest fires in Canada during this period as well, but the only scheduled mission to be cancelled due to a natural disaster was the Indonesian mission to Canada in the autumn of 2003 when Halifax and other parts of Nova Scotia experienced Hurricane Juan—a Category 2 hurricane, which was the most damaging storm in the modern history of Halifax. Awareness of the impact of human activities on climate change and natural disasters grew in both our countries.

One thing that never changed was the warmth and humour of the Indonesian people we worked with and encountered. The same could be said for the basic cultural values of harmony, discussion, consensus building, unity, and respect for age and authority that I observed in the early years of our cooperation.

Agung realized his dream of holding a senior political position. In 2016, he was appointed interim governor of Kepulauan Riau (Riau Islands) province. Kepulauan Riau is a province of two million people on 1,796 islands scattered between Sumatra, the Malay Peninsula and Kalimantan (Borneo) in the Malacca Strait.

I can't say it was ever my dream, but I had reached a point in life where I seldom distinguish myself from the Javanese by showing anger in stressful situations. I'd like to think it was because of my twenty-year exposure to Indonesian society but it could also be from the wisdom and maturity that sometimes comes with age. What may have been my realized dream was to learn more about the world and my place in it. I grew up in a peripheral part of the world that was shaped by world history (economic, political, religion) and reacted to changing world events, but rarely drove them. Through the Indonesia project and other international project opportunities (Europe, Africa, Asia) that came about through my Indonesian involvement I was able to gain knowledge and a better understanding of the wider world.

EPILOGUE / AFTERWORD

(2018–2024)

"Each new friend represents a world in us, a world possibly not born until they arrive, and it is only by this meeting that a new world is born."

– Anias Nin, French-Cuban-American writer

While I was writing this book, I read the *Journal of Southeast Asian Economies* (Vol. 38, No. 3, December 2021), which featured a number of articles on the impact of two decades of decentralization reforms in Indonesia. Although decentralization continues to be widely supported, the results of the review are mixed with progress in some areas and lots of work still to be done in others. What stood out when I read the material was that most of the topic areas and issues raised in these peer-reviewed journal articles were ones that had been part of IPAC's twenty-year cooperation with Home Affairs. In some cases, the reforms had progressed along the lines our cooperation supported, in others they hadn't yet due to capacity issues, and in a few cases the decision-makers had other ideas.

Our first initiative was improving the process for obtaining licences, permits and other services. This was done through the promotion of one-stop shops to provide these services. In addition to a seminar on the topic in Halifax in 1996, roundtable discussions on one-stop service provision were held in two locations, Jakarta and Jatinangor, in 2011. A visit to one or more one-stop shops was included in two of the missions to Canada and most IPAC missions to Indonesia. In 1997, we were asked to formally assess the performance of one of them. While there have been some positive local government licence- and permit-approval process initiatives (and improvements) through decentralization, they weren't sufficient for President Jokowi and he reclaimed national responsibility for issuing some of them. I wasn't surprised by this as the decentralization pendulum had quickly swung quite far out and the central government hadn't thought through the extent of the change. Plus, the *Economist*[77] recently pointed out that

---

77 The *Economist*, November 19, 2022, p.21, shares the World Bank's report suggesting that Indonesian exporters faced a combined 117 hours of checks and paperwork for each consignment of goods leaving the country, far higher than the figures from India, Malaysia, Thailand or Vietnam.

Indonesia still has a long way to go to match the approval time of other countries in the region.

One of the early study missions to Canada focused on local government revenues and stressed the importance (from a local government autonomy perspective) of having sufficient own-source revenues. In 2006, IPAC and Home Affairs coordinated a Jakarta roundtable on local government fiscal decentralization. The 2011 mission to Canada was dedicated to financial planning for local governments. The following year in Indonesia a seminar on local asset management and another on local government finance, budgeting and taxation, were held in Jakarta and Bukittinggi. The journal researchers found that fiscal decentralization lagged behind the political and administrative dimensions. Local governments were still heavily reliant on central government transfers although they have added new taxes and user fees.

Capacity building was covered in different ways during our missions. It started with improving the management of local government enterprises in the 1990s and followed up through an international workshop on the topic in Jakarta in 2003. The 1999 mission to Canada covered the roles and responsibilities of elected officials. The seminar topic for the 2000 mission was on good governance topics related to decentralization (procurement, ethics, public engagement, and codes of conduct for elected and appointed officials). There were missions to both Canada and Indonesia to study and experience the training for newly elected local government councillors. The journal researchers found varying degrees of local government capacity. Positive initiatives in areas such as regulation, infrastructure, and more participatory decision-making processes in urban planning were identified in cities and districts that had higher capacity levels.

Service provision, service standards, and service delivery were a major part of our work in the last six years of our cooperation. In 2009, a Jakarta roundtable looked at decentralization and public service provision. We added an academic stream and undertook a Canadian—Indonesian comparative study to identify areas for improvement in Indonesian service standards and service delivery methods. Once these areas were identified we discussed solutions based on the

Canadian experience and the Indonesian capacity to initiate improvements. Several of the missions to Canada and Indonesia between 2012 and 2014 focused on minimum service standards and service delivery options. Certain services (health, education, water, infrastructure, fire) were identified as priority areas by Home Affairs and teams made up of Indonesian and Canadian experts in these areas were formed and tasked with developing programs for improving them. The journal research found that the capacity of local governments to deliver development outcomes (measured by per capita income, poverty levels, educational attainment) had increased but not in all local governments. Education was identified as a key government service that contributed to poverty reduction.

One of the areas where we involved Canadians with expertise was education. Site visits were included in the missions to Canada in 2012 and 2013 and the missions to Indonesia in 2013 and 2014. Canadian experts made presentations on the topic at seminars in both countries and worked with education colleagues in Indonesia. The journal researchers found a significant effect of education expansion from primary to higher levels for reducing poverty and highlighting the importance of improving the level of education. At present, the quality of education (measured by learning outcomes) varies across local governments, and students enrolled in low-quality schools are at a disadvantage.

Our program workshop topics and discussions included local—central government relations and the need for service coordination at the regional level. They also covered financial programs that could enable all regions and local governments to provide a basic standard level of service. Under the decentralization reforms the role of Indonesian provinces was mainly to coordinate the services provided by the cities and districts. The journal research found that this role is becoming stronger. Some policy making has been recentralized at the national level. There is also a need for improvements in the national grant programs, both to ensure local governments have the resources needed to provide minimum services and that they contribute to economic growth.

The assessments provided by these journal articles demonstrate the relevance of the work IPAC and Home Affairs undertook. As for the results, Canadian direct involvement was limited to short periods of time each year, so it was up to our Indonesian colleagues to use the knowledge gained from our cooperation to implement, or promote, components of the Grand Design decentralization plan. IPAC mainly worked with public servants (and a few politicians) who, like their Canadian colleagues, could influence and advocate for change but did not make the final decisions.

In 2024, I went back to Indonesia and met with several of the people I had worked with on the project. Three of them asked me to meet with staff at their offices and exchange information on contemporary public sector issues related to local governments in Indonesian and Canada. During this time, I read *Governing Urban Indonesia*[78] the latest book (2024) in the Indonesia Update Series organized by the Australian National University Indonesia Project. The information my colleagues shared was in line with the observations made in the *Journal of Southeast Asian Economics* in 2021 and in *Governing Urban Indonesia* in 2024.

The central government had reassumed responsibility for issuing licences and permits for minerals, mines, and natural resources to better serve national interests and policies and achieve national goals. Indonesia is moving away from exporting raw materials, such as nickel and bauxite, in favour of adding value by processing them at home.

Political decentralization has made the most progress when compared with financial decentralization and service delivery, where progress has been slow. Local governments with greater financial and staff capacity have done better in these last two areas by generating a greater share of own-source revenue and using technology to improve service delivery. For example, Tangerang city uses e-government technology to enable online transactions that result in quicker service and promote clean government.

During our cooperation we discussed classifying municipalities based on size and capacity and allocating different responsibilities and

---

78 *Governing Urban Indonesia*, edited by Edward Aspinal and Amalinda Savirani, 2024 ISEAS—Yusof Ishak, Singapore. The book chapters were presented as papers at the fortieth annual Indonesia Update Conference held at the Australian National University in September 2023.

revenue sources to each category. This idea is gaining momentum. Unlike Canada, where each province sets its own governance and service responsibilities for its local governments, in Indonesia they are set at the national level and there is a wide variation in regional capacity. At present all local governments must use a set percent of their budgets for some priority services and report on those set standards when submitting the required reports. A classification system that recognized different economic and resource capacities, as well as different needs, would help set more realistic targets for local governments with varying capacities. Government-led research on asymmetric decentralization is currently underway.

Interest in expanding the coordination role of provinces continues, as does national government efforts to provide clearer directives to local government. Both the Indonesian colleagues I spoke with and chapters in *Governing Urban Indonesia* referred to cities that have embraced the positive aspects of decentralization and improved services, increased opportunities for public engagement, and promoted clean government. Local government enterprises were seen as a means for contributing to local government own-source revenues but large differences in financial and resource capacity have resulted in uneven results.

Indonesia had a poor score on the Transparency International Corruption Index when Suharto was in power. The reform-minded leaders wanted to improve it and we included two workshops related to clean government and codes of conduct as part of our cooperation during Indonesian missions to Canada. The Corruption Eradication Commission (Indonesian: Komisi Pembertasan Koripsi or KPK) was established in 2003 to combat corruption but changing a culture can take time. Several of the contributors to *Governing Urban Indonesia* refer to the close informal relations that link powerful business and political actors at all levels of government in Indonesia. Terms such as corruption, collusion, predatory elites, and money politics are often used when referring to these links. The contributors also provide examples of good governance at the local level where strong leadership and the inclusion of input from civil society has reduced opportunities for corruption. In chapter 7, one of the authors provides an example of a local government with significant local income from taxes and charges that continued with predatory behavior while at the same time improved the delivery of health care, education and other services to the public.

Other authors discuss cities that have become virtual laboratories of political change for the country as a whole, pioneering new methods of services to residents, improving amenities, tackling long standing urban problems and in some cases taking action to reduce entrenched corruption and increase citizen participation. I had thought the Indonesian mayors and regents who participated in the study missions to Canada and hosted workshops in Indonesia were among that group. I was surprised when I learned that one of them, Rita Widyasari former regent of Kutai Kartangera District had been sentenced to ten years in prison after being found guilty of committing graft. Rita had been an active participant in our cooperation and had implemented several service improvements in her district following her exposure to Canadian practices. She was on an upward political career path, had announced her intention to run for governor, and held a prominent position in the Golkar party. I didn't expect corruption and unethical behavior to be eliminated in Indonesia and I knew there were limits on using Canada as a shining example of good governance. A Canadian sponsorship scandal mentioned earlier had already shown Canada was not immune from misusing public funds. But I did expect a higher standard of conduct from the Indonesian elected officials who implemented reforms based to our work together, and on several occasions, Rita had spoken publicly about the positive results in her district. My conversations with Rita were mostly about service delivery and always in group settings. A discussion about predatory elites might have provided some insight on what motivated her actions.

In summary, the decentralization reform process has slowed after a certain amount of rebalancing took place. Prabowo Subianto was elected as Indonesia's eighth president in February 2024, and welfare is one of his priorities. His signature policy is a free school-lunch program that would cost $28 billion per year.[79] Self-sufficiency in agriculture

---

79 *The Economist*, October 26, 2024 p.28.

(rice in particular) is also one of his priorities. It's likely that welfare will come before governance as a priority for the Prabowo government and progress in achieving the remaining Grand Design decentralization goals will be gradual.

As a result of the goodwill built over the twenty-year cooperation between Indonesians and Canadians, Indonesian leaders have often expressed interest in renewing our cooperation through new initiatives. During my 2024 visit with colleagues in Jakarta, some of them expressed interest in reactivating our cooperation to share experiences and best practices.

In addition to observations on the progress of decentralization and government, there were other changes I observed, or heard about, during the 2024 visit. One was the considerable investment that had been made in infrastructure projects like highways, train travel, and other transportation links during Jokowi's presidential terms. Indonesia's first high-speed train service, operating between Jakarta and Bandung and owned by Kereta Cepat Indonesia China, opened in October 2023. High-rise buildings dominate the greater Jakarta / Tangerang skyline and construction cranes are a common site. The economy is strong and Indonesia's 2024 growth as measured by GDP is forecast to be 5.1 percent, which is higher than China's.[80]

Consumer habits and open spaces are changing in Jakarta too. Pasar Baru was a place I always made a point of visiting to experience the real Jakarta—the one for everyday people. In the early years, I'd buy gifts and was often the only visible minority there. Two Indonesian colleagues had told me it wasn't as busy these days because during the Covid-19 pandemic people had switched to online shopping and stayed with it. On a Sunday afternoon I went to see for myself. There was still a lot of activity (and feral cats) but it was greatly reduced from the earlier years. There were several shops for lease at the near end of the street and parked cars in front of empty shops. The mid-street vendor stalls were only in the last few blocks, the mall at the end of the street had several vacant spaces for lease, and the top floors were barricaded. The same

---

80 Economic and financial indicators table in *The Economist* November 2, 2024.

combination of goods (textiles, clothes, watches, music, shoes, etc.) were for sale. A shoe store called Toronto that features a Blue Jays logo was still in business and I saw familiar names on other permanent shops.

On the way back to the hotel I walked through the Lapangan Banteng Park, home of the West Irian Monument (a.k.a. the Incredible Hulk). It had been renovated since I was last there and transformed into an attractive public park with large open spaces, manicured lawns, an outdoor amphitheater, and an attractive pond. Large groups, families, and individuals, were enjoying its tranquil setting. A list of prohibited activities that included vendors and loud noises was posted at the entry points.

Connecting with Friends and Colleagues

I've been back to Indonesia twice since our program ended. In 2018, I made a two-day stop on my way home from a teaching assignment in Papua New Guinea. It had been four years since my previous visit. I let Agung and Arif know I was coming and arranged to see them.

The flight from Brisbane landed in Jakarta shortly after midnight. As agreed, I phoned Agung on arrival. He sounded concerned and asked me to phone him again once I reached the hotel, "no matter how late it was." There was a long line at immigration and it was after 2 a.m. when my taxi pulled up at the Borobudur Hotel. Unlike the early years, instead of driving directly to the entrance, the taxi was stopped for a security check before being allowed to proceed to the main entrance.

After breakfast Agung called and suggested we meet for lunch at the hotel. Lili and their son Arief (who drove) came too, and we had fun reminiscing, catching up on the news, and exchanging gifts. Arief picked up the bill and joked that he was the only one working in the family now. Agung asked about my program and I said it was to visit with him and the next day I would meet colleagues from Home Affairs. When I had corresponded with Agung about my stopover he had suggested we travel to his ancestral village in West Java and spend a few days there. I said I would like to when I had more time.

As he aged Agung put on weight and (like me) his hair turned grey. He started wearing glasses. At our lunch in 2018, both Agung and Lili were formally dressed in *batik* whereas Arief wore a polo shirt. Agung had the appearance of a successful conservative retiree, content with life, his family and his accomplishments. I didn't sense a desire to do more. On my next visit I learned I was wrong about that—he was just taking a break.

There were posters in the Borobudur Hotel and around the city promoting the eighteenth Asian Games being hosted in Jakarta—Palembang. They were underway when Agung came for lunch, and when the games were over Indonesia held the fourth spot in both gold medals and total medals. Only China, Japan, and South Korea had done better. Indonesia was on the move. It had youth, natural resources, a large population and, thanks in part to our twenty-year partnership, the tools to deliver quality public services. After lunch we took photos in front of the Asian Games display in the lobby. As they readied to leave, I asked if they would drop me off at Sarinah department store on their way home.

Arif and I made plans to meet the following day, which was Eid-al-Adha (a Muslim religious day that marks the end of the hajj pilgrimage) and an Indonesian government holiday. I hadn't known it was a holiday when I booked my plane tickets. Nurdin and his wife picked me up at the hotel in their SUV and I climbed in the back seat with Arif and Kuswanto, who had recently completed his doctorate in the Netherlands and was back working at Home Affairs. (Yusharto had called to apologize for not being able to join us and asked when we could start making work plans again.) We had an Indonesian meal at a brightly lit restaurant and then set off to find an open-mic venue. I'd been preparing for this evening for months by taking more voice lessons and learning some of the lyrical mid-twentieth century jazz pieces. We spent the next two hours driving around Jakarta neighbourhoods looking for a club. Arif thought they would be open in some parts of the city but every time we drove up to one it was closed. Apart from the disappointment of not being able to find a venue for singing, it was a wonderful evening of laughter and reminiscing. Yet again, my mission to put my voice lessons to use was thwarted. After Arif and I lost our opportunity to sing together, I stopped taking singing lessons as unlike Arif, I'm not a naturally gifted singer. However, I've been taking music lessons (theory and keyboard) ever since and get a lot of enjoyment from understanding and learning to play familiar tunes. Arif and his colleagues were my inspiration.

In 2024, I made a second post-project visit to Indonesia. This one was longer and involved more planning. I had turned seventy-five earlier in the year and the motivation for making the trip was to take Agung up on his invitation to join him for a multi-day visit to his ancestral village near Cirebon in West Java and do it while we were all in good health. It had been thirty years since Agung had accompanied Sue, Louis and I on our mission to Sulawesi at the beginning of our cooperation. Once we agreed on travel dates, I extended my time so I could also visit with other Indonesian friends and former colleagues. I also wanted to fill some information gaps for this story before submitting it for publication.

The first thing I noticed during the midnight arrival at the Jakarta airport was its newest terminal, number three, which is large and modern. It felt like I could be arriving in Hong Kong or Tokyo and it was so different from the uniquely Indonesian terminal one I experienced when I first entered Indonesia in 1994. Terminal three exuded modern and international rather than traditional Indonesian style. Digital technology was now being used to complete the immigration process, whereas in the past everything was pen and paper. Now it was all done online using QR codes and free airport Wi-Fi. An Indonesian woman from the flight who was on holiday from her work in New Brunswick saw me struggling with the new requirements and guided me through the process. After clearing immigration, I bought some rupiah from a money changer, hailed a Bluebird taxi and arrived at the Borobudur Hotel at 2:30 a.m.. I set my alarm so I wouldn't miss breakfast.

The Hotel Borobudur offers a buffet breakfast featuring multiple food stations. The breakfast experience has evolved since my first start-of-the-day meal there in 1994, and reflects changes in how Indonesia presents itself to the wider world. The breakfast experience in 1994 was like time travelling to an earlier (colonial) era. The staff were uniformed and formal. Guests were escorted to their tables; coffee was served in carafes, and juice requests were filled. A variety of broad-sheet newspapers were available at the entrance. Hotel workers wearing *songkoks* (also known as *peci* hats) moved through the restaurant carrying small chalkboards adorned with tingling bells with the name of the diner they were looking for so a message could be delivered. The diners were foreigners in business attire (except on weekends), Indonesians wearing *batik* who peppered the space with conversation and laughter, and well-dressed families. The food was bountiful, diners could fill their plates as high as they wanted to, and people moved around the food stations at a relaxed pace.

In 2024, there are no newspapers to be found at the entry point where diners' room cards are now scanned. Coffee and juice are self-serve, and at some food stations the counter staff set out plates with standard portion sizes. There is less conversation, less laughter, more smartphone preoccupation at the tables, and more Indonesians are wearing Western-style clothing. The diners' pace at the food stations is rushed. The wait staff are still uniformed and professional but less formal, and none of them are delivering messages. The time-travel experience is limited to jetlag. It's not that different from what I would experience in Canada or another Western nation, other than the Indonesian staff smile more often. It's still a good breakfast.

Agung and his family put a lot of thought and effort in planning the three-day visit to Cirebon and Kuningan. We met at the Borobudur Hotel and Agung's son Arief drove us to Gambir, the main train station in Jakarta. On the three-hour train ride to Cirebon, Agung told me about its rich, diverse history, and about the conquests and intrigues of the sultans of Cirebon. The train was spacious and comfortable and owned by a national government enterprise. Lili and their daughter Anissa, who had recently returned from New Zealand, joined us. Agung was now back in the workforce as the head of the retired civil servants' association. His hours were flexible and he was enjoying the work.

Representatives of the Cirebon history tour company were waiting for us at their train station. They were a young, entrepreneurial group and one of them was fluent in English and made sure I kept up with the tour presentations. The first stop was a local Indonesian restaurant and at the end of the meal Agung surprised me with a cake decorated with the words, "Happy 30th Friendship Anniversary." I was physically six degrees latitude south of the equator, but felt I was on top of the world.

The 30th anniversary friendship cake.

Over the next few days, I learned how Cirebon (nicknamed Shrimp City) had been shaped by the Sultanates, Arabs, Portuguese, Dutch and Chinese. The tour company van transported us to the local palaces, museums, mosques, churches, and markets related to this history and took photos, which they sent to us. In nearby Kuningan, the main attraction was the Linggarjati Museum—the building where negotiations leading to Indonesian independence took place in 1946. Kuningan is Agung's ancestral village and we stayed at his sister's guesthouse that looks on Mount Ceremai, West Java's highest mountain at 3,078 metres. We ate relaxing breakfasts and shared photos of our grandchildren. There was always something going on but we were never rushed. Heavy rainfall slowed the afternoon train ride back to Jakarta, so night had fallen by the time our shared taxi dropped me off at the Borobudur Hotel.

With Agung in Cirebon where we celebrated our thirty-year friendship.
November 2024.

The night before I left Jakarta Agung, Lili, Anissa, Arief, and his wife Reza joined me at the hotel for our farewell dinner, a tradition carried over from our project mission days. Arief and Reza were newlyweds, and it was my first opportunity to talk with Reza. Both Arief and Reza work for the World Bank so I may get to see more of them if they are ever posted to the headquarters in Washington. Agung and Lili both wore traditional *batik* while the younger generation were dressed in Western styles.

When I got back to Jakarta I made plans to meet with Jeffrey Ong and his son at a coffee shop in Plaza Senayan. Jeffrey retired from his work at the Canadian embassy in 2019 and enjoys spending more time with Defrey, his adult son who has Down syndrome. Jeffrey spends a lot of his time advocating for improved services for people with disabilities. We talked a lot about the status of the decentralization reforms and, as always, Jeffrey was up to date on what was happening and generous in sharing his knowledge.

Over the next week, I connected with four other colleagues in both office and social settings. Yusharto is still involved in implementing the decentralization reforms and now is the head of National Policy Strategic Agency at Home Affairs. When I visited his office in 2024, Nurdin was acting mayor of Tangerang, the capital city of Banten province with two million inhabitants. Arif left Home Affairs and now holds a senior position with the Ministry of Manpower. Kuswanto is involved in the logistics of moving the national capital from Jakarta to Nusantara in Kalimantan. The move was initiated by former two-term president Jokowi. I was also in touch with Yuswandi, who served as secretary general of the Ministry of Home Affairs before he retired, but we were unable to meet as he was visiting his daughters in the United States.

Arif is still mistaken for a young professional at times although he's only a few years away from retirement. He is often called on to sing at official gatherings and sends me YouTube links to his performances. During two of the evenings I was in Jakarta, Arif and some of his colleagues met me at the Pendopo Lounge at the Borobudur Hotel for a meal and to listen to the talented trio (saxophone, guitar, vocalist) performing there. We took a table near the stage, made requests, and talked about music with the trio during the breaks. On the second evening, Arif was accompanied by a young colleague, originally from Sulawesi, who had been working with him that day. The young man was bright-eyed, fluent in English, and very engaged in our conversation, both about work and music. He told me he was optimistic about receiving a government sponsorship for post-graduate studies overseas. He had grown up in the post-Suharto era when Indonesia was focusing on improving trade and economic opportunities through good governance and decentralization. There were opportunities for dedicated public servants to contribute and incentives for doing so. Before he left, he told me he was grateful that things had worked out well for him. "I come from a small place in a small province, yet I have all these wonderful study, travel and work opportunities. It's hard to believe my good fortune." When he said this, I did a doubletake and quickly realized why a light had just come on in my head. That was me in Canada fifty years ago in a country that was growing and prospering. When I entered the public sector, opportunities for young graduates to make meaningful public sector contributions were valued and abundant. Now this young person saw the same opportunities in twenty-first century Indonesia. I hope his studies and work in public service bring him satisfaction, both personally and professionally, as my domestic and international work, more than a generation before, did for me from my birthplace, Canada.

BIBLIOGRAPHY

(The) Economist. A Golden Chance: A Special Report on Indonesia. September 12, 2009.

Governing Urban Indonesia, edited by Edward Aspinall and Amalinda Savirani, Singapore: ISEAS Publishing, 2024.

Hannigan, Tim. A Brief History of Indonesia: Sultans, Spices and Tsunamis. First Edition. Rutland, Vermont: Tuttle Publishing, 2015.

IPAC International. Democratic Governance Program: Policies and Procedures Guide. Toronto: Institute of Public Administration of Canada, updated.

Journal of Southeast Asian Economics Volume 38, No.3. Edited by Siwage Dharma Negara and Francis E Hutchinson. Special Edition: The Impact of Indonesia's Decentralization Reforms Two Decades On. ISEAS Publishing , Yusof Ishak Institute, December 2021.

Nasution, Anwar. Government Decentralization Program in Indonesia. ADBI Working Paper Series No.601, Asian Development Bank Institute, October 2016.

Periplus Adventure Guides. Bali. Edited by Eric Oey. Singapore: Periplus Editions, 1995.

Periplus Travel Guides. Java. Edited by Eric Oey. Singapore: Periplus Editions, 1994.

Periplus Travel Guides. Sulawesi. Edited by Toby Alice Volkman and Ian Caldwell. Singapore: Periplus Editions, 1992.

Pisani, Elizabeth. Indonesia Etc: Exploring the Improbable Nation. First edition, New York: W.W. Norton & Company, 2014.

Rasyid, M Ryass. The Policy of Decentralization in Indonesia. International Studies Program Working Paper 02-31, Andrew Young School of Policy Studies, Atlanta: Georgia State University, December 2002.

Ribot, Jesse. Democratic Decentralization of Natural Resources: Institutionalizing Popular Participation. World Resources Institute. Washington DC, 2002.

Schwarz, Adam. A Nation in Waiting: Indonesia in the 1990s. Sydney: Allen and Unwin, 1994.

USAID Democratic Reform Support Program (DRSP) with support from the Donor Working Group on Decentralization. Decentralization 2006: Stock Taking on Indonesia's Recent Decentralization Reforms. August 2006.

USAID Democratic Reform Support Program (DRSP) with support from the Donor Working Group on Decentralization. Decentralization 2009: Stock Taking on Indonesia's Recent Decentralization Reforms Update March 2009.

Van Reybrouck, David. Revolusi: Indonesia and the Birth of the Modern World. Translated from the Dutch by David Colmer and David McKay. W.W. New York: Norton & Company, 2020 and 2024 (translation).

Ziv, Daniel. Jakarta Inside Out. Jakarta: Equinox Publishing, 2002.

Appendix 1: Maps
(showing locations where activities took place)

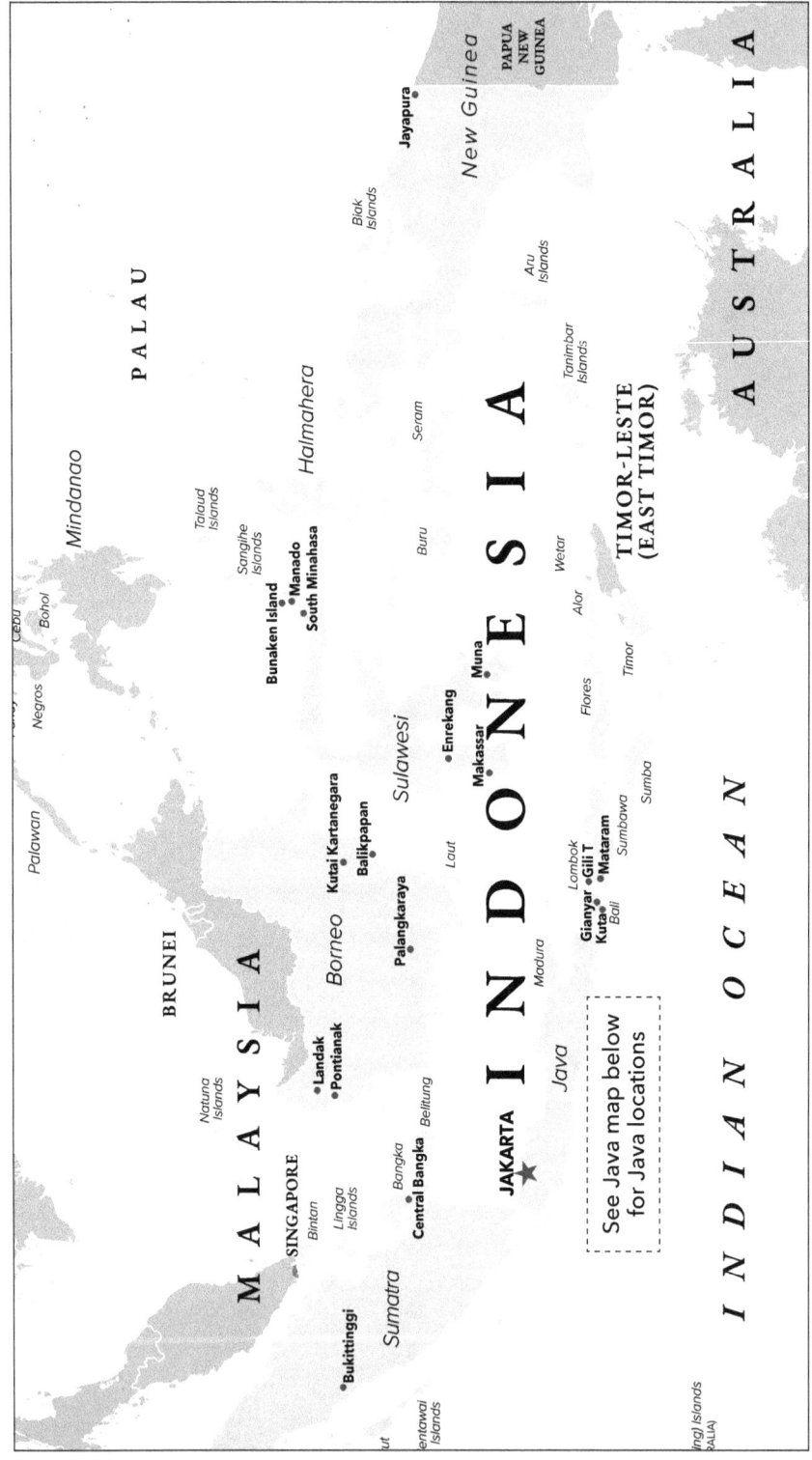

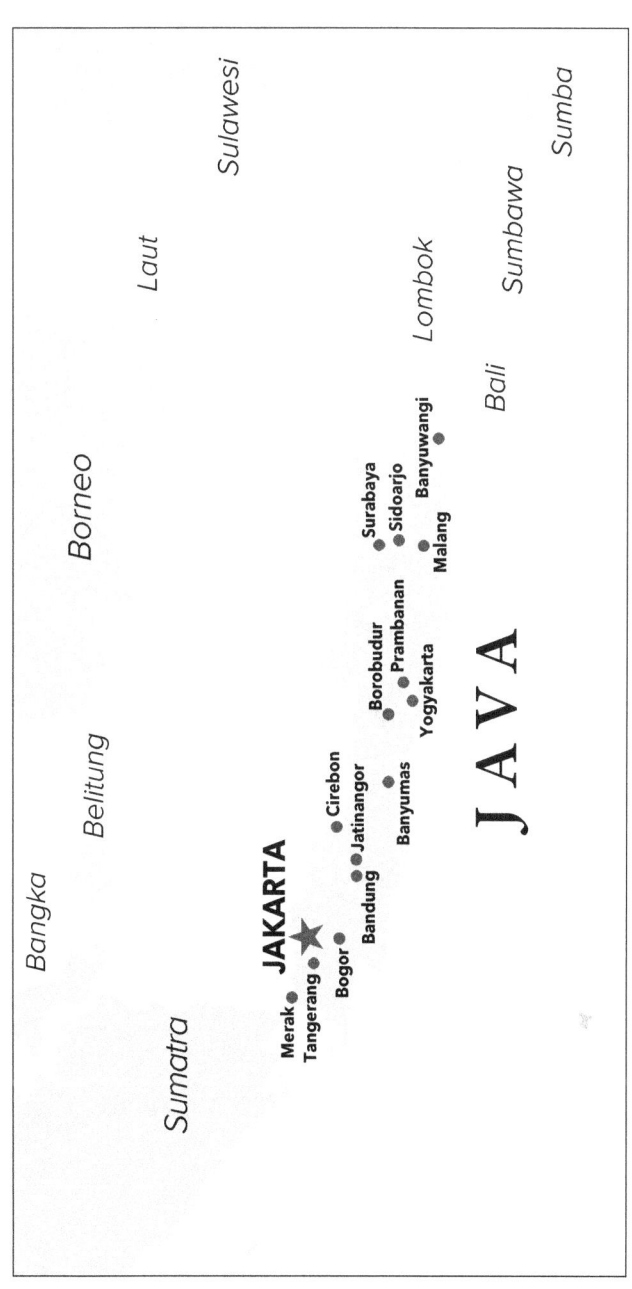

See Nova Scotia map below for NS locations

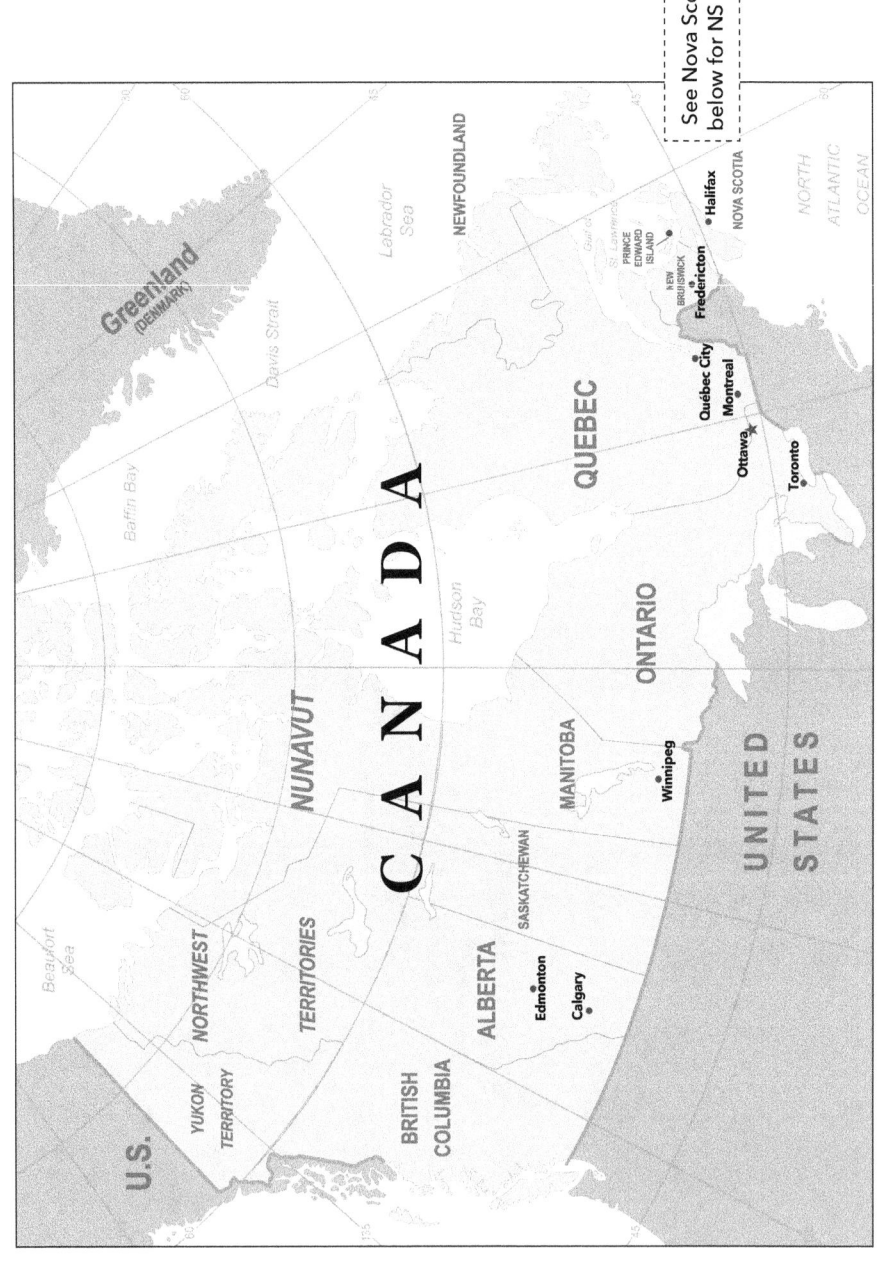

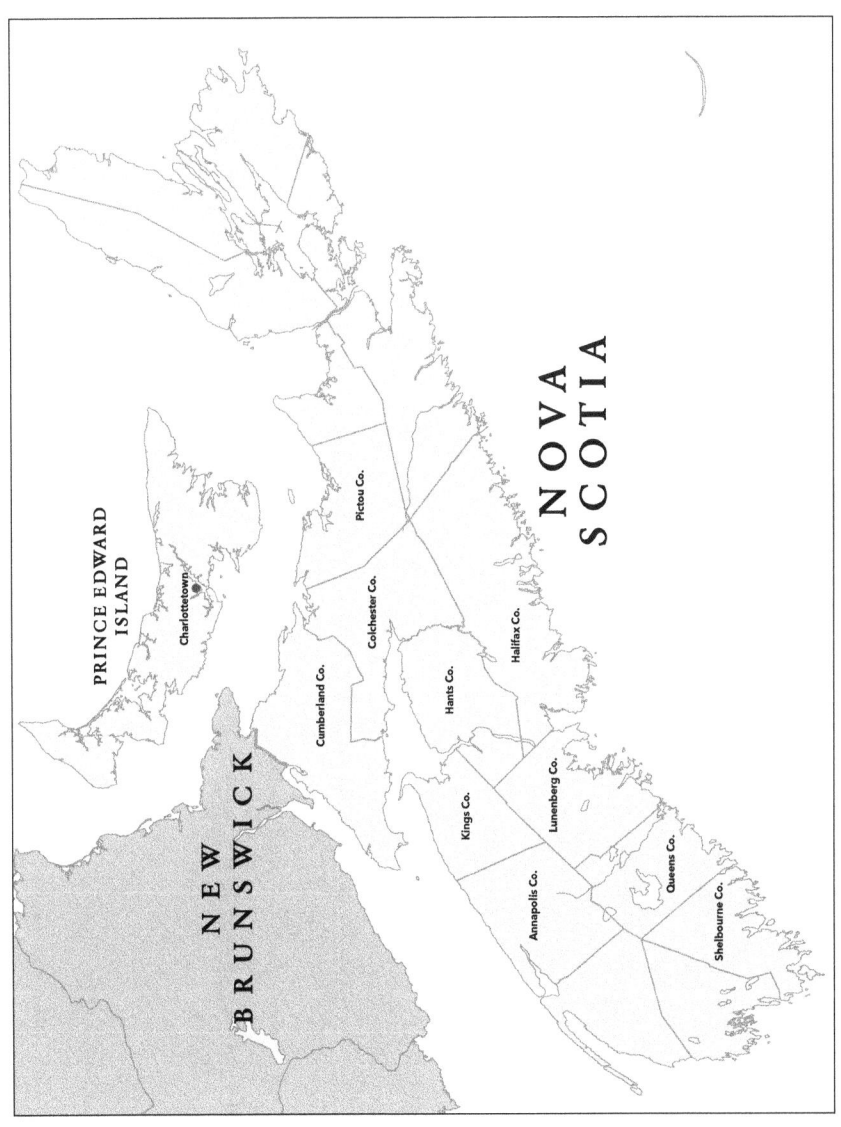

Appendix 2: Presidents of Indonesia

Indonesia had seven presidents between its founding as a nation and the end of our cooperation in 2014/15. Six of the seven served during the period of our cooperation. The presidents and their term dates are:

- Sukarno 1945-1967
- Suharto 1967-1998
- BJ Habibie 1998-1999
- Abdurrahman Wahid 1999-2001
- Megawati Sukarnoputri 2001-2004
- Susilo Bambang 2004-2014
- Joko Widodo 2014-2024

Appendix 3: Country Comparison Statistics

These comparisons of Canada and Indonesia are taken from *The Economist* 2014 Edition, Pocket World in Figures. 2014 was the last year of our cooperation.

Category	Canda	Indonesia
Land area '000 sq. km	9,971 (#2)	1,904 (#15)
Population millions	34.3 (#36)	242.3 (#4)
Biggest cities	Toronto (#60)	Jakarta (#26)
Population living in urban areas	27.4 (#26)	119.7 (#5)
Economy GDP USD billion	1,736 (#11)	847 (#16)
Economy by purchasing power	1,394 (#14)	1,123 (#16)
% of all world exports	2.45 (#11)	0.86 (#33)
Current account $ million	-52,993 (#6 deficit)	+2,070 (#42 surplus)
Big Mac index – currency	overvalued 24%	undervalued 35%
Household debt % disposable income	146% (#10)	not listed
Arable land % of total	4.8	13.0
Largest agricultural output	$37 B (#14)	$125 B (#4)
% GDP from agriculture	1.7%	15%
Global competitiveness	#7	#39
Foreign direct investment	$40 B (#12)	$18.9 B (#18)

Largest global producers: Agriculture, commodities, and energy

- Canada: wheat #7, copper #8, lead #10, zinc #7, nickel #4, aluminum #3, gold #7, platinum # 3, oil # 5, natural gas #5, oil reserves # 3, energy #6, caro #15

- Indonesia: cereals #5, fruit #6, rice # 3, tea # 8, coffee #3, cocoa #3, nickel #3, gold #10, rubber #3, natural gas #10, coal #4, energy #7, caro #20

People and Public Services Statistics

Category	Canada	Indonesia
Population Growth 2000-2010	10.9%	12.4%
Population under 15	16.3%	26.7%
Population over 60	20.0%	8.9%
Life expectancy M/W	78.9/85.3	68.3/71.8
GDP per head	$50,340	$3,500
Health spending % of GDP	11.2%	2.7%
Education spending % of GDP	5.5%	2.8 %
Enrolment tertiary education	62%	23%
Religion	Christian 69% non- religious 24%	Muslim 87.2% Christian 9.9% (5 religions recognized in constitution)

More Comparative Statistics

Category	Canada	Indonesia
Road networks km	1,409,016 (#5)	501,521 (#14)
Air travel annual passenger km	118,933 mil (#7)	39,560 mil (#24)
Railway network '000 km	64.3 (#5)	4.7 (#33)
Tourist arrivals '000	15,976 (#18)	7,650 (#32)
Emitters of CO_2 million tons	513.9 (#8)	451.8 (#12)
Carbon dioxide per person	15.2 tons (#12)	not on top 44 list
Air quality – matter concentration	not in top 23	#20 Jakarta #16 for cities
Telephone lines per 100	53 (#15)	15.9
Mobile subscribers per 100	79.7	103.1
Computers per 100 people	129 (#1)	n/a
Broadband subscribers per 100	31.8 (#16)	1.1
Facebook users '000	17,809 (#15)	47,971 (#4)
Structure of employment		
Agriculture	2%	36%
Industry	22%	21%
Services	76%	43%

<u>Partnership Arrangement</u>

The Institute of Public Administration of Canada
and
Ministry of Home Affairs of the Republic of Indonesia
and
The Province of Nova Scotia

PREAMBLE

WHEREAS a similar cooperative arrangement between Indonesia and the Institute of Public Administration ("IPAC") was made in January 1995 and extended in February 1998; and

WHEREAS there are considerable similarities between the democratic values, structures, and processes of Indonesia and the Province of Nova Scotia; and

WHEREAS the Government of Canada has established contribution programs designed to encourage support and sustainable development in countries seeking to develop their own capacity; and

WHEREAS the Institute of Public Administration administers international programs aimed at strengthening public administration and management and has entered into an agreement with the Canadian International Development Agency ("CIDA") to administer a program known as the Good Governance Program (the "Program"), a part of which includes a governance project or projects in Indonesia; and

WHEREAS IPAC, and Province of Nova Scotia, and the Ministry of Home Affairs of the Republic of Indonesia (collectively the "Parties") wish to share their knowledge and experience on a range of governance matters.

Partnership Principle

Therefore, IPAC, the Province of Nova Scotia and the Ministry of Home Affairs of the Republic of Indonesia agree to use the Program activities as a mechanism for sharing information, experience and skills, to foster responsive, democratic governance, and enabling an environment for sustainable social, economic, and environmental development.

Purpose of the Arrangement

The purpose of this document is to formalize the partnership arrangements between the Province of Nova Scotia and the Ministry of Home Affairs of the Republic of Indonesia, and IPAC.

Partnership Statement

Signatories to this arrangement share a commitment to support and engage in cooperative activities, which foster responsive, democratic governance, and an enabling environment for sustainable social, economic, and environmental development of Indonesia (the "partnership activities"). By collaborating, sharing innovation, best practices, and principles, IPAC, the Province of Nova Scotia, and the Ministry of Home Affairs of the Republic of Indonesia aim to maximize the effectiveness and efficiency of the partnership activities. The Parties will support implementation of partnership initiatives in accordance with the Good Governance Program.

Commitment of the Participants

Commitments of IPAC

IPAC shall be responsible for the successful management and implementation of the partnership initiatives.

To this end, IPAC shall:

1. Effectively manage and implement the partnership activities in accordance with the terms and conditions of its Contribution Agreement with CIDA.

2. Ensure active participation of both Canadian and Indonesian partners in planning, implementing, preparing, and submitting mission work plans, semi-annual and annual reports required by CIDA.

3. In accordance with the conditions outlined in the Contribution Agreement with CIDA and in accordance with the Treasury Board of Canada, Travel Directives, pay for all travel and partnership activity-related landing costs (accommodation; meals; emergency travel, medical and kidnap & ransom insurances; and incidentals) of individuals approved for participation in specific activities.

4. Fund exchanges, workshops, conferences, and/or other activities that are consistent with the above noted goals and purposes of the Program and are approved by the program manager or director.

5. Document and monitor the progress, effectiveness and results of partnership activities.

6. Provide reports to CIDA on project work plans, progress and financial status.

7. Support any audits, evaluations or other reviews initiated by CIDA.

8. Cooperate with the Ministry of Home Affairs of the Republic of Indonesia to ensure that IPAC representatives:
   a. Observe, respect, and comply with the laws and regulations, and policies of Government of the Republic of Indonesia;
   b. Conduct partnership activities in line with Indonesia National Interest;
   c. Respect the integrity of the Unitary State of the Republic of Indonesia and refrain from supporting any separatist movement;
   d. Refrain from involving in any intelligence/clandestine activities;
   e. Refrain from conducting any activities relating to regulation in Indonesia other than those relating to partnership activities;
   f. Respect the customs, traditions, and religions of the local community;
   g. Refrain from engaging in any political and commercial activities;
   h. Refrain from conducting any religious propagation; and
   i. Respect the right of the Indonesia Government regarding the formulation of regulation.

Commitments of the Province of Nova Scotia

The province of Nova Scotia shall be responsible for the successful management and implementation of partnership activities.

To this end, the Province shall:

1. Designate a provincial coordinator to be the main contact.

2. Develop annual work plans that support the RBM (results based management) accountability framework, as well as the priorities, goals, and objectives of the Ministry of Home Affairs together with its partners and IPAC.

3. Have the annual work plans approved by senior provincial officials and IPAC prior to implementation.

4. Ensure active participation in planning, implementation, and monitoring partnership activities and in preparing and submitting mission, semi-annual, and annual reports to the IPAC program manager.

5. Indicate in its plans and reports to the IPAC program manager and Indonesia, the expected impact of project activities on gender equality; the manner in which women were involved in the planning and implementation of governance activities; any special measures undertaken to ensure the full participation of women and actual results related to gender equality.

6. Track in-kind contributions to the partnership activities.

7. Support any audits, evaluations, or other reviews initiated by CIDA.

8. Ensure all Canadian citizens associated with the partnership project register with the Canadian Embassy or High Commission upon arrival in Indonesia.

9. Cooperate with the Ministry of Home Affairs of the Republic of Indonesia to ensure that Nova Scotia representatives:
   a. Observe, respect, and comply with the laws and regulations, and policies of Government of the Republic of Indonesia;
   b. Conduct partnership activities in line with Indonesia National Interest;

   c. Respect the integrity of the Unitary State of the Republic of Indonesia and refrain from supporting any separatist movement;

   d. Refrain from involving in any intelligence/clandestine activities;

   e. Refrain from conducting any activities relating to regulation in Indonesia other than those relating to partnership activities;

   f. Respect the customs, traditions, and religions of the local community;

   g. Refrain from engaging in any political and commercial activities;

   h. Refrain from conducting any religious propagation; and

   i. Respect the right of the Indonesia Government regarding the formulation of regulation.

Commitments of the Ministry of Home Affairs of the Republic of Indonesia

The Ministry of Home Affairs of the Republic of Indonesia shall be responsible for the successful management and implementation of partnership project activities. To this end, the Ministry shall:

1. Designate a project coordinator to be the main contact.

2. Develop annual work plans that support the RBM (results based management) accountability framework, as well as the priorities, goals, and objectives of the Ministry of Home Affairs together with its partners and IPAC.

3. Have the annual work plans approved by senior officials and IPAC prior to implementation.

4. Ensure active participation in planning, implementation, and monitoring partnership project activities and in preparing and submitting regular reports to the IPAC program manager and Canadian project coordinator.

5. Indicate in its plans and reports to the IPAC program manager and Nova Scotia, the expected impact of project activities on gender equality; the manner in which women were involved in the planning and implementation of governance activities; any special measures undertaken to ensure the full participation of women; and actual results related to gender equality.

6. Track in-kind contributions to the partnership activities.

7. Support any audits, evaluations, or other reviews initiated by CIDA.

Complementary to Other Efforts

The partnership activities and this arrangement are complementary to other initiatives and arrangements that may exist between the Ministry of Home Affairs and Canadian provinces and between initiatives and arrangements that Indonesia may have with other donors.

Respect for Ongoing Needs of Governing

IPAC, the Province of Nova Scotia, and the Ministry of Home Affairs are participating in the partnership activities and the Program on a voluntary basis in addition to the ongoing work. The extent of work plans, reports and the number, kind, timing, and duration of activities will depend on the capacity of each partner to participate, while at the same time responding to the needs and pressures of their own governments.

Selection of Canadian Participants

The Province of Nova Scotia agrees to identify public servants and others who have the combination of knowledge, experience, and abilities that are best able to enhance the capacity development requirements of Indonesia and, when required, to release staff identified for the project from their duties without loss of employment pay or benefits for the duration of their assignments. Where possible, the Province agrees to ensure that the persons identified and assigned to the partnership activities are physically capable of performing their duties and have the necessary information prior to the their departure to maintain their health and have adequate health and travel insurance coverage.

All participants are required to work with their project coordinator and the coordinator of Indonesia in the development of objectives, activities, and tasks for specific assignments and to prepare reports of the results of the assignment upon completion.

Selection of the Country Participants

The Ministry of Home Affairs agrees to identify public servants who are best able to integrate and apply knowledge and skills shared by their Canadian colleagues and to release the individuals identified from their duties without loss of employment pay or benefits for the duration of their assignments. The Ministry agrees to ensure that the persons identified and assigned to the partnership activities are physically capable of performing their duties and have the necessary information prior to their departure to maintain their health and have adequate health and travel insurance coverage.

All participants are required to work with their project coordinator and the coordinator of the partner in the development of objectives, activities, and tasks for specific assignments and to prepare reports of the results of the assignment upon completion.

Emphasis on Application
The Parties will make every effort to ensure that work plans and activities are feasible, deliverable, and practical.

Duration of the Arrangement
This arrangement shall continue throughout the duration of the Program. Termination of the arrangement will require six months written notice to the non-terminating parties. The initiatives developed by the participants can be maintained after the arrangement has expired.

Amendment to the Arrangement
Any amendments to this arrangement will only be made after consultation and jointly consented in writing to by each of the Parties through a duly authorized representative.

Dispute Resolution
Any dispute arising from the interpretation or application of this arrangement shall be resolved amicably by consultation and communication among the Parties.

Communication, Trust, and Respect
The Parties and their respective representatives will respect all confidences, including all information shared with them or to which they have gained access in the course of carrying out responsibilities related to the partnership activities.

Confidentiality and Projection of Privacy

All requirements respecting confidentiality and protection of privacy of provinces participating in twining relationships and of non-twinned provinces participating in partnership activities will be respected.

Appropriate Acknowledgement

The funding agency (Canadian International Development Agency), executing agency (IPAC), as well as the partners will be acknowledged in news releases, speeches, publications, and other forms of public communication. The following text will be utilized:

"The Ministry of Home Affairs would like to acknowledge the financial support for this (activity or report) of the Canadian International Development Agency (CIDA), provided through the Good Governance Program and managed by the Institute of Public Administration of Canada (IPAC)."

IN WITNESS WHEREOF, the Participants hereto have caused this PARTNERSHIP ARRANGEMENT to be signed as of this 19th day of November 2008.

Signed on behalf of the **PROVINCE OF NOVA SCOTIA**
Jamie Muir, Minister
Service Nova Scotia and Municipal Relations

Witnessed by
Mark Gilbert
Provincial Co-ordinator

Signed on behalf of the **GOVERNMENT of INDONESIA**
Pak Nuryanto
Head, Centre for Management of Overseas Cooperation
Ministry of Home Affairs

Witnessed by
M Arif Hidayat
Program Participant, Ministry of Home Affairs

Signed on behalf of the **INSTITUTE of PUBLIC ADMINISTRATION of CANADA**
William Greenlaw, President

Witnessed by
Norma MacIsaac, Past Chair
IPAC Nova Scotia Regional group

TERM of REFERENCE

MoHA-IPAC Roundtable Discussion on
Building Local Competitiveness through
One Stop Service (OSS) Provision
Sari Pan Pacific Hotel Jakarta, Indonesia
21st of June, 2011

I. BACKGROUND

The implementation of regional autonomy is essentially a manifestation of national development in order to achieve a righteous and prosperous society. In line with that intention, regional development is an integral part of national development. Regional autonomy has provided a challenge for the government particularly at local level in order to carry out an effective governance to cope with increasingly dynamic environment changes. The principles of autonomy that are vast, real and responsible have opened the opportunities as well as challenges for local governments to manage the development in their regions based on the principle of decentralization.

Decentralization and regional autonomy has transformed the system of governance in Indonesia, particularly local government. With the authority to manage certain government's affairs, local government is expected to create innovations in governance in the region, particularly in the provision of public services for the society. In this regard, decentralization should be an instrument for local government to provide better public services to the society. New paradigm in the provision of good public service is a society-oriented services, in terms of the provision of public services must be able to meet the interests and expectations of society as citizens in accordance with the laws and regulations. One of the things that can be done as an effort to manifest it is through one stop service delivery.

Based on Ministry of Home Affairs Decree (Permendagri) Number 24 Year 2006 on Guidelines for Implementation of One Stop Service, the Implementation of One Stop Service is the activity of licensing and non licensing requirements that the management process from the application stage until the publication stage of the document is through one place. The purpose of the One Stop Service (OSS) is to improve the quality of public services and provide wider access to the public to obtain services. In addition, OSS is a form of bureaucratic reforms that aims to improve bureaucratic service performance that ensures clarity on procedure, certainty of time and cost of service.

Implementation of OSS is expected to become one of the stimuli for enhancing regional competitiveness through increased investment interest in the area by giving greater attention to the role of micro, small and medium enterprises to increase the pace of regional economic growth. In general, competitiveness shows the ability of a region in determining the exact strategy in improving the society welfare, so that local governments are required to seek and recognize the potential that will be developed. One of the efforts that can be done is to create new ideas, improvements that could encourage the growth of new businesses, new industries, and employment.

Data from Directorate General of Regional Development states that until the year 2010 there has been 394 units of OSS in provinces and regencies/cities in Indonesia. A total of 394 units consist of 15 provinces, 292 regencies and 87 cities. This suggests that as many as 60% of provincial and regency/city has adopted an integrated one-stop service. In quantity it is quite satisfactory, but the quality still has to be evaluated further. Some provincial and regency/city governments have shown better performance than other regions, indeed some areas have been able to reform the public service with the implementation OSS and promote innovations that encourage regional competitiveness and economic growth in their regions. However, there are areas that still have problems in implementing OSS in the region. With reference to this, it is necessary to hold a Roundtable Discussion on Building Local Competitiveness through One Stop Service Provision.

This Roundtable Discussion is expected to expand the horizons of local government in the implementation of OSS in Indonesia and Canada as well as encourage innovation and learning from the experiences as lessons learned. Furthermore, this Roundtable Discussion is expected to open opportunities for local governments to learn and exchange ideas/knowledge sharing in providing OSS as a way to build local competitiveness in the era of globalization.

In addition, Canada has become one of the pioneers in the provision of good public services, particularly through the implementation of OSS with the experience of implementing decentralization for over 100 years. Therefore, in this Roundtable Discussion the Indonesian government expects to learn many experiences from the Government of Canada in the field of OSS provision.

II. PURPOSE

The purposes of the Roundtable Discussion are:

1. Provide insights to local governments on policies and implementation of OSS through learning/sharing knowledge and experiences that exists in both Indonesia and Canada as lessons learned.

2. Encourage local governments to innovate in the provision of public services through the implementation of an effective and efficient OSS in order to enhance regional competitiveness.

3. To support close cooperation between the governments of Canada and the Government of the Republic of Indonesia and the relevant organization.

III. SUBSTANCE & METHODOLOGY

Substance

Roundtable Discussion will discuss the following issues:

1. OSS provision in general in Canada (OSS establishment, the type of services provided, and local authorities).

2. OSS provision policy in Indonesia.

3. Evaluation of OSS provision in Indonesia (developments and problems in implementing in the region).

4. Impact of OSS provision in promoting local investment.

5. Implementation of OSS in Canada.

6. Sharing experience and best practices on the innovation and successful implementation of OSS in Indonesia and Canada, including its impact on local revenue.

Methodology

The Roundtable Discussion will be conducted as follows:

1. Each speaker is required to present their paper.

2. After the presentation by each speaker, the panel will be invited to respond, guided by the moderator/facilitator.

3. The other participants are given an opportunity to contribute after the panel discussion.

Each speaker is expected to:

1. Share their experiences and present their ideas based on their background of their expertise.

2. Elaborate on their presentations and respond to questions from the panel and the other participants and summarize and consolidate contributions.

IV. SPEAKERS & PARTICIPANTS

Speakers

1. Speakers are policy makers/practitioners, academics that represent the relevant government institutions and representatives of local governments in Indonesia and Canada which are related to the public services/OSS provision.

2. Speakers from Indonesia are expected to be 6 (six) persons and speakers from Canada are expected to be 4 (four) persons.

Participants

1. Government officials: participants are representatives from central and local governments who have competence in the field of public service/OSS provision.

2. Non Government officials: participants are representatives from International NGO's, International Organizations, and International Donors that are currently have cooperation with MoHA.

3. Participants from the local government are expected to be the Regional Secretary/Head of Department related to the theme.

4. The total numbers of participants are estimated approximately 100 participants.

V. DATE & VENUE

The one-day roundtable discussion will be held on the 21st of June, 2011, in Sari Pan Pacific Hotel Jakarta, Indonesia.

VI. EXPECTED RESULTS

Expected results from the MoHA/IPAC Roundtable Discussion on Building Regional Competitiveness through One Stop Service Provision are:

1. Increased capacity of local governments in implementing an effective and efficient OSS in order to enhance local competitiveness.

2. Identification of issues related to the Implementation of One Stop Service, including the development and problems so that positive recommendations could be generated for local governments.

3. Expand the insight and knowledge of local governments from the discussions, exchange of information/knowledge sharing and best practice through an effective and efficient OSS provision.

VII. FORMAT OF THE PROGRAM

This Roundtable Discussion will be using Bilingual language. In order to achieve the most productive output, format of the roundtable discussion would be managed as follows:

PROGRAM SCHEDULE
MoHA - IPAC Roundtable Discussion on Building Local Competitiveness through One Stop Service Provision

Date	Session	Time	Program	Remarks
Tuesday 21 June 2011		08.45 – 09.00	Notes	Mrs. Diah Anggraeni, Secretary General, Ministry of Home Affairs (tentative)
		09.00 – 09.15	Welcome Speech	The Canadian Ambassador, To be confirmed (Tbc)
		09.15 – 09.30	Welcome Remarks	Mr. Gamawan Fauzi, Minister of Home Affairs (Tbc)
		09.30 – 09.35	Prayer Session	Tbc
		09.35 – 09.45	Nutrition Break	
	Session 1: OSS Provision in Indonesia and Canada	09.45 – 10.05	Topic 1 "OSS provision in general in Canada"	Speaker 1: IPAC Dr Mark Gilbert, Professor, Dalhousie University, Halifax, Canada
		10.05 – 10.25	Topic 2 "OSS provision policy in Indonesia"	Speaker 2: Director of Regional Economic Development, Directorate General of Regional Development, MoHA,
		10.25 – 10.45	Topic 3 "Impact of OSS Provision in promoting local investment."	Speaker 3: Director of Investment Deregulation, Deputy of Investment Climate Development, Investment Coordinating Board (BKPM)
		10.45 – 11.05	Topic 4 "Evaluation of OSS provision in Indonesia, (developments and problems in implementing in the region)"	Speaker 4: Director of Capacity Building and Evaluation of Local Government Performance Directorate General of Regional Autonomy, Ministry of Home Affairs
		11.05 – 11.25	Topic 5 "Implementation of OSS in Canada"	Speaker 5: IPAC Canadian speaker
		11.25 – 12.35	Discussion: discussant will respond to each presentation and discuss with participants	Facilitator: Tbc *) Facilitator will guide in all OSS Provision in Indonesia and Canada. *) Speaker 1, 2, 3, 4, and 5 will be in one panel.
		12.30 – 13.30	Lunch Break	

Date	Session	Time	Program	Remarks
Tuesday 21 June 2011	Session 2 : Best Practices from Indonesia and Canada	13.30 - 13.50	Topic 5 for Speaker 6, 7, 8, 9,10 and 11: " Best Practices in OSS Provision in Indonesia and Canada".	Speaker 6: IPAC, Mark Gilbert
		13.50 - 14.10		Speaker 7: Head of Regional Investment Board of North Sulawesi Province.
		14.10 - 14.30		Speaker 8: Head of Licensing Service Board and Regional Investment of Palembang City, North Sumatera Province
		14.30 - 14.50		Speaker 9: Head of Integrated Licensing Board of Sragen Regency, Central Java Province
		14.50 - 15.10		Speaker 10: Head of Integrated Licensing, Service Board of Sidoarjo, Regency, East Java Province (Tbc)
		15.10 - 15.30		Speaker 11: Canadian Facilitator: Tbc
		15.30 - 15.50	Coffee Break	
		15.50- 17.00	Discussion: Discussant will respond to each of presentation and discuss with participants	#) Facilitator will guide in all Best Practices from Indonesia and Canada". #) Speaker 5, 6, 7, 8, 9, 10 and 11 will be in one panel.
		17.00 - 17.15	Notes	Tbc (From MoHA)
		17.15 - 17.30	Closing Remark	Mrs. Diah Anggraeni, Secretary General, Ministry of Home Affairs (Tbc)

VIII. FUNDINGS

To support the implementation of MoHA/IPAC Roundtable Discussion on Building Regional Competitiveness through One Stop Service Provision requires funds that occur from Budget Allocation List (DIPA) in the Centre for Management of Overseas Cooperation for Fiscal Year 2011.

IX. CLOSING

Thus TOR MoHA/IPAC Roundtable Discussion on Building Regional Competitiveness through One Stop Service Provision was created as a guide for the implementation of activities.

Jakarta, April 2011
HEAD of
CENTER FOR MANAGEMENT OF OVERSEAS COOPERATION,
Drs. H. Harunata, MM

Appendix 6: IPAC Democratic Governance Program Mission Report

IPAC IAPC

The Institute of Public Administration of Canada   L'Institut d'administration publique du Canada

DEMOCRATIC GOVERNANCE PROGRAM (DGP) MISSION REPORT

PURPOSE: to gather information in order to monitor and evaluate the partnership project.

TO BE COMPLETED BY: all International and Canadian mission participants collectively on the last day of the mission.

Partnership Project: INDONESIA-NOVA SCOTIA	Country: CANADA	Dates: November 21 – 25, 2011

1. Using the chart below, please specify the team members who participated in the mission and any key officials met:
   See attached mission agenda for list of key officials met.

Name	Gender	Job Title	Organization
Indonesia (MoHA/IPDN) Participants			
Saut Situmorang	M	Advisor for the Minister of Home Affairs in Development and Community Field	Secretariat General, MoHA

Name	Gender	Job Title	Organization
Norman Muhdad	M	Head of Centre for Functional Position Development and Standardization of Education and Training Agency	MoHA
Muhammad Arif Hidayat	M	Head of Division for Non-Governmental Organization Cooperation, Centre for the Administration of Foreign Cooperation	Secretariat General, MoHA
Nurdin	M	Head of Standardization and Overseas Collaboration Division, Education and Training Agency	MoHA
Professor Sadu Wasistiono	M	Senior Vice Rector	IPDN, MoHA
Bayi Priyono	M	Head of Bureau for General Administration and Finance	IPDN, MoHA
Indonesia (Local Government Officials) Participants			
A. ACEH			
Husin Yusuf	M	Regent of South Aceh	South Aceh Regency, Aceh Province
Teuku Raja Fahsul Falah	M	Head of Income Office for the Local Financial and Asset Management (DPPKAD)	South Aceh Regency, Aceh Province
Masriadi	M	Head of Sub Division for Economic Affairs	South Aceh Regency, Aceh Province
B. RIAU			
H. Achmad	M	Regent of Rokan Hulu	Rokan Hulu Regency, Riau Province

Name	Gender	Job Title	Organization
Jaharuddin	M	Head of Income Office for the Local Financial and Asset Management (DPPKAD)	Rokan Hulu Regency, Riau Province
C. LAMPUNG			
Bustami Zunaidin	M	Regent of Way Kanan	Way Kanan Regency, Lampung Province
Edward Antony	M	Head of Income Office for the Local Financial and Asset Management (DPPKAD)	Way Kanan Regency, Lampung Province
D. DKI JAKARTA			
M. Djunaidin	M	Head, Division of Local Financial Management Board (BPKD)	Local Government Development Planning Board (BAPPEDA), DKI Jakarta Province
Sulistyowati	F	Head, Division of Planning Supervision	Local Government Development Planning Board (BAPPEDA), DKI Jakarta Province
Tuty Kusumawati	F	Head, Division of Research and Statistics	Local Government Development Planning Board (BAPPEDA), DKI Jakarta Province
E. KALIMANTAN			
Ogi Fajar Nuzuli	M	Vice Mayor of Banjarbaru	Banjarbaru City, South Kalimantan Province
F. WEST JAVA			
Muhamad Noor Hanafie Zain	M	Head of Local Development Planning Board (BAPPEDA)	Sukabumi Regency, West Java Province
Nova Scotia Participants			
Mark Gilbert	M	Professor	School of Public Administration, Dalhousie University

Name	Gender	Job Title	Organization
Bob Houlihan	M	Chief Executive Officer	Nova Scotia Municipal Finance Corporation
Nancy Bray	F	Senior Policy Analyst	Service Nova Scotia and Municipal Relations
IPAC Participants			
Mel Sweetnam	F	Program Manager	International

2. For meetings held with multiple people beyond the project team, please specify the total number of men and women who attended *Men: 100, Women: 25*

    These total figures included the delegates from Indonesia, the Nova Scotia and Dalhousie presenters, and the IPAC representative.

3. Did the mission achieve all the objectives as specified on the mission agenda? If yes, please elaborate. If no, please elaborate and recommend how the mission may have been changed to meet its objectives. List any factors that contributed to meeting the mission objectives.

    Most mission objectives were achieved, including learning on federal, provincial and municipal roles, responsibilities and approaches to strategic financial planning and management; financial performance measurement, budget cycle including expenditure and revenue sources; use of integrated community sustainability plans; financial aspects of capital assets; accounting for capital assets; long-term borrowing; capital grants programs; debt affordability models; inter-government relations; council-staff relations; public engagement/participation; Masters of Public Administration course development curriculum approaches; business and government relations courses; lecture exchange.

    Some mission objectives were substantially exceeded. While the mission was planned around the core project team and its priorities, IPAC was able to create a larger impact by leveraging the CIDA funding to also integrate a concurrent study tour by local government officials from Indonesia. The local government officials' participation was organized by Indonesia's Ministry of Home Affairs to complement and augment the IPAC-MoHA partnership priorities, and enabled capacity development to take place at the national, regional and local levels of Indonesia's public service.

The only objective not met was the detailed exposure to multiple Nova Scotia municipalities approaches to financial planning and management. This had to be deferred due to a sudden winter storm that prohibited the group's ability to travel to the relevant municipalities outside of Halifax. However, the Halifax Regional Municipality made a presentation and led a discussion on the approaches used by that municipality.

4. What types of knowledge (e.g. policy development, gender mainstreaming etc) and tools (e.g. Canadian government templates, guidelines, manuals, curriculum etc.) were shared during the mission?

   Provincial and municipal policy, program design and delivery knowledge was shared. In addition, the Province of Nova Scotia's templates, tools and guidelines related to debt affordability calculation and capital asset management were shared. Dalhousie University's Master's of Public Administration course catalogue was also shared. In addition, the first deliverable of a joint research project (between Dalhousie and IPDN) was shared – it is the comparative analysis of public services delivered in Nova Scotia at the federal, provincial and municipal levels.

   During the study tour wrap up session, the participants identified the following **lessons learned***.*

   - *Competent and credible public service is defined by:*
     - *transparency and public accountability at all levels of government;*
     - *the separation of political and professional public servants reporting lines/accountabilities (i.e. firewalling the professional public service from inappropriate political influence);*

- *professionalism in the public service – highly trained staff, with the skills and experience required to develop relevant policy and to deliver effective programming;*
- *reciprocal accountability – citizens must be prepared to pay (i.e. through taxation) for the infrastructure and services they want from government;*
- *commitment to long-term planning not necessarily tied to election cycles;*
- *commitment to sustainability (financial, environmental, social, economic, etc.); and*
- *evidence-based decision making.*

- *In addition to the core project focus areas, some opportunities for ongoing collaboration of interest to the participants include:*
  - *service delivery at the local government level, and how to measure results;*
  - *provincial supervision of local government;*
  - *the strategic role of the municipal Chief Administrative Officer (CAO);*
  - *exposure to public hearing/consultation processes in Canada; and*
  - *short-term work/study opportunities in Canadian municipal physical and financial planning.*

5. Were there any products created during the mission, such as strategy documents, frameworks, templates, guidelines, curriculum, manuals etc.? If yes, please specify and indicate how your team will use them.

   None were created during the mission, but the discussions that took place will be reflected in a refined MoU between the project partners that more clearly defines agreed upon partnership activities.

6. Did your team use the DGP's gender mainstreaming checklist to analyze any products created or processes undertaken? If yes, please specify what was evaluated, which checklist was employed,

whether a gender issue was identified, and any further action required to address the issue.
No.

7. Have there been significant changes to the project since the last mission? If yes, elaborate and indicate how these changes might affect the achievement of the project's objectives.
No significant changes since the last mission.

8. Were any changes to the project's work plan made since the last mission? If yes, describe the nature of and rationale for these changes.

   Greater clarity and agreement on next steps for the project activities was achieved, including agreement on topics, roles and responsibilities, timelines and deliverables for joint research projects. In addition, a greater understanding of the capacity development needs of Indonesia's local government officials, and those working in central government with responsibility for local government oversight – particularly as they relate to financial management responsibilities and minimum service standards responsibilities – was achieved and will form the basis of planning for the relevant Canadian expertise to participate in the next training mission to Indonesia. Additionally, the project team further explored ways to leverage the partnership to access additional funding (i.e. potentially from Indonesian philanthropic foundations) to expand the academic training opportunities for Indonesia's public servants (such as through MPA and/or shorter term training partnerships with Dalhousie University).

9. Has your team experienced any challenges with/delays in implementing your project (e.g. elections, change in team members etc.)? If yes, what were they and how did you mitigate them?
No.

10. What are the next steps for the project and who is responsible for moving these steps forward?
The immediate next steps and responsible parties are as follows.

Next Step	By	Responsible Party
Confirmation of specific dates for next mission to Indonesia (in April, 2012)	Dec 31, 2011	Pak Saut, MoHA/Pak Arif, MoHA
Completion of the Indonesian portion of the local government comparative study	Jan 31, 2012	Professor Sadu, IPDN
Preparation of a detailed agenda for the next mission to Indonesia, including: • Identify research activities to be undertaken while in Indonesia and identification of relevant Canadian and Indonesian experts to participate • Indentify topics for joint lectures to IPDN students and faculty • Identify training/capacity development topics and activities to be undertaken while in Indonesia and identification of relevant Canadian and Indonesian experts to participate, and identification of target audience	Jan 15, 2012	Professor Mark Gilbert, Professor Sadu, Pak Saut, Pak Arif, Pak Norman, Dr Taylor (IPAC)
Provision of a list of Indonesian philanthropic funding sources to IPAC	Jan 31, 2012	Pak Arif, MoHA
Initial follow up with Indonesian philanthropic foundations in regards to potential funding for joint IPDN/Dalhousie University training opportunities	Feb 29, 2012	Mel Sweetnam, IPAC
Confirmation of the Indonesian team's participation in the 2012 IPAC Annual Conference in St John's, Newfoundland	Feb 29, 2012	Pak Arif, MoHA
Ongoing feedback to IPAC and Canadian partners on how study tour materials and activities are being used in shaping Indonesia's legislation, policies and regulations as they relate to decentralization	Ongoing	Pak Saut, MoHA

MINISTRY OF HOME AFFAIRS (MOHA) – THE INSTITUTE OF PUBLIC ADMINISTRATION OF CANADA (IPAC) ROUNDTABLE DISCUSSION ON IMPLEMENTATION OF ALTERNATIVE SERVICE DELIVERY STRATEGIES IN CANADA AND INDONESIA: OPPORTUNITIES AND CHALLENGES JAKARTA, 30 APRIL 2013

I. BACKGROUND

Indonesia has been implementing decentralization or regional autonomy since the enactment of Law Number 22 Year 1999 regarding Local Government and effectively implemented in 2001 as a response to public demands for reform that emerged in 1998. It changed Indonesia from the most centralized government to the most decentralized one. According to the Law No. 32/2004 on Local Government, all authorities have been transferred to local administration level except in the area of foreign policy, national defence, national security, judicial, religious affairs and national fiscal and monetary. In this law, Indonesian government system consists of three levels of governments which are national government, provincial government and regencies/municipalities government. Decentralisation is weigthened in the regency's level, so that the regencies or municipalities become the major administrative unit providing most government services. It based on the assumption that decentralization will bring government closer to the public so the service will be better for people.

After more than a decade in implementation, public service is still a big issue in Indonesia even for the basic services such as education and health. For example, many people still do not have access to health services. Hospitals are only utilized by 39.1 % of poor people in Indonesia as the health expenses that are unaffordable for them. Thus, only 18.7% of people in Indonesia are covered by health insurance.[81] In addition, medical or paramedic workers in Indonesia are still far from sufficient. According to data of Ministry of Health, ratio of doctor to population is 27:100.000; ratio of nurse to population is 158:100.000; and ratio of midwife to population is 44:100.000.[82] Another example is education services are still not accessible for all children in this country. Fasli Djalal, Deputy Ministry of Education stated that in 2010, there are about 29 million toddlers, and 52 million children have no access to education services.[83] The education issue is not merely on education services access but also its system.

In order to deal with those issues, improvement in public service delivery system has been made. Public service tasks are decentralized to lower level of government. In regard to decentralization, the central government is obliged to provide guidance by developing the minimum services standard. Based on that standard, each local government should deliver public services directly to citizens. The decentralization is expected to make services deliveries are faster and simpler. The central government has enacted the Government Regulation No. 65 Year 2005 of Guidance for Development of Minimum Standard of Service Delivery. Then, in accordance to that regulation, all ministries enact a Minimum Standard of Services guideline in their area. Currently, the central government has enacted Minimum Services Standard for basic education services, housing services, health services, social services, governance services, child and women protection services, environmental protection services, workforce services, land use planning services, food security services, family planning program services, art

---

81 Bappenas, *Indonesian National Medium Term Development ,2009–2013*

82 Ibid

83 http://www.republika.co.id/berita/pendidikan/
    berita/10/05/19/116125-duh-jutaan-anak-indonesia-belum-dapat-akses-pendidikan

and communication services, etc. After the standard has been made, local government should implement it. It is called minimum standard, so local governments are allowed to achieve beyond that but must fulfil that standard.

After implementation, the evaluation has been done. Based on the evaluation, in some areas, even the basic standard services have not been fulfilled yet. Furthermore, local governments face obstacles such as lack of financial resources, institutional capacities and human resources capacities in delivering good services. Financial limitation is found in many local governments. According to data from Ministry of Finance, most local governments do not have enough fiscal capacity so they are very dependable to the central government. In aggregate level, 80% of total revenue of local governments is granted from central government. Additionally, most local governments are burdened by obligation to pay civil servants' salary which spends more than 51% of total budget.[84] Other obstacle is institutional capacities limitation. Big size of organization and lack of coordination are hampered local governments to deliver of service efficiently. For example, in some local governments, waste management is done by some agencies but not well coordinated. Another example is in the transportation system development some cities build their own system without coordinates with their neighbour cities so the system is not well connected. Human resources capacity limitation is another important obstacle that is faced by local governments. Before reform era, the development is very centralized. Local governments have little involvement in the development project as all development projects are managed by central government. Currently , after decentralization local governments have to manage the development by itself. In result, human resources capacity is not ready yet. While local governments face those obstacles, our world becomes more dynamic and public demands on good quality of services is increased.

Due to those limitations, a new approach of public service delivery should be introduced. Dynamic situation is also enforced local

---

84 Ministry of Finance, Local Budget Data 2011

governments to adapt, by using innovative approach despite its limitation. While the governments' capacities in delivering public services are limited, involvement of other stakeholders should be encouraged. The new paradigm of public services that is "steering rather than rowing" is appropriate to be introduced in this current situation. It means that the government is expected to act more as a director rather than a rower. One approach that might be appropriated and it is proven successfully implemented in Canada is Alternative Service Delivery (ASD). Fored and Zuman refers ASD as "*a creative and dynamic process of public sector restructuring that improves the delivery of services to clients by sharing governance functions with individuals, community groups and other government entities.*"[85] In simple term, ASD mean the government deliver public service through distribute its function to other stakeholders such as community group, private entity or independent agencies as its limited resources. Since the early 1990s, political and public service leaders worldwide have increasingly pursued improved service to citizens by adopting alternative service delivery (ASD) arrangements. In the framework of regional autonomy, Indonesia has several potential ways to do in delivering public services. These ways also have been done by some local governments in Indonesia which are having partnership with other regions, partnership with private sectors and partnership with non-governmental organisations, and created assigned public service delivery to local government enterprises (LGE's). In order to introduce the new approach in delivering public services, the MOHA through Centre for Management of Overseas Cooperation is planning to hold a Discussion involved all Head of Regions in Indonesia.

As in Indonesian government system, role of local governments as services provider, increasing of local governments' capacity is necessary. Ministry of Home Affairs (MOHA) of Indonesia has created some programs that aim to enhance local governments' capacities in improvement of public services delivery. Aiming to enhance local capacities, (MOHA) which is coordinated by the Centre for

---

85 Robin Ford and David Zussman. *Alternative Service Delivery: Transcending Boundaries.* (Toronto: KPMG and IPAC, 1997), 6.

Management of Overseas Cooperation (Pusat AKLN) cooperated with the Institute of Public Administration of Canada brought a delegation of local governments, Education and Training Agency MOHA (Badan Diklat), the Institute of Public Administration (IPDN) MoHA to study visit to Canada. The delegation has been introduced on the implementation of Alternative Service Delivery (ASD) system in Nova Scotia Province. As a result, seven chief of regencies/municipalities that participated in that study show their commitment to improve public services in their area. Focusing on the area of health, education, and waste management, they have developed a strategic plan on pursuing international standard of services in their regions. Motivated by their eagerness to improve services in their regions, MOHA pays special attention to those areas in term of implementation of Minimum Service Standard.

Continuing the study mission above and also in line with Democratic Governance Program, a joined program of MOHA, IPAC, Nova Scotia Province and Dalhousie University, MOHA invited delegations of Canada to visit to Indonesia this year. The visit will be beneficial for Canadian Government and also Indonesian Government. Canadian Government through IPAC will have more insightful lessons from Asia perspectives in public administration area. Current practices of public administration that has been implemented in Indonesia will be explored from the practitioner and from the field directly. Furthermore, several expectations from this program for Indonesia Government should be achieved. *Firstly*, in order to support those seven chief of regencies in implementing their commitment to improve public services, efforts to change civil servants' mindset and to increase their skill in services are necessary. MOHA expects Canadian local government's officer (operator) who experiences in each area of health, education and waste management services to come and give training/supervision to employees in those areas. The training/supervision is focused on technical or experiences in delivering services at operational level, so it can be useful for them. MOHA also expects that one of members is also private entity or agency which is assigned by Province of Nova Scotia to manage waste in Canada to come to Indonesia. We expect those regencies to discuss possible cooperation with them that can be managed in the future. *Secondly*, to discuss about ASD, MOHA is holding Roundtable Discussion. The Roundtable Discussion provides an opportunity to learn from both Indonesian and Canadian experiences in the field alternative service delivery of public services. The Government of Indonesia is looking forward to a focused and intensive exchange of ideas, perspectives and experience with our friends and colleagues from Canada. Issues to be covered include: minimum service standard, public service delivery in the perspective of regional autonomy, and ASD in particular service areas such as education, health care and waste management. Moreover, the Roundtable Discussion will be followed by a series of Seminars at Regional Institute of Public Administration (IPDN) to bring opportunities for academia and students to broaden their perspective about public service alternatives. It is important to broaden perspective and strengthen their quality of education and research.

As explained above, In order to improve public service delivery with current limitation a new approach in service deliveries should be introduced to local governments and enhancement of local government capacities in public service delivery should be done. Under Democratic Governance Program, Indonesian Government cooperates with Canadian Government invites delegation of Canadian Government to visit to Indonesia as part of the effort. The visit is beneficial for both governments. Several activities are set

such as training/supervision to employees in seven areas to support implementation of chief of regencies' commitment to improve public services, roundtable discussion, and seminars at Regional Institute of Public Administration (IPDN).

II. AIMS FOR THIS ROUNDTABLE

This one-day intensive and interactive Roundtable aims to provide an opportunity for "innovative" thinking to:

1. Provide insight to local governments on delivering an efficient and effective public service strategies through learning / sharing

knowledge and experiences that exists in both Indonesia and Canada as a lesson learned;

2. Introduce alternative approaches in delivering public services which might be able to be more effective;

3. Encourage local governments to improve the public service delivery through the implementation of effective and efficient alternative service delivery strategies;

4. To support the implementation of Minimum Service Standard in the local governments.

5. To provide a practical summary of a methodology and practical experiences in the implementation of Alternative Service Delivery models. This will empower local government officials to apply similar practices in their respective areas;

6. To support close cooperation between the Government of Canada and the Government of the Republic of Indonesia as well as related organization.

III. THEME

The Democratic Governance Program event that will be held in the year of 2013 uses theme: **"Implementation of Alternative Service Delivery Strategies in Canada and Indonesia: Opportunities and Challenges"**

IV. SPEAKERS, PARTICIPANTS AND TOPICS

MOHA invited speakers from Canada and Indonesia which are:

1. Prof. Mark Gilbert, Academia from Dalhousie University, with topic of presentation: **"Concept of Alternative Service Delivery in Canada in Order to Improve Service Delivery and Efficiency in Financing. (Concepts, Principles, Models, and Types of ASD)."**

2. Dan McDougall, Associate Deputy Minister, Service Nova Scotia and Municipal Relations, with topic of presentation: **"Best Practice of Alternative Service Delivery Implementation in Nova Scotia, Canada."**

3. Robert Taylor, Chief Executive Officer, IPAC; with topic presentation: **"Best Practice: Alternative Service Delivery Implementation across Canada and International Country Program."**

4. Saut Situmorang, The Minister of Home Affairs Advisor on Governance Affairs with topic presentation: **"Concept of Alternative Service Delivery in Indonesia (Minimum Service Standard and Cooperation between Local Governments and Stakeholders)."**

5. Dr. Ir. Bastary Pandji Indra, MSP, Director of Public Private Partnership Development, National Development Planning Agency (Bappenas), with topic presentation: **"Public Private Partnership in Public Service Provision."**

6. Hj. Airin Rachmi Diany, SH, MH, the Mayor of Tangerang Selatan, with topic presentation: "Best Practice: Alternative Service Delivery Implementation in South Tangerang City: **"Upgrading the quality of Community Health Centre (Puskesmas) and General Hospital and also Schools."**

7. Abdullah Azwar Anas, M.Si, Head of Banyuwangi Regency , with topic presentation: **"Best Practice: Alternative Service Delivery Implementation in Banyuwangi Regency: "Digital Society and Argo Tourism Program."**

8. H.M. Riban Satia, S.Sos, M.Si, Mayor of Palangkaraya City, with topic presentation: **"Best Practice: Alternative Service Delivery Implementation in Palangkaraya City: Shared Service Program for Waste Management and Education Special Area Program."**

9. Rita Widyasari, S.Sos, MM, Head of Kutai Kartanegara Regency, with topic presentation: **"Best Practice: Alternative Service Delivery Implementation in Kutai Kartanegara Regency: "Gerbang Raja Self Reliance Village Development Program and Increasing the Quality of Services in General Hospital."**

Participants

The roundtable discussion invites about 100 people that consist of:

1. Government officials of central government. We invite government official from Ministry of Home Affairs, Ministry of Health, Ministry of Education, Ministry of Public Works and Ministry of Environment.

2. Regional Secretary/Head of Department of all Provinces and selected Regencies/Municipalities in Indonesia as part of local government's stakeholders, and also the alumni that visited Canada on Study Mission last November.

3. Non Government officials: participants are representatives from International NGO's, International Organizations, and International Donors that are currently have cooperation with MoHA, and private agencies.

IV. DATE and VENUE

The Roundtable Discussion will be held on April 30th, 2013 in Aryaduta Hotel, Jakarta.

V. COMMITEE

The events are held by Ministry of Home Affairs through Secretary General c.q. the Centre for Management of Overseas Cooperation cooperated with the Institute of Public Administration of Canada.

VI. BUDGET

The budget for Roundtable Discussion event is funded by the Centre for Management of Overseas Cooperation Budgeting.

VII. CLOSING

The event is a part of cooperation between Indonesian Government and Canadian Government to promote good governance and support decentralization in Indonesia. All programs and activities are aiming to support those missions that finally will strengthen Indonesia-Canada partnership in the future.

SCHEDULE
MoHA-IPAC Roundtable Discussion
"Implementation of Alternative Service Delivery Strategies in
Canada and Indonesia: Opportunities and Challenges"
Hotel Aryaduta, 30 April 2013

Session	Time	Activities	Source Speakers
1	2	3	4
Session 1. **The Opening**	08.30 – 08.45	Registration	
	08.45 – 09.00	Indonesian and Canadian National Anthem	
	09.00 – 09.15	Report from the Head of Committee	Ibu Diah Anggraeni, SH, MM General Secretary, MoHA
	09.15 – 09.30	Remarks from Canadian Government	Ambassador of Canada for Indonesia
	09.30 – 09.45	Opening Remarks from Indonesian Government	Bapak Gamawan Fauzi, Minister of Home Affairs
	09.45 – 09.50	Praying Session	
	09.50 – 10.00	Coffee Break	
Session 2. **The Concept and Policy of Alternative Service Delivery in Indonesia and Canada**	10.00 – 10.20	Topic 1. **Concept of Alternative Service Delivery in Canada in Order to Improve Service Delivery and Efficiency in Financing. (Concepts, Principles, Models, and Types of ASD)**	Prof. Mark Gilbert Professor Dalhousie University, Canada
	10.20 – 10.40	Topic 2. **Concept of Alternative Service Delivery in Indonesia (Minimum Service Standard and Cooperation between Local Governments and Stakeholders)**	Saut Situmorang Advisor for the Minister of Home Affairs in Governance Fields
	10.40 – 11.00	Topic 3. **Public Private Partnership in Public Service Provision**	Dr. Ir. Bastary Pandji Indra, MSP Director of Public Private Partnership, National Development Planning Agency (Bappenas)
	11.00 – 12.00	Open Discussion	Facilitator: Jeffrey Ong Senior Development Officer Development Cooperation Embassy of Canada
	12.00 – 13.00	**Lunch time**	

Session	Time	Activities	Source Speakers
1	2	3	4
Session 3. **Best Practice** **The** **Implementation** **of Alternative** **Service Delivery** **in Indonesia and** **Canada**	13.00 – 13.20	Topic 4. Best Practice: **Alternative Service Delivery Implementation in Nova Scotia Province, Canada**	Dan McDougall Associate Deputy Minister, Service Nova Scotia and Municipal Relations
	13.20 – 13.40	Topic 5. Best Practice: Alternative Service Delivery Implementation in South Tangerang City: **"Upgrading the quality of Community Health Centre (Puskesmas) and General Hospital and also Schools"**	Airin Rachmi Diany Mayor of South Tangerang
	13.40 – 14.00	Topic 6. Best Practice: Alternative Service Delivery Implementation in Palangkaraya City: **" Shared Service Program for Waste Management and Education Special Area Program."**	H.M. Riban Satia, S.Sos, M.Si Mayor of Palangkaraya
	14.00 – 15.00	Open Discussion	Facilitator: Ms. Helen Vanwel Country Director Care International Indonesia
	15.00 – 15.15	**Coffee Break**	
Session 4. **Best Practice** **The** **Implementation** **of Alternative** **Service Delivery** **in Indonesia and** **Canada**	15.15 – 15.35	Topic 7. Best Practice: Alternative Service Delivery Implementation in Kutai Kartanegara Regency: **"Gerbang Raja Self Reliance Village Development Program and Increasing the Quality of Services in General Hospital."**	Rita Widyasari, S.Sos, MM Regent of Kutai Kartanegara
	15.35-15.55	Topic 8. Best Practice: Alternative Service Delivery Implementation in Banyuwangi Regency: **"Digital Society and Argo Tourism Program."**	Abdullah Azwar Anas,M.Si Regent of Banyuwangi
	15.55 – 16.25	Topic 9. Best Practice: **Alternative Service Delivery Implementation Across Canada and International Country Program**	Robert Taylor, Chief Executive Officer, IPAC
	16.25 – 17.15	Open Discussion	Facilitator: Mr. Bruce Douglas Walker, Program Manager Partner Aid International (PAI)
	17.15 – 17.30	Wrap up and Closing Remarks	Ibu Diah Anggraeni, SH, MM General Secretary, MoHA

Appendix 8: IPAC Letter of Appreciation

May 22, 2015

Dr. Mark Gilbert
Professor
School of Public Administration
Dalhousie University
Kenneth C Rowe Management Building, Room 3039
6100 University Avenue
Halifax, Nova Scotia B3H 3J5

Dear Mark,

Re: Letter of Appreciation – Democratic Governance Program

On behalf of the Institute of Public Administration of Canada (IPAC), we would like to thank you for your valuable contribution to the Democratic Governance Program (DGP), funded by Canada's Department of Foreign Affairs, Trade and Development, Partnerships for Development Innovation Branch. As you know, this five year project began in 2010, and will officially come to an end in June, 2015. We truly believe that the success of this project could not have been achieved without the strong relationships that were developed amongst the Canadian and international participants along with the dedication and commitments that were made by all. Your collective efforts have helped in achieving the goals of the DGP to enhance institutional capacity to address a variety of socio-economic priorities.

Over the past five years, the DGP has proven itself to be an effective results-oriented program that has provided sustainable and practical development assistance worldwide. The project has connected multiple public sector institutions in partnership arrangements in 10 countries - Ghana, Kenya, Malawi, Mali, Uganda, Tanzania, Indonesia, the Philippines, Vietnam and Namibia - and has also linked public sector associations in Africa, Asia, Europe, the Americas and Canada. Our success was forged around four program components: Partnership Building, Technical Assistance, Knowledge Sharing/Public Engagement and Gender Mainstreaming.

Although the project is ending, the results and relationships will continue. In particular, the plans for sustainability incorporated into the overall plan of the DGP and the strong focus on the hand-over process with our international partners during the final year of the project will allow help to ensure that our work in building institutional capacity will continue to show results for the foreseeable future. In an effort to share our experiences more broadly, we will be sending you a copy of our most recent book, "Results through Rapport" which is a collection of international case studies which document the many benefits of and lessons learned using the partnership model. The depth, insight and knowledge transfer potential of the case studies included in this volume will be of value to public servants, academics and students in both Canadian and international contexts.

1075 rue Bay Street, Suite/Bureau 401, Toronto ON M5S 2B1
1-416-924-8787 • ntl@ipac.ca / ntl@iapc.ca • www.ipac.ca / www.iapc.ca

Dedicated to Excellence in Public Service   Voué à l'excellence dans la fonction publique
www.ipac.ca   www.iapc.ca

On behalf of the Domestic and International Program team here at IPAC, we would like to express our sincere appreciation for all of your hard work and wish you all the best for the future and we look forward to working with you again.

Yours truly,

Robert P. Taylor, BA, M.Pl., PhD.   Ann Masson
Chief Executive Officer   Director, Domestic and International Programs

c.   Steve Jaltema, Deputy Director/Manager, DFATD
        Vlad Ionescu, A/Senior International Development Officer, DFATD

1075 rue Bay Street, Suite/Bureau 401, Toronto ON M5S 2B1
1 416-924-8787 · ntl@ipac.ca / ntl@iapc.ca · www.ipac.ca / www.iapc.ca

Dedicated to Excellence in Public Service   ·   Voué à l'excellence dans la fonction publique
www.ipac.ca   www.iapc.ca

Appendix 9: Chronology of Missions to Indonesia and Canada by Year and Location

Missions to Indonesia by Canadians

1994 February *Jakarta, Makassar, Enrekang*

1995 January *Jakarta, Surabaya, Sidoarjo, Bogor, Manado*

1996 January *Bali, Jakarta, Bandung, Manila (IPAC sponsored conference)*

1997 February Jakarta, *Bandung, Yogyakarta, Kuta, Gianyar*

1998 February *Jakarta, Bandung*

1999 February *Jakarta, Banyumas, Surabaya, Sidoarjo*

2000 February *Jakarta, Yogyakarta, Malang*

2001 September *Jakarta*

2002 February *Jakarta, Manila, Panay*

2003 March *Jakarta, Manila*

2006 February *Jakarta, Manila*

2006 November *Jakarta, Tangerang*

2007-2008 October – December & January – February: Separate project Jakarta

2008 April *Jakarta*

2009 June *Jakarta*

2010 November *Jakarta, Jatinangor*

2011 June *Jakarta, Bandung, Jatinangor*

2012 April *Jakarta, Bukittinggi, Mataram, Makassar*

2013 April *Jakarta, Pontianak, Palangkaraya (Central Kalimantan), Kutai Kartanegara (East Kalimantan), Banyuwangi (East Java), Manado, Bunaken Island*

2014 February *Jakarta, Jayapura, Muna, Central Bangka, Landak, South Minahasa, Balikpapan*

2015 October *Jakarta, Jatinangor, Hanoi (EROPA conference)*

2018 August *Two-day stopover in Jakarta*

2024 November *Two-weeks in Indonesia: Jakarta and Cirebon*

Missions to Canada by Indonesians

1994 May *Winnipeg, Quebec City, Halifax, Annapolis Valley*

1995 October *Montreal, Halifax*

1996 October *Halifax*

1997 October *Halifax and other parts of Nova Scotia*

1998 September *Calgary, Montreal, Halifax*

1999 September *Halifax, Prince Edward Island*

2000 October *Halifax, Montreal*

2002 September *Halifax*

2004 February *Halifax (during White Juan)*

2007 August *Winnipeg, Toronto, Halifax*

2008 August *Quebec City, Halifax (Partnership Arrangement Signed)*

2009 August *Fredericton, Halifax*

2010 August *Ottawa, Halifax*

2011 November *Halifax and local governments in Nova Scotia*

2012 November *Halifax and local governments in Nova Scotia*

2013 August *Halifax and local governments in Nova Scotia*

2013 December *Halifax and local governments in Nova Scotia*

2014 June *Halifax, Edmonton*

GLOSSARY AND ACRONYMS

AKLN – centre for management of overseas cooperation

ASD – alternative service delivery

Big Bang – A fast-paced Indonesian government initiative to decentralize most government services and transfer the responsibility for providing them to local governments

Blackberry – A smartphone manufactured by a Canadian company that was popular in both Canada and Indonesia in the mid aughts and early 2010s

Borobudur Hotel – hotel in Jakarta near the Ministry of Home Affairs offices frequented by the IPAC team

BUMD – Badan Usaha Milik Daerah – Indonesian term for local government enterprise

Bupati – head of kabupaten (district)

CIDA – Canadian International Development Agency

CIRDAP – Centre on Integrated Rural Development for Asia and the Pacific

Decentralization – the transfer of decision-making authority and responsibility for delivering and financing public services from central government to subnational governments.

DGP – Democratic Governance Program

DIKLAT / ETA – Home Affairs Education and Training Agency

EROPA – Eastern Regional Organization for Public Administration

Gado- gado – An Indonesian salad with vegetables, eggs, tofu, tempeh and peanut sauce

GGP – Good Governance Program

Golkar – A political party comprised of functional groups founded in 1964. It dominated Indonesian national politics during the Suharto era.

Grand design – a multi-year initiative to coordinate the decentralization reforms at the regional and local levels.

GTZ – a German development agency that provides international development cooperation services

Gus Dur – Abdurham Wahid Indonesia's 4th president

Habibie – Indonesia's 3rd president

Hatta – Indonesia's first vice-president

Ibu – Madame or Mrs.

Indonesian – national language of Indonesia

IPAC – Institute of Public Administration of Canada

IPDN – Institut Pemerintahan Dalam Negeri – a degree granting institution within the Ministry of Home Affairs or Kementerian (department) Dalam Negeri often shortened to Home Affairs in the book

Jokowi – Joko Widodo Indonesia's 7th president

Kampung – village within a city

Medan Merdeka – a square in Central Jakarta where 'Monas" the national monument is located.

Megawati Sukarnoputri – Indonesia's 5th president and daughter of its first president

MENPAN – Ministry of State Apparatus Utilization and Bureaucratic Reform

MOHA – Ministry of Home Affairs or Kementerian (department) Dalam Negeri

MOU – Memorandum of understanding

MRP – Peoples Consultative Assembly which consists of two chambers: the DPR-RI (House of Representatives) and DPD (Regional Representative Council)

MSOP – Public sector Capacity Building for Governance and Social development Program

MSS – minimum service standards

Pak – mister

Pasar Baru – one of the oldest shopping markets in Jakarta

Sekwilda – chief administrative office of a District

Soekarno – first Indonesian president

Suharto – Indonesia's second and longest serving president

SBY – Susilo Bambang Yudhyono Indonesia's 6th president

SOCSEA – sub regional office of CIRDAP

UNDP – United Nations Development Programme

Wali kota – mayor

ACKNOWLEDGEMENTS

This book started out as a COVID-19 stuck at home project. I'd been wanting to organize the records, notes and reports on the IPAC-Indonesia twenty-year project and put it in chronological order. This was an ideal time to do it. Once completed, I realized I had enough material for a book that could be of interest to public sector colleagues engaged in international development projects.

I am thankful to the late Burris Devanney, a Nova Scotia educator and author of two fabulous books on his international project experiences in African countries. He was the first to provide editing and structural advice on the early chapters of this book. David Smith, a former colleague now living in Regina, provided valued feedback on several of the earlier drafts of the book. I wanted it to be both the story of an international project and my story as it related to the project. Both Burris and David helped me find a framework and a voice that would make the 'memoir plus' possible.

For her commitment to quality publishing and her dedication to serve the writer and the reader I give thanks to Anne O'Connell of OC Publishing. The editing work undertaken by Anne and Jon Tattrie added immensely to the readability of the book. A big thank you to David Edelstein for his role in the production and design of the book and its cover.

I am grateful to IPAC for providing me with the opportunity to contribute to a worthwhile project and gain exposure to a wider world, and the IPAC staff that provided support to the project and missions. Thanks to the Province of Nova Scotia for the support they provided for my involvement in the initiative, its significant contribution to the project itself, and its openness to international collaboration and opportunities. Dalhousie University is recognized for its support and willingness to host missions and join our Indonesian colleagues in curriculum development and joint research. And last, but not least, a thank you to the Indonesia Ministry of Home Affairs, and our colleagues there, for formalizing and sustaining the partnership during the twenty years of our cooperation.

The program's many achievements are a credit to the Indonesians and Canadians, several of whom are mentioned in the book, who contributed to our cooperation during its twenty years. Over one hundred Canadian public servants and academics joined or hosted study missions, made presentations, shared knowledge, showcased their operations and areas of expertise, and provided logistical support. Hundreds of Indonesians did the same while a few thousand attended the workshops, roundtables, and seminars held in government buildings, hotels, and university campuses in Java, Sumatra, Sulawesi, Kalimantan, Papua, and Lombok.

This book was also made possible through the support and encouragement of my wife Lise who always looked forward to spending time with our Indonesian colleagues and learning about their country and culture. My daughter Carla completed her MFA in Writing while I was involved in the Indonesia cooperation and she was truly the first person who inspired the writing of this book.

Most of the photos in the book were taken by the author or individuals using the author's camera. Some were contributed by project participants for inclusion in this book.

ABOUT THE AUTHOR

Mark Gilbert's career as a local government specialist included work as a practitioner, an international consultant, and an academic. Highlights included twelve years as CEO of a provincial crown corporation, two years as a financial advisor on a post-apartheid local government capacity-building project in South Africa, a twenty-year involvement in public sector reform in Indonesia, and a professorship at Dalhousie University. He served as a national director of the Institute of Public Administration of Canada (IPAC) for six years and a board member of the Government Finance Officers Association (GFOA) of the United States and Canada for three years. He served as co-chair, and later academic advisor, to the GFOA Committee on Canadian Issues. Dr. Gilbert holds an MBA and PhD and has published articles in academic journals and professional association publications. He has also contributed to projects in Eastern Europe, the Baltic States, West Africa, Oceania, and South Asia through short term assignments. He has travelled extensively throughout the Indonesia archipelago and feels at home there. He lives in Halifax, Nova Scotia.

www.ingramcontent.com/pod-product-compliance
Lightning Source LLC
Chambersburg PA
CBHW061558120626
46550CB00004B/1536